Casebook for Business, Government, and Society

Casebook for Business, Government, and Society

SECOND EDITION

Originally Published as *Casebook in Business and Society*

GEORGE A. STEINER

Harry and Elsa Kunin Professor of Business and Society
and Professor of Management
University of California, Los Angeles

JOHN F. STEINER

Associate Professor of Business Administration
and Director of the Center for the Study of Business in Society
California State University, Los Angeles

RANDOM HOUSE
BUSINESS DIVISION
NEW YORK   TORONTO

Second Edition
98765432
Copyright © 1975, 1980 by Random House, Inc.

Library of Congress Cataloging in Publication Data

Steiner, George Albert, 1912–
  Business, government, and society.

  Previous editions published under title: Business and society.
  Bibliography: p. 583
  Includes index.
  1. Industry—Social aspects—United States. 2. Industry and state—United States. I. Steiner, I. Steiner, John F., joint author. II. Title.
HD60.5.U5S8 1980   658.4'08   79–22719

ISBN: 0-394-32566-4

Manufactured in the United States of America

PERMISSIONS

Excerpt on pp. 71–76 ("Firestone's Radial Recall"): Reprinted from the August 28 issue of *Fortune Magazine* by special permission; © 1978 Time Inc.

Excerpt on pp. 77–78 ("Lift Controls on Trucking?"): Copyright 1979 by U.S. News and World Report, Inc.

Excerpts on pp. 90–91 and 94 from "Sullivan's Follies" by Thaddeus H. Spratlen. Reprinted by permission from *Business and Society Review*, Number 26, Summer 1978. Copyright © 1978, Warren, Gorham, and Lamont, Inc., 210 South Street, Boston, Mass. All rights reserved.

Excerpt on pp. 91–92 from "It Takes More Than Good Intentions to Overcome an Evil Like Apartheid" by Ernest Conine. Copyright 1971 by *Los Angeles Times*. Reprinted by permission.

Excerpts on p. 91 from "Whitewash for Apartheid from Twelve U.S. Firms" by Timothy Smith. Reprinted by permission from *Business and Society Review*, Number 22, Summer 1977. Copyright © 1977, Warren, Gorham, and Lamont, Inc., 210 South Street, Boston, Mass. All rights reserved.

Excerpts on pp. 94 and 96 from "Reflections on Divestment of Stock: An Open Letter to the Harvard Community" by Derek Bok. Published in the *Harvard University Gazette*, April 6, 1979. Reprinted by permission of the author.

Excerpts on pp. 182 and 183 and exhibit on p. 185 from *Energy Future: Report of the Energy Project at the Harvard Business School*, edited by Robert Stobaugh and Daniel Yergin. Copyright © 1979 by the editors.

Excerpts on pp. 205, 206, 207, 208, and 209 from "Nestlé and Infant Formula: Facts and Fallacies." Reprinted with permission.

Excerpt on pp. 215–217 from "Pro and Con Mandatory Wage-Price Controls?" by Robert Lekachman in *U.S. News and World Report*, June 18, 1979. Copyright 1979 by U.S. News and World Report, Inc.

PREFACE

Teaching courses in business, government, and society is more an inexact art than a rule-bound science. Many different teaching approaches are possible and are used by professors across the country. In our opinion, some approaches work better than others, and, in particular, we find that in teaching our courses case studies are invaluable for stimulating student expression of thoughts and attitudes.

This book of cases is designed to accompany our basic text, *Business, Government, and Society*, third edition, Random House, 1980. We have included many cases we have found to be well-received in the classroom in the past. We have written a number of new cases designed to bring out discussion of current problems in the business-society relationship. We have written many of the cases to provide in-depth information and factual detail about issues that, because of space problems, could not be fully spelled out in the text. We have taken considerable care in selecting the mix of cases, trying to include cases on major controversial issues that we believe will be of high interest to students. In addition, we have tried to choose an appropriate mix of long, medium, and short cases.

The fundamental purpose of each case in this book is to provide a basis for spirited dialogue about an important issue or problem. The focus of the cases is primarily, although not exclusively, on the way that changing forces in the environment affect the manager's job. An underlying purpose of many of the cases is to make clear to students that equally objective and knowledgeable people can come to widely different conclusions depending on the way they marshall facts and emotions and apply different values.

Another major purpose of the cases is to emphasize student learning rather than instructor lecturing. In our courses in this area we do a minimum of lecturing because we think the students get much more out of discussing basic issues among themselves. These cases will help in this learning process.

Classical case writers do not like to put questions at the end of their cases be-cause they believe this brings in the writer and destroys the illusion of reality. The student, they say, then becomes aware that the case is only an artificial teaching device. For certain types of cases used in teaching traditional policy courses we suppose this is so. For teaching and learning in the business, government, and so-ciety area, however, we do not believe these objections are valid. Furthermore, it is a time-saver to focus attention on specific issues, and this can be done by asking specific questions. Thus, most cases have questions at the end.

The cases may be used in many different ways. For example, responses may be solicited by the instructor from students in the class. These responses may be to questions at the end of the case or to a general invitation by the instructor to com-ment on the case. Following any responses an exchange may be generated between the instructor and a student or among students in the class. Instructors may choose to get involved in a class discussion or remain silent except to correct errors of facts in student discussion.

For some cases an instructor may ask one student or a team of students to pre-pare a presentation to the class on their approach to a case. In other instances students may be asked to be knowledgeable about the case and to act as a resource for general classroom discussion.

One instructor who has used the case method in this field finds the following procedure to be highly effective in stimulating discussion in class. His classes range between twenty-five and thirty-five students. Early in the term he separates them into groups of five or six and assigns a number of cases to each group. It is the responsibility of the group to determine how each case can be presented best in class (with the counsel of the instructor) and to arrange the class discussion.

It is rewarding to students to have someone from the business community visit the class and participate in the discussion of a case. There are many different ways to make such a visit interesting and useful. For example, in some cases the person from business may interact with students. The businessperson may comment after the class discussion about the issues. Or, the businessperson may be asked to play a business role in a role-playing case.

Sometimes it is helpful for an instructor to present background information to a case and to build a climate for discussion. Generally, however, it seems better to stimulate students to debate without the instructor standing between them or serv-ing as the authority for answers to individual questions.

While there are many cases for some chapters, there are few or none for others. This reflects our evaluation of the relative interest in and typical emphasis likely to be given to different subjects in the average classroom in this area. For each chapter there are questions that may serve as guides to classroom discussion of the material presented in the chapter in the basic textbook. "Mind-stretching" questions are also included for each chapter. They raise issues that go beyond the substance of the material in the text. In those chapters where no cases are presented, the questions on chapter content and the mind-stretching questions are, perhaps, enough for classroom discussion. We have also included several field study exercises.

ACKNOWLEDGMENTS

We wish to express our gratitude to others who have helped in the preparation of this volume. We are very grateful to those who prepared cases, and their names appear on the cases they have written. We extend thanks to T. K. Das of UCLA for drafting chapter questions; to George Engler of California State University, Los Angeles, for comments on parts of the draft; and to Alan Stein of the John F. Kennedy Memorial Library at California State University, Los Angeles, for help in finding references. We also extend particular thanks to all those who generously gave their time to be interviewed. Michele Black of the Center for the Study of Business in Society, California State University, Los Angeles; Betty Smith, and Barbara Tennison did an excellent job of typing and helping to prepare the manuscript.

George A. Steiner

John F. Steiner

Los Angeles

September 1979

SOME ADVICE
FOR STUDENTS

Let's assume that your instructor has assigned you to prepare either a written or an oral presentation of a case from this book. We would like to offer some advice to help you prepare the case with minimum wasted effort and maximum positive results.

First, remember that in most of the cases there are no final answers, so don't waste time looking for any. Rather, the best course of action for you is to open a range of views to your understanding so that you will be prepared to discuss the case in class. How can you do this?

One way, of course, is to read the case carefully and think deeply about the issues that are raised. This process can be supported by your general knowledge as well as background material bearing on the case which appears in the basic text, *Business, Government, and Society*.

Another way is to do some further reading. On many of the cases we have listed references, which are either books or articles in journals and magazines. These are easy to look up in your school's library; they give you much additional basic information about the case. On other cases there are footnotes. The references in these footnotes will also include books and articles you can find in your library.

You may have been assigned a case in which events have occurred after the time the case was written. This gives you a chance to look more efficient by bringing the class up-to-date. What's the best way to do this? There are two basic approaches you can take.

One is to go to your school library and use some commonly available reference tools. For example, you can look up recent newspaper articles in the *New York Times Index* or, since most of these cases involve business, the *Wall Street Journal Index*. These indexes will direct you to microfilms that you can put in an easy-to-use machine and read. Some libraries even have microfilm machines that allow you to make photocopies of the articles to take home. Your library may also carry other newspapers and have indexes for them. In California, for example, libraries will have the *Los Angeles Times* and an index for it. Ask your librarian at the reference desk about this. If you are interested in reading magazine articles too, the *Reader's Guide to Periodical Literature* and, in the case of business, the *Guide to Business Publications,* will have indexed articles from several hundred magazines on the subject you are researching. You should find much help here if you pick the right subjects to research.

Two, you can get some very original views and updates on particular cases by contacting people in business. You can write or call a company involved in a case and talk to its public relations department. Part of its job is to familiarize the pub-lic—and that includes you—with what the company is doing to be socially responsible. If you cannot contact somebody in a particular company, or if no one company is mentioned in the case, you can call another firm in the industry. The public relations department there will be familiar with the basic problems in the case. You can get information nobody else has by taking this approach. A word of caution: It is harder to do research at the last minute through business contacts than it is to do library research. So plan ahead. It may be a day or two or even a week before a person in business returns your call. It may be two or three weeks before brochures, annual reports, copies of speeches, and other information you request arrives. So be forewarned that advance planning is needed. You can, however, get a lot of information and literature sometimes through a simple phone call. If you want to explore the company further, ask if there is anyone there you can interview and arrange a meeting.

Naturally, you can use these two research methods simultaneously for best results.

Good luck.

CONTENTS

Casebook for Business, Government, and Society

INTRODUCTION

1

THE STUDY OF BUSINESS, GOVERNMENT, AND SOCIETY

DISCUSSION GUIDES ON CHAPTER CONTENT

1. Define business, businessperson, business ecology, government, and society.

2. Using Exhibit 1-1 as a guideline, illustrate differences in impact of several major forces on two distinctly different business entities (such as a large and a small company).

3. Discuss the widespread misunderstandings about the relationships between business, government, and other elements of society. Why do they arise?

4. Discuss the major deficiencies in the Dominance and Market Capitalism conceptual models. How does the Business Ecology model succeed in providing more insight into the nature of the interrelationships among business, government, and society?

5. Comment on the manner in which dominant influences on business have changed over the last five decades.

6. Do you agree with the book's approach to the study of business-government-society relationships? Why?

7. Discuss the range of issues involved in the business-government-society interrelationship.

8. When the right issues are identified, and all the facts are available, how can reasonable people arrive at vastly different conclusions? Explain.

MIND-STRETCHING QUESTIONS

1. What curriculum center would be able to give the most comprehensive course and the maximum objectivity on business-government-society interrelationships? Consider such departments as political science, business management, philosophy, and sociology. Should objectivity be the principal consideration for designing a comprehensive course in business, government, and society?

2. Do you believe that a continuous study of the environment is a necessity for students, government officials, and business executives?

2

THE CHANGING ENVIRONMENT OF BUSINESS AND THE CHANGING ROLE OF BUSINESS IN SOCIETY

A) POWER TO THE PEOPLE*

As the crusades of vigilantes in the old West illustrate, America's common people have long taken the law into their own hands to secure justice. This is a story of clashing values between farmers and two large electric distribution cooperatives in rural Minnesota. The farmers are rebelling against what they see as imperious political and economic power. Their views, reminiscent of colonial views of English government, have led to a sort of electrified Boston Tea Party in which a 435-mile power transmission line has been vandalized repeatedly. This sabotage is a last resort for people who feel confronted with an unresponsive political and economic establishment. Here are the basic facts underlying the conflict.

Rural Minnesota Faces a Power Shortage

The story begins in mid-1972, when the two cooperative utilities, United Power Association (UPA) of Elk River, Minnesota, and Cooperative Power Association (CPA) of Minneapolis, began discussing the possibility of jointly constructing a major power generating complex to supply power for their customers. Together, UPA and CPA supply electricity to 34 rural electric distribution co-ops which in turn distribute it to over one million rural residents in territory comprising two thirds of Minnesota.

Rural consumption of electricity was rising seven to eight percent a year as farmers used more and more electric cow-milking machines, barn cleaners, feed grinders, grain dryers, and irrigation water pumps. The two utilities faced a severe projected power deficit of 665 megawatts by winter 1978 and other suppliers in the

*Prepared by John F. Steiner

4

midwest power pool could not give assurance that surplus electricity would be for sale then. Even if electricity was on the market the price might be sky-high.

Because energy demand was increasing, UPA and CPA decided that construction of a new power plant was necessary and planned a joint venture to take advantage of economies of scale available through pooled resources. They hired an engineering firm to undertake feasibility studies for power plant sites. The company recommended a location in a rural area near Underwood, North Dakota, 50 miles north of Bismarck. The power generated at this plant could be transmitted by power lines over 400 miles to the areas of Minnesota where it was needed. Power lines like this are not uncommon. As demand for electricity has increased in recent years, utilities across the United States have opted to transmit more and more power using high voltage transmission lines. For example, an 834-mile line between the Columbia River in Oregon and Los Angeles has been operating since 1971.

Billion-Watt Power Plant Constructed

The Coal Creek Station, as the power plant is known, is a gigantic symbol of an energy-mad society. Rising abruptly out of the North Dakota plains, this $711 million behemoth is dominated by two 650-foot-tall stacks towering above twin 20-story steam boilers. Other large structures in the complex are cooling towers, antipollution equipment, and converters to change the alternating current electricity produced by the plant into direct current electricity for the transmission lines.

The two 550-megawatt generating units, capable of producing a billion watts during peak operation, are powered by low-grade, low-sulfur, lignite coal from North American Coal Corporation's Falkirk Mine. The mine consists of 11-foot-thick seams of lignite at depths of 35 to 150 feet throughout a 27,000-acre area next to the plant. The coal is strip mined, crushed, and fed into the maw of the power plant by a 1.4-mile long conveyor belt. In full operation the plant uses 19,000 tons of coal daily.

This ready source of coal is one key to economical operation of the plant. Lignite coal has a 40 percent moisture content and is too moist and sticky to be shipped by railroad. Therefore, to utilize this vast but isolated reserve the power plant had to be built nearby. According to planners, exporting power via a direct current transmission line was more efficient and economical than transporting coal. Using coal for power generation, of course, cuts reliance on increasingly expensive oil and natural gas. Construction near the mine also reflects an agreement between the utilities and the coal company that makes coal available at a stable, long-term price for the projected life of the plant. It is estimated that the Falkirk coal reserves will last 35 years and that nearby reserves would last another 35 years if they were developed.

Water used at the plant is pumped from the Missouri River six miles away, purified to remove minerals that might cause harmful deposits, and fed into giant boilers where it becomes steam to power the two turbine generators. The plant's permit allows extraction of 15,000 acre-feet of water per year.

In building the Coal Creek plant UPA and CPA adhered to federal and state environmental guidelines. Air, water, and sludge pollution control equipment added $150 million, or about 21 percent, to the plant's cost. Operation of this equipment also decreases the plant's efficiency.

Ground was broken for the Coal Creek Station in 1974 and the first generating unit, scheduled to begin operation in November 1978, finally went on-line in the summer of 1979. Construction of the entire complex was accomplished with little regulatory delay or public criticism.

Power from the plant was to be carried over 435 miles of double-circuit ($\pm$) 400 kilovolt direct current transmission line to a converter station near Minneapolis. There it would be reconverted to alternating current and carried out over two other lines totaling 115 miles to be made available to the 34 member co-ops. The power line was the $350 million spine of a $1.2 billion project.

Official Approval of Power Line Sought

In the early summer of 1973, when the engineering report on the generating station site was being completed, the Minnesota Legislature passed a law creating the Minnesota Environmental Quality Council (MEQC). The MEQC was given power to require environmental impact statements for power plants and high voltage transmission lines, but only for projects begun after July 1, 1974. Projects starting before July 1 could be grandfathered out of the costly and time-consuming compliance requirements.

Noting this, UPA and CPA rushed to get started. On August 23, 1973, a meeting with state leaders and members of Minnesota's congressional delegation took place at a St. Paul restaurant. It was well attended. The UPA/CPA presentation of the project was followed by a frank question-and-answer session. A similar meeting was held in Washington, D.C., four months later for congressional representatives from Minnesota and North Dakota. During this period the utilities also applied for a low-interest loan from the Rural Electrification Administration (REA) to facilitate construction of the line. The REA assembled a massive, federally required environmental impact statement, gained approval for it, and in February 1974 granted initial loan approval in the amount of $537 million. By July 1, 1974, the utilities had acquired land in an area near Minneapolis for a converter station which would be needed to change direct current from the $\pm$400 kV line to alternating current for the two shorter transmission lines. The utilities had also done survey work and made substantial progress in planning for line construction. They believed that the project met the July 1 deadline to be grandfathered out of the new environmental protection requirements and the MEQC subsequently agreed.

The Selling of the Power Line Begins

After July 1974, UPA and CPA began holding public meetings about the $\pm$400 kV DC power line in the areas where zoning permits and easements over private farmland were needed. Between 1974 and 1977, thirty-four such meetings were held in

North Dakota and Minnesota. Many of these meetings, especially those early in 1974, were poorly attended even though they were announced in newspapers.

By the fall of 1974 opposition to the lines appeared as county planning commissions, under pressure from local farmers, opposed routes through their territories. Over 48 local meetings were held in the next year and a half. Hundreds of local people participated. It soon became apparent, however, that dialogue-oriented public relations efforts could not overcome opposition to the power line, and the utilities asked the MEQC to determine the route of the line and to remove the project's grandfather status. Exemption of the project from MEQC approval was waived. UPA and CPA hoped this move would bestow government legitimacy on the project and prevent further delays and opposition once MEQC approval was granted. About this time a Citizen's Route Evaluation Committee composed of 47 people active in their local communities was set up as required by the state's Power Plant Siting Act. This committee held eleven public hearings through 1975. Over 80 witnesses paraded before it and the typed transcript of proceedings has 1,792 pages. The committee concluded that the power line planning had been sensitive to farmers' needs and overall environmental concerns. The committee's report was adopted officially by the MEQC in October 1975.

Following issuance of this report, which supported the line's construction, UPA and CPA undertook an ambitious public relations campaign of appearances on local radio and TV stations throughout rural Minnesota, made speeches at civic and fraternal organizations, and distributed information through newspapers and other publications. Slide shows were produced and special literature was published to explain the line.

After getting MEQC blessing for the line, UPA and CPA filed for approval by the Minnesota Energy Agency (MEA). New hearings were held by the MEA beginning in December 1975. Thirteen days of hearings saw 22 witnesses and produced a typed transcript of 1,151 pages. The hearing officer concluded that "there are no reasonable and prudent alternatives to the proposed facility that will meet the demand placed on the applicants for electricity . . ."[1] However, some rural opponents were further alienated because all but one of the formal public hearings were held in Minneapolis. Early in 1976 a reconstituted Citizen's Route Evaluation Committee, made up of new volunteers from all walks of life, was set up to evaluate proposals for the final route of the ±400 kV DC line and a revised environmental impact statement. The committee met 24 times at meetings that were open to the public and well attended. Both in these hearings and in subsequent hearings by the MEQC it was determined through expert testimony that no adverse health effects to humans or animals would result from construction of the line. Normal farm operations such as irrigation and plowing could proceed directly under the line.

During the summer of 1976, the utilities embarked on still another big public relations push emphasizing radio commercials and newspaper advertisements. As this campaign was progressing they attempted to gain easements from farmers along the route. As they did so, resistance began to stiffen. Opponents of the line threatened to disrupt surveying activities. They marched on the MEQC and on the governor's office. Rumors about health and environmental problems from operation of the line began to fly. UPA and CPA representatives were held against their will by farmers at easement negotiating sessions. These sessions were voluntary. When the farmers were stubborn, the utilities asked for and got use of the state's eminent domain, since state agencies had sanctioned the project.

Causes of Protest Against the Transmission Line

The cooperative based forecasts and plans for the transmission line on rational economic analysis, and from that point of view it made sense. The line would transport the electrical energy equivalent of 1.6 million gallons of fuel oil to Minnesota each day with 94 percent efficiency over its 435-mile course. Construction costs for the Coal Creek Generating Station and the power line would result in a doubling of the price of electricity for the million customers of UPA and CPA. However, higher costs were preferable to running out of electricity if demand rose to projected levels.

The planners, however, did not reckon with the recalcitrance of the farmers through whose land the line had to pass. As public meetings and the media spread information about the line, opposition perversely increased rather than decreased. Although 98 percent of North Dakota farmers willingly signed easements for power line construction, by 1977 fewer than one third of Minnesota farmers had done so. After construction began, vandalism reached epidemic proportions in some counties.

Why, in light of the public relations campaign, was there so much opposition? There is never any strict rule or formula explaining such social phenomena, but it is known that farmers had a number of complaints.

First, there was aesthetic pain caused by the lines and towers. The farmers considered them eyesores that violated peaceful vistas of rural life. The utilities had anticipated this objection and gone to considerable trouble to make the line unobtrusive. On the 435-mile DC line there are approximately four latticed steel towers for each mile. The towers are 41 feet square and 145 feet high. All the towers in the line together take up only 32 acres, much of it untillable. On some sections of alternating current line the towers are painted sky blue, and graceful, single-shaft poles are used instead of the busy-looking latticed towers. The power line itself is kept 50 feet above the ground at its lowest point.

This was not enough. Farmers saw the line as visual pollution. Robert Sheldon, manager of public relations for CPA, explains it this way:

> Most of the farms we crossed are prosperous farms. If not wealthy, most of the farmers are comfortable. With all their basic needs satisfied, aesthetics become more important to them.
> I've heard this comment a hundred times: 'I don't care if you offer me a million dollars, it isn't worth it if I have to look at that ugly power line the rest of my life.'[2]

Second, the farmers also objected to anticipated adverse health effects when the line went into operation. It was alleged that the line would produce ozone and nitrogen oxide when in operation, that it would cause harmful shocks, and that the electromagnetic field produced by power coursing through the line would have deleterious health effects. Birds landing on the wire would be fried and cows would give less milk. Crops would be stunted by a corona current that singed the tips of leaves. Radio and TV interference would be a problem. People with cardiac pacemakers would be endangered, and a loud buzzing noise would be present.

In fact, scientific literature on the effects of high voltage lines and studies of operating power lines give no support to these fears. One recent overview of available evidence, for example, says this:

> In summary, neither animal and plant experimentation nor clinical studies nor 25 years experience with operating EHV transmission lines have to date provided convincing evidence for a harmful effect of exposure to electric and magnetic fields associated with transmission lines, in spite of numerous attempts to find such effects.[3]

While no recent clinical or scientific evidence shows the existence of health or environmental problems from operation of a DC line, there is a grain of truth in the charges sufficient to keep scare stories circulating. Some ozone and NOX is produced by operating power lines, but in concentrations barely detectable at ground level. Photochemical oxidation of O_3 and NOX has negligible effect on the atmosphere, though under unusually extended conditions of dead calm, ozone could be hazardous to birds sitting on the line. Likewise, some shocks are felt by humans and animals near the line, but an unpleasant sensation is the only adverse effect involved. The line does make some noise but falls well within the limits of Minnesota noise standards. Still, rumors of scientific studies showing health problems circulated, and like a Gresham's law of gossip, a few methodologically questionable studies were emphasized by opponents more than recent and comprehensive ones. Efforts at enlightenment by the utilities were regarded as self-serving and met with little success.

Third, farmers felt that the high voltage line would disrupt farming. Studies of crop growth showed that electromagnetic radiation from the line would have little effect, but farmers were afraid to operate equipment or irrigate near the line. The utilities assured them this was possible without danger. Other problems existed, however. During surveying, soil sampling, and construction, vehicles and equipment had moved over the soil and compacted it. Compression of loose soil reduces crop growth along the power line right-of-way. This problem was real.

Fourth, farmers felt their rights were violated by the utilities and state government. According to Donald G. Jacobson, manager of public relations for UPA, "Any time government gets involved, as it did in the permitting and siting process, people begin to feel alienation and this may bring out the protest."[4] And it did. Farmer's wife Alice Tripp, who ran for governor in 1978 and got 20 percent of the Democratic primary vote on an anti-power line ticket, argues that:

> The government is under steady pressure from the utilities. They have access to the government and access to the media. . . . Government has acceded to the demands of the utilities. It is just like the oil industry, which has control over government, the media, and public policy. A citizen can hardly face up to a big conglomerate like this, let alone fight it.[5]

Teacher and environmental activist Mary Stackpool of Glenwood feels that the farmers "are being denied basic rights by having their land taken away from them."[6] George Crocker, former Vietnam protestor, writes in *Hold That Line*, a rambling mimeographed anti-power line newsletter for farmers and protestors, that farmers are "all guinea pigs in the corporate laboratory."[7] Attitudes like this give rise to dark theories of conspiracy and corruption. Mary Stackpool believes, for instance, that there is no real need for the line and that North American Coal Corporation talked the utilities into building the power plant near its lignite reserves since there was no other way to sell the coal. Now electricity costs in rural Minnesota will double and the little people will pay. "The utilities," she says, "have been had by the coal company."[8]

Other farmers and protestors believe that CPA and UPA are being manipulated by big private utilities in urban areas so that the latter can take advantage of low-cost federal loans available through the REA. The new ±400 kV DC line will tie into the Mid-Continent Area Power Pool, an electric grid dominated by a large Minneapolis investor-owned utility, and the farmers wonder if electricity will go to the city and profits to the urban utilities.[9] UPA and CPA, on the other hand, state that no electricity from the line will go to the Minneapolis-St. Paul area, with the exception of a small suburban area served by one member co-op. When the Coal Creek Generating Station goes into full power production in 1980 it will have some excess capacity that can be sold in the Midwest. However, power demand increased over seven percent in both 1978 and 1979. If this trend continues UPA and CPA will sell less and less power. Some early excess capacity was planned for the new system.[10]

Still, conjectures about utility greed and manipulation have led protestors to challenge the statistical projections of CPA and UPA. Many feel they were contrived to show a need for the power project. Crocker, for instance, challenges utility statistics in *Hold That Line:*

> . . . NSP [a utility publication] was lying through its Readdy Kilowatt when they were facing brownouts and blackouts, and running out of electricity. Just ask Mike Belford of the Minnesota Energy Agency. During the summer peak in 1978 there was a 29 percent reserve margin in the region. There was a 48 percent reserve margin during the winter peak when UPA/CPA experience their biggest load. 29 percent amounts to about 6,000 megawatts. Comparatively, the CU power line project is supposed to be able to carry about 1,000 megawatts.[11]

However, a news release from CPA on June 29, 1979, announced that CPA customers had increased their demand for electricity by almost 10 percent during the first six months of 1979 as compared to the same period in 1978. The release also stated that CPA currently had a generating deficit of about 30 percent and was forced to purchase expensive electricity from other utilities in Minnesota and the midwest power pool.

Finally, the farmers simply have different values than the utilities. Most have been paid well for use of their land. In Stearns County, where protest has been heaviest, for example, farmers averaged $33,000 per mile of right-of-way even where condemnation proceedings were necessary. The utilities have also paid for other damages. When a farmer broke his tractor axle on ruts left by construction equipment, the utilities offered to reimburse him. "Their attitude is that money pays for everything," says Alice Tripp, the farmer's wife.[12] For the farmers, physical and aesthetic damage to land produces scars money cannot heal. Money cannot be equated to loss of pristine quality any more than virginity can be restored by cash payments. Public relations work cannot resolve this clash between the land ethic and business decision making.

Opposition and Sabotage Delay Completion of the Line

During 1976, letters were sent to farmers asking for easements on their property. Response from counties where organized protest existed was not good. In March 1977, letters went out to all landowners who had not voluntarily signed easements stating that for the line to be completed on time, condemnation proceedings must begin. Farmers had little legal recourse; the utilities used the power of eminent domain if an agreement could not be reached.

At about the same time, Governor Perpich of Minnesota asked the protestors and utilities to get together with Josh Stulberg, a New York mediator. Five meetings were held and the utilities agreed to cooperate further. The protestors, however, maintained they had little to mediate until questions of health and safety were cleared up. Negotiations broke off. Shortly thereafter the Minnesota legislature held hearings on a moratorium bill, favored by protestors, which would have stopped construction on the line. Lobbying took place on both sides, but after the hearings the bill was killed. Utility lobbyists were blamed. Protestors and their attorneys then challenged the MEQC procedures in seven lawsuits. On September 30, 1977, the Minnesota Supreme Court upheld the actions of the MEQC, thereby effectively closing legal opposition to the power line on grounds of bureaucratic ineptitude. A month later, the Minnesota Health Department completed a study of the potential health effects of the line and concluded that, "As yet, there is no evidence whatsoever suggesting any effect on health or a sense of well being from the intermittent exposure experienced in the transmission line environment."[13] This was another blow to the anti-power line struggle, but much spirit for opposition remained.

By this time construction was underway across Minnesota and vandalism reached epidemic proportions. Governor Perpich sent in the state highway patrol to keep order. At one point, more than 300 private security guards were hired by UPA and CPA, but vandalism continued at a cost of millions of dollars.

The protestors established a "Rumor Control," or telephone message center into which farmers could call to report construction activities. If surveyors or workers appeared somewhere, Rumor Control would send out a call for help via a telephone chain and within 15 to 20 minutes as many as 75 protestors would appear at the work site, standing in the way, dancing on the hoods of trucks, demonstrating, and even urinating on towers and equipment. Some violence took place and over 200 arrests were made between 1977 and 1979 for such offenses as resisting arrest and failure to obey a lawful order.

Vandalism was hard to stop. A small, hard-core group of protestors roamed the vast right-of-way area with slingshots, smashing nearly 5,500 glass insulators on the line as of July 1979. During one week, 69 of the 12-inch-diameter insulators were destroyed on a single tower in Pope County. The insulators cost an average of $256 each to replace. Six towers were also toppled by "bolt weevils" with replacement costs ranging from $51,000 to $200,000.

The utilities started regular aerial patrols to count the broken insulators, and pushed local law enforcement officers to catch vandals. They also established a vandalism "Hot Line." As a bonus to the loquacious, CPA and UPA in newspaper ads offered a reward of $50,000 for information leading to the arrest and conviction of persons responsible for toppling the towers and $1,000 for information about persons destroying insulators.

Not a single arrest has, however, been made for vandalism, prompting the utilities to complain: "CPA and UPA will be paying approximately $7,000 in taxes per mile of the line to the affected counties. This should certainly provide enough revenue to finance a comprehensive law enforcement program."[14] The utilities estimate that not only has vandalism delayed completion of the project by several months, but its total cost has been $141 million, or $141 for each man, woman, and child served by CPA and UPA.

Is the end in sight? Not likely. Line opponent Mary Stackpool says that sabotage will go on "forever and ever," and estimates that protestors number "in the hundreds and hundreds and hundreds."[15] Protestors have organized into an *omnium gatherum* of colorfully named groups, including the Southern Landowners Alliance of Minnesota (SLAM), the General Assembly to Stop the Powerline (GASP), Determined Runestone Electric Association Members (DREAM), and an umbrella group including all others named Counties United for a Rural Environment (CURE). Group members meet at barbecues, wiener roasts, barn dances, and film showings to raise money and build camaraderie. An example from *Hold That Line:*

> June 30: Is our big "No Line On Line Party." The festivities will take place at Ronnie Stoon's west of Lowry. There will be music, an auction, possibly a film, refreshments, food and by the way, it will be Ronnie's birthday party as well.[16]

The cooperatives, on the other hand, think the trouble is being caused by a small number of activists. Diane Bishoff of CPA estimates there are "a couple dozen hard-core protestors."[17] Donald Jacobson of UPA blames part of the difficulties on interference from outside groups. He says that groups from Washington, Illinois, and other areas have poured in financial support. In addition:

> One person who was arrested and tried was a popular singer in the Soviet block countries and his trial brought *Tass* newsmen and a TV crew from the German Democratic Republic. Now, I'm not saying that was a conspiracy, those are just the facts.[18]

The Line Goes On

During 1978, as construction progressed in the face of vandalism and outspoken opposition, UPA and CPA continued public relations efforts. In March they sponsored a tour for 93 landowners, journalists, and environmentalists to Oregon and California to visit the operating Bonneville Power Administration ±400 kV DC line. Protest leaders were invited by personal letter to make the trip, but none did. During the tour there was opportunity to stop and talk with homeowners, farmers, and business owners working near the line. Time was allocated to let the tour members knock on doors and talk with anyone they wished in a Los Angeles subdivision at the southern end of the line.

Governor Perpich in 1978 wanted to convene a "science court" with morally binding force to decide health and safety issues. Protestors were in favor of this action but UPA and CPA refused to participate when protestors made stopping construction of the line a condition for participating. Thus, no "science court" to resolve difficult technical conflicts was possible.

In August 1979, the line was completed and went into operation for the first time. But when the utilities cut off the power during a 10-day period for routine maintenance, two more towers were felled. Some thought that protest had died down with the juicing up of the line, since the first weeks of operation were completed without significant vandalism. However, newspapers ran stories that the Coal Creek Plant would shut down for routine maintenance for the week of August 19, 1979, and speculation is that protestors were less afraid of cutting the line when there was no electricity flowing through it. Following the incident, CPA and UPA doubled the reward for information on tower vandals from $50,000 to $100,000.

Insulators continue to be broken and no end to vandalism is in sight. *Hold That Line* still advocates "creative removal" of the line. Many opponents still hope it can be turned off permanently. Farmers in the area have threatened to begin using their own small electrical generators to avoid reliance on the expensive electricity brought via the power line. However, the price of diesel fuel may make their use uneconomical.

Some opponents claim to have observed adverse health effects. According to one resident of farmland traversed by the line:

> People have suffered nose bleeding. My husband had the first nosebleed of his life. Rashes that lasted a long time have refused to go away. People have headaches, bronchitis. There has been a lot of trouble with cows. They are feisty and hard to handle. Milk production is down after the line began to operate. A veterinarian told us that cows have a lot of trouble with the line because they have four legs with sharp hooves and have good contact with the earth. There have been numerous cow abortions where the calves are lost.[19]

During the power line's first few weeks of operation, however, the cooperatives and the Minnesota Health Department received only 10 health-related complaints from residents near the line, with no discernible pattern. Diane Bishoff points out that no health complaints at all have been received from residents under other

Minnesota power lines.[20] It is possible that health complaints may be the result of mass hysteria, hypochondria, or psychosomatic illness induced by anger over the line.

Lessons from the Power Line?

Utility executives recognize that this is a situation in which the environment of an economically rational organization contains hidden and treacherous shoals. Donald Jacobson, PR manager for UPA, says that, "If we had it to do over again, we would spend even more time and energy selling the project. We would go out to the people earlier. We would try to provide even more information."[21]

As a result of the controversy surrounding this case, the Minnesota legislature has enacted some significant changes in statutes governing the siting and construction of high voltage transmission lines.[22] Yet the policy process will remain open to delays caused by environmental groups and values will not likely be changed. Twenty years ago a project like this could have been built from a rational economic standpoint with ease, as were the Bonneville power transmission lines in Washington, Oregon, and California. Today, executives must spend more and more time working with new forces and values. One new need illustrated in this case is to inject uncertain ethical, social, and aesthetic criteria into traditional quantitative management decisions. Whatever the lessons to be learned, they must be learned quickly; CPA forecasts that new power lines will be needed in 1989 and 1990 to meet future electricity demands.

CASE QUESTIONS

1. Should the electricity transmission line be put into operation?
2. Are the farmers' objections to the power line important enough to merit the costs that protest has brought about?
3. What actions could the utilities have taken to stop protests, vandalism, and widespread opposition? Did they make any mistakes during construction of the line? What can be done now?
4. Were farmers and protestors justified in taking the law into their own hands when state government agencies and state courts repeatedly approved of the power line project?
5. What are some other examples of value conflicts between business and elements of society that pose problems similiar to those in this case?

Notes

1. "CU Project Summary," United Power Association, 1979, p. 16.
2. Letter to John F. Steiner, August 6, 1979.
3. Morton W. Miller and Gary E. Kaufman, "High Voltage Overhead," *Environment,* Vol. 20, No. 1 (January/February 1979), p. 33.

4. Interview, August 27, 1969. This interview and all others in this case are with John F. Steiner.
5. Interview, August 29, 1979.
6. Interview, August 27, 1979.
7. *Hold That Line,* May 7–20, 1979, p. 5.
8. Interview, August 27, 1979.
9. Harvey Wasserman, "Revolt of the Bolt Weevils," *Rolling Stone,* No. 297, August 9, 1979, p. 39.
10. Interview with Diane Bishoff, CPA public relations, September 13, 1979.
11. *Hold That Line,* May 7–20, 1979, p. 2.
12. Interview, August 29, 1979.
13. "Public Health and Safety Effects of High Voltage Overhead Transmission Lines," a study by the Minnesota Health Department for the Minnesota Environmental Quality Council, October 1977, p. 33.
14. "Power Line Vandalism Report," United Power Association, May 15, 1979, p. 1.
15. Interview, August 27, 1979.
16. *Hold That Line,* May 7–20, 1979, p. 1.
17. Interview, August 27, 1979.
18. Interview, August 27, 1979.
19. Interview, August 29, 1979.
20. Interview, September 13, 1979.
21. Interview, August 27, 1979.
22. Lawrence B. Hartman and Terry Simmons, "Public Issues and Regulatory Change: A Minnesota Experience," Minnesota Environmental Quality Council, 1979, pp. 13–21.

DISCUSSION GUIDES ON CHAPTER CONTENT

1. Give a summary of the environmental forces influencing the interrelationships of business, government, and society.

2. Explain how the forces identified above affect particular business environments.

3. Discuss how the changing values of people lead to new demands on business. Give illustrations.

4. What are the major criticisms leveled at today's businesspeople? How do they contrast with past criticisms?

5. Discuss the dynamics of governmental regulation of business and the power of business in the political process. How does each affect the other?

6. It is said that ours is a pluralistic society. What does this mean with reference to business and its interactions with government and its role in society?

7. What do the authors say are the fundamental, underlying forces that are changing the environment of business?

8. Do you agree with the authors that business success is dependent more and more upon how a business relates to its environment? Explain.

MIND-STRETCHING QUESTIONS ————————————

1. Would you accept the thought that today's business environment is making the task of managing a company far more complex than ever before? Explain.

2. Do you agree or disagree with the notion that the very complexity of today's business environment gives the large company an advantage over the small one? In what ways?

FIELD RESEARCH: THE ENVIRONMENTAL IMPACT ON THE MANAGEMENT TASK OF THE CHIEF EXECUTIVE OFFICER

Ten years ago a study of how chief executive officers of large companies spent their time showed that they said they devoted approximately 20 percent to environmental forces such as government regulation, community affairs, environmental groups, and so on. Today the percentage is 50 and rising.

Interview a local CEO of a fairly large corporation and prepare a report on how much time top executives devote to environmental forces. Contrast it with their past experience. Find out from them how such attention to the environment is changing the ways in which they manage their companies.

II
A SURVEY OF PAST BUSINESS-GOVERNMENT-SOCIETY RELATIONSHIPS

3
ANTECEDENTS TO CAPITALISM

DISCUSSION GUIDES ON CHAPTER CONTENT ——————

1. Compare and contrast the role of the people engaged in business in ancient Greece, ancient Rome, the medieval world, and mercantilist societies.
2. Discuss the implications of the Protestant Reformation for the development of business.
3. What were the major events that led to the decline of mercantilism and the rise of capitalism?
4. Discuss the principal ideas regarding the position of individuals in economic and social life, which were generated in parallel with the Industrial Revolution and the advent of capitalism.

MIND-STRETCHING QUESTION ——————————

1. Why be concerned with historical patterns and profiles? Is history relevant to current issues? Are there lessons to be learned from a quick review of the history of the business-government-society interrelationship?

4
THE THEORY OF CLASSICAL CAPITALISM

DISCUSSION GUIDES ON CHAPTER CONTENT

1. Explain briefly the operation of the classical individual-enterprise system and the underlying institutions upon which it was presumed to operate.
2. Define *liberalism* as used in the classical theory of capitalism.
3. What was the function of government from the classical viewpoint?
4. Comment on the quotation: "Adam Smith did not accept a rigorous laissez-faire policy."
5. How valid are the underlying assumptions of the classical individual-enterprise system today? Explain in detail.

MIND-STRETCHING QUESTIONS

1. The publication of Adam Smith's *Wealth of Nations* and the Declaration of Independence both occurred in the year 1776. Is this a mere coincidence, or were the two events intellectually related?
2. Do you agree with the authors that it is important for students of business-government-society interrelationships to understand the classical capitalist theory? Explain.

5
THE AMERICAN EXPERIENCE

A) THE CONSTRUCTION OF THE CENTRAL PACIFIC

The term "Robber Baron," as popularly applied, refers to a small group of coevals who began conspicuous and controversial business careers about the time of the Civil War. The members of this group, the most famous of which are Andrew Carnegie, Jay Gould, J. P. Morgan, and John D. Rockefeller, took advantage of new business opportunities and expanding national markets. Though many of the Robber Barons were deeply religious, they separated business affairs from personal morality and employed tactics in business that were questioned at the time and continue to be questioned.

The Robber Barons were buttressed in their actions by values of the time which extolled the virtues of ruthless competition. Particularly popular were the works of Herbert Spencer (1820-1903), an English philosopher who popularized the doctrine called Social Darwinism. Spencer's philosophy provided a moral basis for the accumulation of large fortunes through economic operations which, in the words of historian Henry Demarest Lloyd, made "the Black Flag the emblem of success on the high seas of human interchange . . ." Spencer argued that life was a continuing process of adaptation to a harsh, external environment. Businessmen were engaged in a competitive struggle for survival in which the fittest survived. The strongest competitors benefited the human race by their survival and prosperity. This idea enabled the Robber Barons to justify any effective business tactic, no matter how harsh or cruel, as contributing to a positive end result in the evolutionary process.

The construction of the Central Pacific Railroad is one of many examples of the infamous commercial activities of the time. Matthew Josephson, left-wing historian and author of a widely read book entitled *The Robber Barons*, describes the actions of three shopowners in California named Collis Huntington, Mark Hopkins and Leland Stanford.

In 1860 the three combined with a gold miner named Charles Crocker to form a group called the Pacific Associates. The four raised $200,000, which Huntington carried to Washington in a trunk in 1861 and handed out liberally to congressmen and senators in pursuit of a federal charter for a railroad in California. After expending all the money, Huntington came home with the charter and promises of land grants and federal financial support for the fledgling railroad construction project.

In 1863, after Leland Stanford became California's governor, the Central

Pacific was able to invoke the power of state government. In May of that year elections were held in San Francisco for a $3 million bond issue to finance further construction of the railway. Leaving nothing to chance, Leland's brother Philip Stanford arrived at the polls in a buggy filled with bags of gold pieces and tossed them liberally into the outstretched hands of the crowd. The bond issue passed.

Later, the Central Pacific raised funds by demanding bond subscriptions from towns through which the roadbed was to pass and by threatening to build elsewhere and cut towns off from "progress." In 1868, for instance, the Pacific Associates extracted five percent of the assessed valuation of all of Los Angeles County as the price for connecting the residents there with a rail line to the east. Such a levy was not unusual. In the meantime, Huntington attended to government relations in Washington by expending $200,000 to $500,000 each legislative session to secure political favors.

Construction of the Central Pacific proceeded utilizing back-breaking labor of up to 10,000 Chinese coolies who were paid $1 a day. The four Pacific Associates received a total of $79 million in bonds, government subsidies, and investor cash during construction of the railroad. Experts have estimated that almost half this amount was in excess of that needed for legitimate construction costs and made its way into the pockets of the four principals. The railroad, however, was built and in operation.

CASE QUESTIONS

1. Judged by the standards of the 1980s the behavior of the Pacific Associates is corrupt. Is it corrupt when judged by the standards of their time?

2. In recent years a theoretical case has been made for "functional corruption," or corrupt behavior that serves the public interest or benefits society at the same time that it promotes selfish gain. Some scholars argue that corruption of this type is valuable in rapidly developing countries. Was the business behavior of the Robber Barons "functional corruption"?

3. Do changes in our social structure and business ideology make today's business environment hostile to business people who use tactics similar to the Robber Barons of yesteryear? Were the motives of the Robber Barons different from those of executives who engage in corrupt behavior today?

References

These three books provide useful perspective on the Robber Barons and their times.

Thomas B. Brewer, ed., *The Robber Barons: Saints or Sinners?* (New York: Holt, Rinehart and Winston, 1970).

Peter d'Alroy Jones, ed., *The Robber Barons Revisited* (Boston: D. C. Heath and Company, 1968).

Matthew Josephson, *The Robber Barons* (New York: Harcourt, Brace & World, Inc., 1934).

For contrasting views of corruption see:

George C. S. Benson and Thomas S. Engeman, *Amoral America* (Stanford, California: Hoover Institution Press, 1975), chapter 4.

Samuel P. Huntington, *Political Order in Changing Societies* (New Haven: Yale University Press, 1968), chapter 1.

DISCUSSION GUIDES ON CHAPTER CONTENT

1. What major forces led to the rise of the modern corporation?

2. It has been said that the modern corporation is one of the world's great social inventions. Do you agree?

3. To what extent has business been responsible for the remarkable economic growth of the United States? How has government contributed to this growth?

4. What major forces have led the government to interfere more and more in the economic sphere?

5. The authors discuss a number of social and religious values that have been important in the business-government-society interrelationship. Which ones have been *most* critical in stimulating business?

6. Explain briefly how major economic depressions in our history have affected business.

7. Throughout the nineteenth century and well into the present one, the Supreme Court's decisions have been highly favorable to business. Briefly explain why this is the case. Has this trend changed recently?

MIND-STRETCHING QUESTION

1. Do you think the pace of change in the business-government-society interrelationship is more rapid, about the same, or slower today than in previous eras in United States history? Explain.

III
UNDERLYING FORCES IN TODAY'S INTERRELATIONSHIPS

6
CHANGING VALUES IN SOCIETY

A) INK DATING AND THE RIGHT TO PRIVACY

Since 1970 the Treasury Department's Bureau of Alcohol, Tobacco and Firearms (ATF) has been promoting a National Ink Tagging Program. The proposal dates back to 1968 when the ATF first started an ink identification program. The purpose of the program is to expose fraudulent documents prepared with inks not available on alleged signing dates. The method of analysis involves examination of inks and comparisons to standards provided by ink manufacturers. The effectiveness of the program relies primarily on frequent formulation changes in ink batches by ink manufacturers.

Since 1970 the Bureau has attempted without success to interest the ink companies in a national program. In 1971 the Anja Engineering Company, a vendor of inks to small pen manufacturers, did add a tag to its ink batches for identification purposes which allowed ATF to determine the manufacturer and year of production. (The paper industry has been using a similar tagging procedure for years.) This voluntary move has been overshadowed by the refusal of the largest ink manufacturers to even consider the plan.

Why are the manufacturers reluctant to comply? First, from a purely financial point of view, tagging would cost a company about one cent per pound of ink and approximately $10,000 for analytical instrumentation to detect trace elements. There would also be salary and laboratory costs to bear. Also, companies run the risk of loss of sales and a tarnished public image should consumers who value their right to privacy object to the tagging. Second, the confidential tagging program poses a threat to individual freedom and the right to privacy. It requires that the private sector join forces with government in an effort that could theoretically lead to further constriction of the sphere of individual liberty.

On the other hand, it is estimated that white-collar crimes cost the public at least $50 billion each year. Aside from the cost, such crimes cause incalculable injustices to people and threats to our national security. Ink dating can be very helpful in controlling such crimes.

CASE QUESTIONS

1. Suppose that you are the president of a large ink-manufacturing company, and the government asks you to take the following actions:
   a) Add trace amounts of a chemical tag to all inks.
   b) Change the tags each year.
   c) Maintain strict confidentiality about the tag between ATF and respective manufacturers.
How would you respond to the request?

2. Does the proposed ink tagging program pose a threat to individual liberty? Should the private sector be encouraged to cooperate with government in an activity that resemples wiretapping, bugging, or other forms of government "snooping"?

3. If an ink manufacturer did tag batches of ink would it be morally obliged to reveal this act in order to protect the consumer's right to privacy?

B) TWO-WAY TELEVISION AND SOCIETY'S VALUES

Two-way television with a camera in the home, hooked to a central processing center by cable that permits verbal and visual communications in either direction, is now feasible and is being tried in selected geographical areas. At the present time, however, the costs of such a system are high for the average homeowner. It is estimated, for example, that the costs to a subscriber would be $20 a month for service, with an initial equipment cost to each homeowner of about $1,000.

Suppose, however, that the cost of such a system could be drastically reduced so that the majority of homeowners in the United States could afford such a system. Most of the homeowners could choose, if they wished, to stay home all of the time. A housewife could visit stores, friends, and business associates, yet never leave the house. Children could get their education at home. If people became ill they could contact the family doctor and get his diagnosis and prescribed treatment without leaving home. Entertainment, of course, could be had at home. Furthermore, with the use of supplemental monitoring screens and sensors located around the house, automatic warning signals could be relayed to appropriate authorities in case of trouble.

CASE QUESTION

1. Assuming that such a system was installed in the great majority of houses in the United States, what primary changes in business practices and individual relationships would you expect? What might be some secondary changes in society's values? Analyze the implications of such changing values for business. (For some thoughts on the impacts of new, cheap communications technology, see J. L. Hult, "Cheap Communications," *The Futurist,* June 1969, pp. 70-72. "The Impact of Interactive Television on Life," *The*

Futurist, October 1973, pp. 200–201. For difficulties in making such forecasts, see Richard N. Farmer, "Looking Back At Looking Forward," *Business
Horizons,* February 1973, pp. 21–28.)

DISCUSSION GUIDES ON CHAPTER CONTENT ————————

1. What is meant by values and value systems?
2. Appraise the worth of Exhibit 6–2 in explaining how values change in a
society. Do you think that technology is a basic cause of changing values?
How does this happen? What other major forces alter the values that people
hold? Compare these forces with those of the past.
3. There is conflicting evidence about the extent to which values have
changed in society today. Do you agree with the authors' assessment of the
situation?
4. If you were asked to forecast changing values that might have an important impact on business, how would you go about doing it?
5. What impact will perceptible changes in values have on the business-
government-society interrelationships over the next ten to twenty years?
6. Discuss how changes in ideas, attitudes, and beliefs of people are affecting their thinking; and what impact shifts in traditional values have on
concepts such as individualism, profit, growth, materialism, equality, and
so on.

MIND-STRETCHING QUESTIONS ————————————————

1. What forces do you think could accelerate the changing values of today's
youth? What forces could slow the rate of change?
2. Can values be measured accurately in surveys?
3. A survey on the value systems of young people conducted by Louis
Harris found that "like their fathers, young people are willing to work, but
they want to enjoy what they do and move around less." If true, what is the
impact on business?

7
CRITICISMS AND CRITICS OF BUSINESS

A) JANE FONDA SPEECH ANGERS DOW PRESIDENT*

What follows is a narrative of events preceding and following a daring and original move by a corporate leader to protect his company from what he considered unjust criticism. His strong stand collided with traditional views of freedom of speech and academic freedom for universities. Therein lies the case presented here for analysis.

Background: The Dow Chemical Company

The Dow Chemical Company is a multinational giant that had net sales of over $6.2 billion in 1977, the year the incident described here took place. Within the chemical industry Dow ranked seventh in total sales but was the most profitable of all companies.

Dow's world headquarters are located in Midland, Michigan, where it produces chemicals and is an important factor in the economic well-being of the region. The organizational structure of Dow in 1977 divided it into five territorial segments. The largest of these was then and is now Dow Chemical U.S.A. Dow U.S.A. had annual sales of $3.5 billion in 1977 and was also headquartered in Midland. Midland has been called a company town because most paychecks there come from Dow. It is also heavily industrialized, and in 1976 two *Los Angeles Times* reporters described Midland this way:

> Winter and summer, clouds of steam rise from five square miles of pipes, tanks and kettles in which Dow Chemical Co. produces chlorine, caustic soda, carbolic acid, bug and weed killers, industrial solvents—a witch's brew of toxic substances that makes the radioactive fuel in most nuclear plants seem tame as lemonade.[1]

Dow is perhaps best known to ordinary consumers for its Styrofoam plastic foam and products such as Ziploc bags and Saran Wrap. Consumer products, however, account for less than two percent of Dow's business. It is mainly a producer of basic commodities. For example, the company makes the chemical ingredients for 90 percent of the world's aspirin, which it sells to others who produce the final

*Prepared by John F. Steiner

product. It also manufactures hydrocarbon-based products, epoxy resins, soil fumigants, herbicides, pesticides, insecticides, chlorine and other chemicals.

During the Vietnam conflict Dow achieved unwanted notoriety as the contractor who was producing napalm for the Air Force. Because of student outrage at Dow during the war years the company's recruiters were often picketed and vilified when they visited campuses. Students chanted slogans like "Dow Shalt Not Kill," and the company was the target of a continuous stream of invective until 1969 when it lost the contract—some say by purposely overbidding.[2]

Since many of Dow's chemical products are toxic and have a potentially adverse effect on the environment, the company was under the intense scrutiny of environmentalists and government regulators. Nonenvironmental regulations were costly as well, too costly in the view of Dow officials. Total costs of compliance with government regulations for Dow U.S.A. in 1977 were $147 million, and of this total $50 million was deemed "excessive" by a Dow study.[3]

However, Dow had earned the reputation as a pioneer in research into the hazards of exposure to industrial chemicals in the workplace and had assiduously worked to protect its employees over the years. For example, the company trained industrial hygienists in its plants, kept detailed records of chemical use and exposure, and offered regular medical examinations to workers. Scientific studies of worker illness and death revealed, among other things, that Dow workers had a lower overall rate of death from cancer than the general public.[4] And company officials believe that while there is much debate in recognized scientific circles concerning what is and is not toxic in regards to the dose level of exposure, the facts demonstrate that, in nearly all cases, chemicals can be used safely and pose no harm to the environment when deployed in the manner and levels recommended.

In sum, in 1977 Dow was caught in a turbulent and threatening social environment of increasing government regulation, a general climate of public opinion in which some pollsters found over 75 percent expressing distrust of big business in surveys, and a collective corporate memory of public censure stemming from napalm production.

Women's Month on Campus

Twenty-eight miles west of Midland lies the town of Mt. Pleasant, the location of Central Michigan University, a former business and normal school that has grown into a multifaceted university of 16,000 students. In the fall semester of 1977 two groups of women students at CMU, the Association for Women Students (representing all female students) and the Women's Health Information Project (a group with particular interest in health issues and representing a more radical element of AWS), decided to sponsor a project called Women's Month.

The month of October was so designated and the student groups applied to CMU's general fund for a lump sum appropriation to cover the cost of planned activities. These activities included workshops, panel sessions, exhibits, and a major address. The university gave the women students an appropriation without asking for all the details of Women's Month and after receiving the money they decided to contact Jane Fonda, a controversial political activist and Oscar-winning actress, to invite her to speak. Ms. Fonda had attained a reputation for radical political views during the Vietnam protest years. In July 1972, for example, she traveled to North Vietnam and, during a two-week stay, made broadcasts over Radio Hanoi appealing to American pilots to stop bombing the Vietnamese. She accepted the invitation to speak and the CMU administration neither approved nor disapproved when it learned that she would. In fact, prior to her speech the matter was not an issue.

Ms. Fonda Attacks Corporations

On the evening of October 10, 1977, Jane Fonda addressed an overflow audience of 1,500 in a two-hour talk and question-and-answer session at Warriner Auditorium on the campus. Opinions differ about the topic on which Ms. Fonda was asked to speak. Newspapers in surrounding communities were notified that Ms. Fonda would speak on "Politics in Film" and announced that the general public was invited. Dr. Charles House, executive assistant to the president at CMU, indicates that it was assumed she would speak on women's issues, and both students and the administration were surprised when she subsequently lambasted multinational corporations and criticized the lack of economic freedom in America.[5] Ms. Fonda says simply that she gave her "standard speech" of that time.[6]

No written transcript of the talk that night exists, but subsequent newspaper accounts report that she said economic freedom no longer existed in America and that the concept of free enterprise was becoming obsolete because the American and world economies increasingly were monopolized by large corporations. She also asserted that big multinationals take unjust advantage of tax shelters and unfairly avoid laws and government regulations. To buttress this point she cited stories that IT&T sold war material to the Nazis during World War II. Multinationals were also alleged to utilize interlocking directorates to dampen competitive forces and to manipulate advertising to create markets for products the public did not need. Ms. Fonda encouraged students to challenge injustice in the business system and to fight for "economic democracy."

The subject of Dow first came up in her speech when she quoted Dow's chairman, Carl A. Gerstacker, from a book entitled *Global Reach.* In the book, which is generally critical of multinationals, the authors attribute the following statement to him.

> I have long dreamed of buying an island owned by no nation, and of establishing the World Headquarters of the Dow Company on the truly neutral ground of such an island, beholden to no nation or society. If we were located on such truly neutral ground we could then really operate in the United States as U.S. citizens, in Japan as Japanese citizens and in Brazil as Brazilians rather than being governed in prime by the laws of the United States . . . We could even pay any natives handsomely to move elsewhere.[7]

Ms. Fonda's recollection of the evening is that her words were greeted with frequent applause and that when she mentioned Dow Chemical the audience "just exploded." At that time she was unaware that Dow's headquarters were located nearby, but soon ascertained the audience's special interest in Dow and made observations in the question-and-answer session about Dow making napalm, manufacturing chemicals that caused sterility in workers, and exhibiting a corporate mentality that led to many of the abuses cited in her earlier remarks.

In addition to Dow's geographical proximity, one likely reason for the volatility of students on the subject may have been an accident that occurred at a Dow plant in Midland only three days earlier. At 9:15 on the Friday morning before Ms. Fonda's speech, a pipe leading to a chlorine tank broke at the Dow chlor-alkali plant in Midland, releasing 20 to 30 gallons of liquid chlorine. The chlorine turned to gas upon contact with air, leading to the formation of a gas cloud that hospitalized eight workers with serious injuries. The airborne cloud began to move and forced thousands to evacuate homes and schools along its path. It reached the Mt. Pleasant campus between 1:30 and 2 P.M. on Friday afternoon and campus workers turned off all intake fan motors into buildings and checked for open windows so that air would not be taken in until the cloud passed. Children and the elderly were especially cautioned to stay indoors. Although no ill effects were reported in the Mt. Pleasant area, students had had a "consciousness-raising" experience making them aware of potential danger from industrial accidents at Dow. State regulatory agencies had begun an investigation of the incident.

Financing Ms. Fonda's Speaker's Fee

For her speech Ms. Fonda was paid $3,500. Part of this money came from the money the women students had been granted from CMU's general fund and part was covered by gate receipts. Students had been charged $1.00 admission for the talk; nonstudents paid $1.50. Dr. House estimates that after all expenses for the evening were totaled, approximately $2,000 from the general fund went to pay Ms. Fonda. The students organizing Women's Month also charged admission to other events, and House estimates that receipts were "very close to the original allocation," adding that the students "didn't make money." In any case, House points out that Dow funds characteristically came as gifts designated for specific projects and there may have been no Dow gift money in the general fund. Even if there was, Dow contributions would have been mixed with funds from other sources and specific dollars spent on projects such as Women's Month could not be labeled by source of donation.

Dow Suspends Support to the University

Because of its location near Dow, the school had many ties to the company. Off-campus classes were conducted by CMU faculty at Dow installations, some professors consulted with Dow, and CMU alumni were employed there. Dow employees attended evening MBA classes at the school. Dow contributed to the school in a variety of ways, including about $70,000 a year in direct, cash grants. In the previous year, 1976, for example, Dow had contributed $73,566 to the university and $70,000 of that had been used by the chemistry department to get a new spectrometer. Dow also contributed through a matching fund program for employees. The company underwrote conferences at CMU, contributed Styrofoam to the art department, provided speakers for the journalism department, and gave surplus equipment to the industrial education and technology department. Dow also supported other universities and in 1977 gave $1 million to institutions around the country. (That amount has since increased.)

Reports of Jane Fonda's speech had, however, disturbed Paul F. Oreffice, 49, the chemical engineer who was president of Dow Chemical U.S.A. Oreffice is a dapper man, extremely intelligent, quick-witted, articulate, and animated by a desire to strike back at predatory critics and tyrannical regulators. Under his aggressive leadership Dow has acquired the reputation of a company that fights attackers in the social arena rather than remaining silent in the fear that assertiveness will bring retaliation. Oreffice, who had been president for one year at the time, decided to derail Dow funding for CMU, and on October 12 sent the following letter to Dr. Harold Abel, its president.

> Dear Dr. Abel:
>
> Yesterday's paper carried a front page story reporting that Jane Fonda was paid a fee of $3,500 to spread her venom against free enterprise to the student body at your university. Of course, it is your prerogative to have an avowed communist sympathizer like Jane Fonda, or anyone else speak at your university, and you can pay them whatever you please. I have absolutely no argument with that.
>
> While inviting Ms. Fonda to your campus is your prerogative, I consider it our prerogative and obligation to make certain our funds are never again used to support people intent upon destruction of freedom. Therefore, effective immediately, support of any kind from the Dow Chemical Company to Central Michigan University has been stopped, and will not resumed until we are convinced our dollars are not expended in supporting those who would destroy us.
>
> In addition, resumption of any Dow aid to Central Michigan is contingent on balancing the scales of what your students hear. I am open to an invitation to give a speech to a group of students similar to the one Ms. Fonda addressed, for the same fee. This fee will be donated to a non-profit organization which supports the free enterprise system.
>
> Yours very truly,
>
> Paul F. Oreffice

It was intended by Oreffice to be a confidential letter, but the secret was hard to keep. Faculty teaching at Dow plant sites and students who were employees at Dow knew something was in the wind. Rumors began. Finally, reporters from *Central Michigan Life*, the university's student newspaper, approached President Abel and asked directly what was happening with Dow. Abel declined comment. At about this time Dow officials decided to publish the letter to dispel rumors. The company released it on October 27. It appeared on the front page of *Central Michigan Life* on October 18 and immediately generated controversy.

With the release of the letter Oreffice made a statement reinforcing his position. "I have nothing to hide," he said, "the letter states exactly how I feel. I have no quarrel with the University's right to have whomever it wants to speak. I am only concerned that the other side is heard equally."[8] On the same day Phillip L. Schneider, manager of media public relations for Dow, told reporters for the student paper that the issue was not one of free speech rights and that funds to the University would be resumed when Oreffice received assurance that ". . . funds given to the University are not used to support those who come to advocate the overthrow of the free enterprise system in this country."[9]

President Abel wrote a letter to Oreffice indicating that he would "welcome the opportunity to talk to him" and to student reporters he added: "I don't know if it's appropriate to go further so I don't know what I'm going to do."[10]

Public Debate Favors Dow

In the meantime, the story was picked up by wire services, and newspapers and television stations editorialized on the issue. As the questions of free speech and academic freedom involved became clear, a rushing cataract of public opinion was released. Dow received the first of more than 3,000 letters it was eventually to accumulate. Schneider estimates that 90 percent of the letters, many from college faculty, favored the Dow funding cut-off. An example is this excerpt from a letter by an attorney.

> I congratulate you and enthusiastically support your moves. I firmly believe that the average American citizen is disgusted by the Fonda types and we should make our thoughts known to the Institutions [sic] of higher learning that are evidently not aware of the "Real World." Your type of move is needed more often and should bring them to their senses. CONGRATULATIONS!

Similarly, House at CMU estimates that about 90 percent of "hundreds" of letters coming to the campus were critical and calls some of them "violently critical." One scrawled note signed by 30 people read: "HOORAY FOR DOW. Sick of Fonda. What's her bitch she's already made her money from free enterprise." Many letters arrived anonymously and at least one writer enclosed a "once cherished alumnus card." Another typical letter read:

> I laud Paul Oreffice . . . for withdrawing support from your university after such a fiasco.
> I also ask the question—why is MY TAX MONEY, which is allocated to CMU by the State of Michigan being used for such purposes—to overthrow the very business which is the lifeblood of this country—free enterprise.
> How many jobs has Jane Fonda created in the United States of America? How many jobs has Dow Chemical created?
> This woman has been known for her sympathies to those nations such as North Korea, which country hates the United States and would like nothing better than to see us fold up.
> If we allow such persons as Jane Fonda to speak their poison among our young people, what can we expect from future generations.

On October 31, an editorial in *Central Michigan Life* took up the defense of the school. It read, in part:

> Like a spoiled child who did not get his way, Dow Chemical Co. U.S.A. has taken all its corporate support from CMU and gone home to sulk. Some people, it seems, just have not learned money cannot buy everything, especially the rights to freedom of expression.
> . . . A University is a place for an exchange of ideas stretching across the vast spectrum of thinking in this world. Speakers should be brought to this campus on the basis of what they have to say and the educational content of the messages. Decisions to bring speakers here should not be based upon whether the speaker will anger some University supporter such as Dow.

President Abel issued a statement the next day expressing his determination to "preserve the freedom of individual expression on the campus and protect the intellectual independence of the University." However, a telephone survey of 626 people in nearby Saginaw by The Saginaw News on November 2, resulted in 67 percent of the respondents favoring Dow's withholding of funds. Jane Fonda, reached in Los Angeles for comment, told a staff writer of The Saginaw News that, "This is a case of corporate blackmail—a giant corporation trying to dictate to a state university who students can invite to speak and what ideas can be discussed."[11]

Oreffice Further Defends His Position

In the wake of press controversy Oreffice granted an exclusive interview to James Reindl, student editor of Central Michigan Life. The Dow president elaborated his position and described how he was born under a dictatorship and how his family fled Italy after the rise of Mussolini. "So I'm a great advocate of free speech," he insisted, "I'd just like to make sure our money is not used to [pay for] those that speak against free enterprise, which I think has made this country great."[12] Oreffice noted that big business gets criticized unjustly and has "no chance for defense."[13] Business, he explained, should look more carefully into what it is supporting and that is not a violation of free speech.

On November 4, Oreffice met with President Abel of CMU and after a meeting that both described as cordial, it was jointly announced that Oreffice had been invited to speak at Central in 1978 and to sponsor a symposium on free enterprise. No promises about future behavior in inviting speakers were made by Abel, and Oreffice did not promise to restore funding, although he emphasized that the funding cut-off applied only to future grants and did not include the employee matching grant program.

Public Controversy Continues

The meeting of the leaders failed to quiet controversy in the press, where people continued to take sides. A letter to The Saginaw News on November 7 read in part:

> Great. Right on. Its about time someone took a stand against kooks who would destroy free enterprise. Withdrawing dollars from CMU may not be enough. Maybe a good look should be taken at curricula which appears to generate an "over-flow" crowd at such talks, or groups that sponsor them.
> A little book-burning in the defense of free enterprise may not be all that bad.

An associate professor from Delta College wrote:

> The leadership of the Dow Chemical Company should be commended . . . . Hopefully, other companies will follow suit and just maybe we can get this great country going again.
> It is a disgrace the way the irresponsible radicals and other liberals have gone unchecked in spreading their anti-American garbage. Many of our campuses have become a breeding ground for this kind of ferment—mainly because they are almost totally lacking in real leadership.

But Edna Garte, assistant professor of art history at CMU, penned a letter in *Central Michigan Life* that echoed the main theme of many who attacked Dow's imperiousness. The last paragraph of her letter of November 7 is:

> As I understood it, the thrust of Ms. Fonda's lecture was that large companies and power blocks have been exercising too much control over our lives. A decision, on the part of Dow, to suspend funding to the University, does not seem to be the most effective way to combat this argument.

John A. Puravs, a columnist with *The Saginaw News*, chided both sides in the affair. His column of November 8 included these paragraphs.

> What Jane Fonda has to say is of little real consequence. The views of the left can be presented far more coherently by other men and women than an actress dabbling in causes she doesn't fully understand.
> What does matter is that for its own sake, American business learns to deal with the public—and that academia learns to stop abusing true academic freedom by claiming a monopoly on the liberty of expression.

Dow Funding Continues as the Issue Quiets Down

Jane Fonda, at the invitation of CMU students and faculty of the department of sociology and anthropology, declared that she wanted an encore. Students and faculty debated the best forum for a return engagement. Some wanted a debate between Oreffice and Fonda. Others wanted them to give separate speeches and answer questions from the audience, either on the same day or in the same week. Ms. Fonda also threatened to sue Dow. Invited for a return appearance on December 5, however, she notified the university that previous film-making commitments would keep her from attending. No more was heard from her about legal action.

During the Abel-Oreffice meeting of November 4, it had been agreed that future funding arrangements between Central and Dow would be subject to an evolving dialogue between them. Two years later, both sides agreed that not a penny of Dow money was ever cut off and presidential assistant House says that relations with Dow are "normalized" and its support continues.

In the spring of 1979, Paul Oreffice spoke to a respectful audience of students in University Center Auditorium, a 310-seat meeting hall much smaller than Warriner Auditorium where Jane Fonda had addressed 1,500 persons. The university administration had scheduled Oreffice there, sensing a decline of student interest and not wishing to face the embarrassment of a half-filled room. However, the smaller auditorium was filled and standees increased the head count to 500. A few students had to be turned away. Oreffice, a compelling speaker, answered questions about his threat to cut off funds and, according to some, won the audience over. A tape of the speech was broadcast later on the University's FM radio station. Oreffice did not receive a fee.

Since the Fonda speech controversy the CMU administration has been more conscious of the need to insure ideological balance among speakers appearing on campus. In the past, lecture and concert programs were turned over to committees, giving the administration little influence over the invitation process. House explains that while the university does not, of course, exercise prior censorship of speakers, it has now started a Platform Series under administrative control. The series, established partly because of the Fonda-Dow affair, began operation in 1978 and the first speaker was invited in 1979. Other groups on campus continue to be free to invite speakers without administrative restriction and the platform series exists to counterbalance inadvertent ideological excess.

More Funding Restrictions in the Future?

In concluding this narrative it may be noted that at Dow's 1979 annual shareholders meeting four resolutions attaching conditions to the corporation's support of colleges and universities were proposed, including one that recommended no funding to institutions that employed avowed Communists, Marxists, Leninists, or Maoists.[14] Dow's management declined to recommend voting for or against the proposal, which received 14.4 percent of votes cast. None of the other proposals passed either, but Dow shareholders gave them higher percentages of support than did shareholders at the annual meetings of duPont and Colgate-Palmolive who were faced with similar votes. Phillip Schneider, manager of media relations at Dow, in 1979 denies any relationship between the appearance of these shareholder resolutions and the Dow-CMU controversy two years before.[15]

Nevertheless, it can be noted that should public criticism of business continue to be present at high levels, other business leaders may take and encourage actions similar to those described in this case. Paul Oreffice's action may be seen as a rare and bold response by the leader of a corporation smarting under radical criticism, excessive regulation, and memories of past public calumny. Similar circumstances, repeated widely in the future, pose the specter of repetition by other corporations.

CASE QUESTIONS

1. Should the university administration have intervened in the decision to invite Jane Fonda to speak?

2. Did Dow infringe upon the academic freedom of Central Michigan University by threatening to cut off funding? Was Dow's action an exercise of free speech?

3. How did the definitions of freedom of speech differ between Oreffice and the university community?

4. Was Oreffice's strong action a public relations plus or minus? Would it be beneficial if other companies followed suit? Are there better ways to fight public criticism?

Notes

1. Richard T. Cooper and Paul E. Steiger, "How One Big Firm Fought Health Perils," *Los Angeles Times,* June 27, 1976.
2. One who does is William G. Capitman in *Panic in the Boardroom* (New York: Anchor Press/Doubleday, 1973), p. 123.
3. Reported in "The Impact of Government Regulation," The Dow Chemical Company, 1977.
4. A published study by Dow researchers which supports this conclusion is Gerald Ott, Benjamin B. Holder, and R. R. Langner, "Determinants of Mortality in an Industrial Population," *Journal of Occupational Medicine,* Vol. 18, No. 3 (March 1976), pp. 171–177. Dr. Holder, in an interview with John Steiner on August 16, 1979, cautioned, however, that a "healthy worker effect" exists in such studies. Because of the screening process for employment at corporations like Dow, workers are healthier as a group than the United States white male population, which is not a screened group.
5. This information and all subsequent quotations attributable to Dr. Charles House are from interviews on July 20 and August 16, 1979, conducted by John Steiner.
6. This quotation and others not otherwise attributed are from an interview with Ms. Fonda on August 6, 1979, by John Steiner.
7. From Richard J. Barnet and Ronald E. Muller, *Global Reach: The Power of the Multinational Corporations* (New York: Simon and Schuster, 1974).
8. Kathy Jennings and James Reindl, "Dow Cancels Aid to CMU," *Central Michigan Life,* October 28, 1979.
9. *Ibid.*
10. Kathy Jennings and James Reindl, "Abel Silent About Amount of Dow Gifts, Grants to CMU," *Central Michigan Life,* October 31, 1977.
11. Holly Hayes, "Dow Withdraws CMU Grants," *The Saginaw News,* October 29, 1977.
12. James J. Reindl, "Dow Chief: Fonda Abuses Free-Speech Right," *The Saginaw News,* November 4, 1977.
13. *Ibid.*
14. Jack Magarrell, "Stockholders Reject Resolutions Aimed at Campus Communists," *The Chronicle of Higher Education,* June 25, 1979.
15. Interview with Phillip Schneider on July 19, 1979 by John Steiner.

DISCUSSION GUIDES ON CHAPTER CONTENT ————————

1. What are the trends in attitudes toward business in America?

2. Discuss the various factors that account for negative attitudes toward American business.

3. Compare and contrast criticisms of American business made by Marxists and radical non-Marxists.

4. What is the nature of the leftist challenge to American business?

5. Do you agree that despite strong criticism of business, there exists considerable support for the American private enterprise system?

MIND-STRETCHING QUESTIONS ——————————————————

1. In what way do you think American business might be changed in the future as a result of public antipathy?

2. As an optimist, could you justify the statement that current public attitudes to business are conducive to the continuing vitality of American private enterprise?

8

THE NEW DEMANDS ON BUSINESS

A) CAMPAIGN GM*

In 1970 the Project on Corporate Responsibility was created by Ralph Nader in Washington, D.C., and leaped into prominence with its "Campaign GM." The broad aims of the Project on Corporate Responsibility concerned such goals as making "corporate decision-makers more responsive to legitimate social demands, such as the need to end employment discrimination and develop the resources of economically disadvantaged communities." The main strategy of the Project was to get proxies from nonprofit institutions to vote proposals prepared by the Project.

Campaign GM was the first significant move of the Project. Two basic demands were made on the General Motors Corporation at its annual stockholders meeting in May 1970, as follows: first, set up a committee on corporate responsibility to study GM's performance in dealing with social and environmental issues and recommend changes "to make GM responsible"; and, second, place three "public interest" directors on the board.

The details of these two proposals as submitted to the stockholders of record, together with management's reasons why stockholders should reject them, are as follows:

The Committee for Corporate Responsibility—Proposal[1]

> Whereas the shareholders of General Motors are concerned that the present policies and priorities pursued by the management have failed to take into account the possible adverse social impact of the Corporation's activities, it is
> Resolved that:
> 1) There be established the General Motors Shareholders Committee for Corporate Responsibility.
> 2) The Committee for Corporate Responsibility shall consist of no less than fifteen and no more than twenty-five persons, to be appointed by a representative of the Board of Directors, a representative of the Campaign to Make General Motors Responsible, and a representative of United Auto Workers, acting by majority vote. The members of the Committee for Corporate Responsibility shall be chosen to represent the following: General Motors management, the United Auto Workers, environmental and conservation groups, consumers, the academic community,

*Prepared by George A. Steiner

38

civil rights organizations, labor, the scientific community, religious and social service organizations, and small shareholders.

3) The Committee for Corporate Responsibility shall prepare a report and make recommendations to the shareholders with respect to the role of the corporation in modern society and how to achieve a proper balance between the rights and interests of shareholders, employees, consumers and the general public. The Committee shall specifically examine, among other things:

    A. The Corporation's past and present efforts to produce an automobile which:

        (1) is non-polluting

        (2) reduces the potentiality for accidents

        (3) reduces personal injury resulting from accidents

        (4) reduces property damage resulting from accidents

        (5) reduces the costs of repair and maintenance whether from accidents or extended use.

    B. The extent to which the Corporation's policies towards suppliers, employees, consumers and dealers- are contributing to the goals of providing safe and reliable products.

    C. The extent to which the Corporation's past and present efforts have contributed to a sound national transportation policy and an effective low-cost mass transportation system.

    D. The manner in which the Corporation has used its vast economic power to contribute to the social welfare of the nation.

    E. The manner by which the participation of diverse-sectors of society in corporate decision-making can be increased including nomination and election of directors and selection of members of the committees of the Board of Directors.

4) The Committee's report shall be distributed to the shareholders and to the public no later than March 31, 1971. The committee shall be authorized to employ staff members in the performance of its duties. The Board of Directors shall allocate to the Committee those funds the Board of Directors determines reasonably necessary for the Committee to accomplish its tasks. The Committee may obtain any information from the Corporation and its employees reasonably deemed relevant by the Committee, provided, however, that the Board of Directors may restrict the information to be made available to the Committee to information which the Board of Directors reasonably determines to be not privileged for business or competitive reasons.

The Stockholder has submitted the following statement in support of such resolution:

Reasons: "The purpose of this resolution is to enable shareholders to assess the public impact of the Corporation's decisions, and to determine the proper role of the Corporation in society. Past efforts by men such as Ralph Nader to raise these issues have been frustrated by the refusal of management to make its files and records available either to the shareholders or to the public. Only a committee representing a broad segment of the public with adequate resources and access to information can prepare a report which will accomplish these objectives."

The Board of Directors favors a vote **AGAINST** this resolution for the following reasons:

This resolution and the Proposal for Directors to Represent Special Interests by the same sponsor are parts of an attack on the General Motors Board of Directors and management and on what General Motors has achieved on behalf of its stockholders and the public. In the opinion of the Board of Directors and management the attack is based on false conceptions and assumptions. It was launched by a stockholder (the Project), composed of seven members, which purchased 12 shares of General Motors stock in January 1970 for the express purpose of this attack. The Project has announced that while General Motors is its first target, similar attacks will be made on other large corporations.

The Project is a nonprofit corporation organized this year under the laws of the District of Columbia. Its formation was announced by Ralph Nader. Although he has stated that he is "not a formal participant in the Project" and that the "program" affecting General Motors is one "undertaken by a number of other young attorneys in Washington," he has promoted the Project and the Campaign to Make General Motors Responsible ("Campaign GM") by press interview, television appearance and otherwise. For many years he has been identified with various campaigns against General Motors and was a prominent participant in a demonstration against the Corporation at the General Motors Building in New York in December 1969.

The names "Committee for Corporate Responsibility" and "Campaign to Make General Motors Responsible" together with this resolution which would establish a Committee for Corporate Responsibility and the statements in support of the resolution suggest that management's decisions "have failed to take into account the possible adverse social impact of the Corporation's activities. . . ." This simply is not true. The true facts in regard to the concern and responsibility with which General Motors has pursued goals of social and public policy are set forth in the enclosed booklet, "GM's Record of Progress." We are proud of this record and all stockholders are urged to read the booklet.[2]

The objective of the resolution is to interpose a body unknown to corporate law or practice (the Committee for Corporate Responsibility)—purportedly investigatory in nature but structured for harassment and publicity—between the stockholders and the Board of Directors. The establishment of such a Committee would seriously hamper the Board of Directors in representing the stockholders and in carrying out its responsibilities to manage the business and affairs of the Corporation.

The proposed Committee, far from achieving "a proper balance between the rights and interest of shareholders, employees, consumers and the general public," is proposed to be appointed "by majority vote" of (i) a representative of "Campaign GM," which is a creature of the proponent of the resolution, (ii) a representative of the United Auto Workers, and (iii) a representative of the Board of Directors. This permits the crucial "majority vote," with power to elect the entire Committee, to be supplied by a representative of "Campaign GM" (which itself owns no General Motors stock) and by a representative of the United Auto Workers. Members of the Committee would not be required to be stockholders of General Motors and would be chosen to represent General Motors management, the U.A.W., environmental and conservation groups, consumers, the academic community, civil rights organizations, labor, the scientific community, religious and social service organizations and small stockholders. It is obvious that the proponent of the resolution seeks this Committee to pursue its special interests.

The proposed method of appointing the proposed Committee makes it clear that its purpose is to harass the Corporation and its management and to promote the particular economic and social views espoused by the proponent of the resolution. The Board of Directors believes that this resolution, if adopted, would do serious damage to General Motors and to its stockholders and, in fact, to the general public.

The Board of Directors favors a vote **AGAINST** this Proposal. . . . Proxies solicited by the Board of Directors will be so voted unless stockholders specify in their proxies a contrary choice.

Directors to Represent Special Interests—Proposal

> Resolved: That Number 15 of the By-Laws of the Corporation be amended to read as follows:

15) The business of the Corporation shall be managed by a board of twenty-six members (an addition of three).

The Stockholder has submitted the following statement in support of such resolution:

> Reasons: This amendment will expand the number of directors to enable representatives of the public to sit on the Board of Directors without replacing any of the current nominees of management. The proponents of this amendment believe that adding representatives of the public to the Board is one method to insure that the Corporation will consider the impact of its decisions on important public issues, including auto safety, pollution, repairs, mass transportation and equal employment opportunities.

The Board of Directors favors a vote **AGAINST** this resolution for the following reasons:

> The Board of Directors finds no valid reason why the number of directors should be increased at the present time. Any suggestion that General Motors Corporation has been deficient in considering the interest of the public in such matters as auto safety, pollution, mass transportation and the like is entirely contrary to fact; the Company's record in this regard is set forth in the enclosed booklet.
>
> The Board of Directors believes that each director, in addition to his responsibility to represent all the stockholders, has a very important responsibility to customers, employees, the public and society generally. This is in accord with the development of the modern American corporation and corporate theory to which General Motors wholeheartedly subscribes and in accordance with which it operates. But that is very different from having as members of the Board individuals, no matter how worthy, who would be elected to represent special interests and who would feel obliged to concentrate attention on those special interests whether or not the effect would be to disrupt the proper and effective functioning of the Board.
>
> Moreover, the Board of Directors continues to believe that for a board of directors to be effective each member must feel a responsibility to represent all the stockholders. In fact, representation of special groups introduces the possibility of partisanship among board members, which would impair the ability to work together, a requirement essential to the efficient functioning of a board of directors.
>
> Stockholders should recognize that the resolution to amend the By-Laws to increase the number of Directors is not a simple, innocuous proposal. The real issue posed by this proposal is whether an opportunity should be created to inject into the Corporation's Board of Directors three additional directors who are selected not on the basis of their interest in the success of the Corporation but rather on the basis of their sympathy with the special interests of the proponent of the resolution. This is proposed under the guise that as "representatives of the public" they would insure that the Corporation "will consider the impact of its decisions on important public issues." The proposal is a reflection upon the service rendered to the Corporation and its stockholders by the present members of the Board of Directors who were elected because of their integrity and broad experience in many fields including public service. The suggestion that they have

not taken into account the impact of their decisions upon the public has no basis in fact. The objective of this proposal is substantially the same as that of the proposal for the Committee for Corporate Responsibility.

If the proponent should be successful in increasing the number of directors and thereafter electing·its nominees, the Board of Directors believes there would be similar internal harassment to the detriment of General Motors, its stockholders and the public.

The Board of Directors favors a vote **AGAINST** this proposal. . . . Proxies solicited by the Board of Directors will be so voted unless stockholders specify in their proxies a contrary choice.*

The Project requested large holders of GM stock to provide proxies to be used at the annual stockholders meeting to enforce its demands. Various university boards of trustees—Harvard, California, Michigan, and Texas, for instance—were requested to give The Project their proxies. Other large holders such as charitable foundations also were solicited. No large holder gave the Project proxies. Some, however, sympathized with its views. The Rockefeller Foundation, for instance, cast its vote with management, but in explaining its position criticized the corporation. Some excerpts follow:

> There are constituents other than stockholders to whom corporations are also obligated. There are battles to be waged against racism, poverty, pollution, and urban blight which the Government alone cannot win; they can be won only if the status and power of American corporate industry are fully and effectively committed to the struggle. What is needed from business today is leadership which is courageous, wise and compassionate, which is enlightened in its own and the public's interest, and which greets change with an open mind. In our judgment, the management of General Motors did not display this spirit in its response to the two proposals offered by Campaign GM [a subgroup of the Committee on Corporate Responsibility].
>
> We recognize that these proposals are, from management's viewpoint, unwieldy and impractical; Campaign GM itself conceded the difficulty it encountered in trying to determine a method of selecting members of a Committee for Corporate Responsibility. Because of these inadequacies we are prepared, this time, to sign our proxy as requested by management. But we are not prepared to let the matter rest there.
>
> We do not share the view which was expressed by management that the Campaign GM proposals represent an 'attack' on the corporation. . . We believe the language of the Campaign GM proposals is more reasonable and temperate than the response of management. We also believe the goals of the proposals have been designed to serve the public good by increasing the corporation's awareness of the major impact of its decisions and policies on society at large.†

The demands of Campaign GM were not met because the overwhelming majority of stockholders gave their proxies to GM's management. Reactions in 1970, however, seemed to portend trouble for GM's management in 1971.

In September 1970 the General Motors Corporation announced that it was responding to criticism that the company's decisions sometimes did not take the

*This portion of the article is reprinted with the permission of *The Wall Street Journal,* © Dow Jones & Company, Inc., 1970.

†From General Motors Corporation, Proxy Statement for Annual Meeting of Stockholders held May 22, 1970. Reproduced with permission.

public welfare into consideration by forming a Public Policy Committee made up of five GM directors. Mr. Roche, chairman of the Board of Directors, said that matters associated with community action and corporate citizenship would have as a result, "a permanent place on the highest level of management." He said that he antici- pated the work of the committee "will demonstrate their understanding of General Motors and its industry, their awareness of the expanding role of business in society and their comprehension of the responsibilities of the board of directors, who are charged with the successful operation of the business." The committee "will inquire into all phases of General Motors' operations that relate to matters of public policy and recommend actions to the full board." None of the members of the committee were officers of GM.

In January 1971 General Motors invited the Reverend Leon H. Sullivan to be- come the first black member of its board of directors. Reverend Sullivan, in com- menting on his appointment, said:

> I told Mr. Roche he should have no illusions about what I am. He knows I'm a man who expresses his opinions, and that I will not be tied to the traditions of the board. I'm more interested in human returns than capital returns. My main concern is helping to improve the position of black people in America. I want to be a voice from the outside on the inside.[3]

At the May 1971 stockholders meeting, Campaign GM advanced new proposals to make GM "accountable to the people their decisions affect." These included a requirement that GM list in the proxy it sends to shareholders the names of sug- gested directors made by nonmanagement shareholders; a proposal to require GM to disclose in its annual report information about such matters as minority hiring, air pollution, and automobile safety policies so that shareholders "may accurately evaluate the performance of management in meeting public responsibilities in these areas"; and a proposal to permit GM's key constituencies—employees, consumers, and dealers—to participate in the election of three of the directors of the company.

These proposals were overwhelmingly defeated. The Project on Corporate Re- sponsibility held only 12 of GM's 286 million shares of stock and were able to gather together less than 3 percent of the shares voted. This was a smaller per- centage than in 1970.

In 1972 The Project on Corporate Responsibility made two new proposals. One would require the directors of General Motors to appoint a committee to study the desirability of dividing the company into several independent corporations. The proposal suggested that GM be broken up because its fear of antitrust action by the government had prevented it from competing for a larger share of the market. The function of the committee, therefore, would be to determine whether breaking up GM was in the best interests of the public and could also maximize profits for the separate companies thus formed. The second proposal called for regular progress reports from GM's Public Policy Committee. These proposals received less than two percent of the votes cast.

In three annual meetings, the overwhelming number of stockholders gave GM's management their vote of confidence and flatly rejected the proposals of the Project. By the size of the vote, it is obvious that even the foundations and nonprofit institutions holding GM stock voted with management.

CASE QUESTIONS

1. Identify the fundamental issues raised in this case study about the business-society relationship and the way corporations are influenced and managed.

2. If you were a shareholder in GM, would you give your proxy to management or to the Project? Explain.

3. Argue the pros and cons of the Project's proposal for the Committee for Social Responsibility. (See Henry G. Manne, "Who's Responsible?" *Barrons,* May 17, 1971.)

4. Who is to determine what are the responsibilities of a company like General Motors?

5. Argue the pros and cons of placing special interest representatives on boards of directors of American corporations. (See Harold Koontz, "The Corporate Board and Special Interests," *Business Horizons,* October 1971, pp. 75–93.) For a succinct yet wide-ranging commentary on the challenge to corporate boards of directors see "The Board of Directors Faces Challenge and Change," *The Conference Board Record,* February 1972, pp. 39–54. For an evaluation of the new liability of boards of directors, see Robert M. Estes, "Outside Directors: More Vulnerable Than Ever," *Harvard Business Review,* January-February 1973, pp. 107–114.

Notes

1. See, "A Proposal on Corporate Responsibility" (Washington, D.C.: Center for Law and Social Policy, and the Washington Research Project, October 20, 1969.) Reprinted by permission of General Motors Corporation.

2. For a more recent report see *General Motors Public Interest Report* (Detroit: General Motors Corporation, 1979).

3. *Business Week,* April 10, 1971, p. 100.

B) CONSOLIDATED INDUSTRIES FORECASTS CHANGING SOCIAL VALUES AND DEMANDS

Consolidated Industries is one of the largest manufacturing companies in the world. The major products that account for the bulk of its sales are chemicals, steel, aircraft, trucks, and consumer-durable goods. It also produces a wide variety of other commodities. Among these are special metals, light agricultural equipment, small office appliances, medical instruments, and scientific toys.

In recent years, the top management of the company has been attacked with unusual force by such various groups as the Sierra Club, Ralph Nader's "raiders," local communities in which the company does business, and student activists.

This company prides itself on the skill with which it develops long-range plans and has asserted repeatedly that its great success has been due in no small part to the quality of these plans. Top management has decided, however, that if its plans are to be effective in the future it is necessary for the company to have a much better understanding of those changing social values that will particularly affect it.

CASE QUESTIONS

You are hired as a consultant to advise the company on how to forecast changing social values and the consequent demands that will be of major concern to the company over the next ten years. What would you suggest?

For a short analysis of major methods see Robert F. Lusch and Gene R. Laczniak, "Futures Research for Managers," *Business,* January-February 1979. For brief discussions of how some companies do this see Burt Nanus, "The Future-Oriented Corporation," *Business Horizons,* February 1975. For a thorough analysis of the state of the art see Wayne I. Boucher, ed., *The Study of the Future: An Agenda For Research,* Washington, D.C.: U.S. Government Printing Office, July 1977. For a detailed analysis of what companies are doing today to identify future issues of importance to them see James K. Brown, *This Business of Issues: Coping With the Company's Environments* (New York: The Conference Board, 1979).

DISCUSSION GUIDES ON CHAPTER CONTENT

1. The authors claim that a major new demand on business is to help society achieve its goals. What does this mean? If a person took this seriously, how might he or she determine what society's goals were?

2. Another major new demand on business is to improve the quality of life. What does this mean?

3. If you were asked by the president of a large company to determine what demands were being made upon the company by its constituents, how would you do it?

4. Which of the critical public issues of the 1980s do you think will provide the greatest opportunities for GM? Which pose the greatest threats to the company?

5. Do you believe that the expectations most people have about what business should do are unrealistic?

6. How have managerial philosophies changed to keep pace with changing business conditions?

7. Do you think the Bank of America's standards for top executives are ones that other companies should adopt?

8. In what major ways are new managerial philosophies and current demands on business changing the way managers manage?

MIND-STRETCHING QUESTION

1. Are there ways in which business organizations could substantially shape the nature of societal demands on them, apart from merely anticipating and adapting to such demands?

9
CORPORATE POWER, PLURALISM, AND LEGITIMACY

A) THE DOW PETROCHEMICAL PROJECT[*]

On January 19, 1977, the Dow Chemical Company announced that it was dropping its plans to build a $500 million petrochemical complex in California. The company's press release said that managers had spent more than two years and $4 million in an attempt to obtain necessary permits to build the complex, and cited excessive delays and costs in the permitting process as the major reason for terminating the project.

Because of subsequent investigations by the California legislature and attendent public statements by legislators and state regulatory employees, the public beyond the San Francisco bay area first became aware of the serious consequences of one of the major industry-environmental confrontations of the 1970s. The controversy was to grow among California lawmakers and regulators and spill over into the national scene, where it would augment pressure on the U.S. Environmental Protection Agency and the U.S. Congress for modification of the Federal Clean Air Act.

At stake are not simply the technical requirements of the act, but the manner of interpretation of those requirements by federal, state, and local officers. Perhaps more importantly, what has come to be known as "the Dow Case" has called into question the entire bureaucratic process by which governmental agencies at various levels evaluate applications for permits to construct and operate industrial facilities.

The "process," it is claimed, is often rife with overlapping jurisdictions, conflicting laws, and widely differing interpretations of federal, state, and local laws, arrived at independently by various agencies. The experience of Dow and other industrial firms with the process had been characterized as being "too long, too costly, and too indefinite." Some have concluded with California State Senator John Holmdahl that for industry "the unwelcome sign is out."

A Business Decision

The long and frustrating experience of the planners at Dow Chemical U.S.A. began with a decision to build a petrochemical complex near Collinsville in Solano County,

*Prepared by C. Wesley Morse

47

California, on the Sacramento River. Dow executives viewed the proposed plant as an expansion of their Pittsburg, California, plant located on the San Joaquin River, in the Sacramento Delta four and a half miles away. The purpose of the new facility would be to produce olefins and their derivatives: basic feedstocks for a wide variety of chemical products consumed on the west coast. Dow was currently supplying olefins from its Texas and Louisiana plants and would at decision time derive a $56 million annual saving in freight alone from west coast production. Stanford Research Institute had estimated that by 1980, Dow would derive a $160 million annual freight saving. North slope Alaska oil was becoming available and west coast refineries were expected to produce an ample supply of naphtha (which together with salt would be Dow's basic raw material) for the company's needs. It was rumored that Dow marketers had their eyes on a 40 percent share of west coast petrochemical demand.

The expansion called for construction of 13 production units which were to be integrated and mutually supportive and which were also to be integrated with the company's existing production facilities at Pittsburg. Land required for this expansion was about 800 acres. The company had only 200 acres of undeveloped land at its 450-acre Pittsburg site and there was no additional land available in the area that could be purchased and would be suitable to accommodate the expansion. Because of this, the company acquired a site in Solano County, located directly across the San Joaquin and Sacramento Rivers from the company's Pittsburg site, and proposed to tie the two sites together with pipelines. The pipelines were to be buried beneath the river beds. The primary production mission of the Solano County plants would be to produce feedstocks to be delivered to the Pittsburg site via the underground pipelines.

The basic feedstock for the new plants is naphtha, a low grade form of gasoline produced from petroleum. Naphtha has an octane rating of about 30, compared to an octane rating of 90 which is required for an acceptable grade of gasoline. Conversion of refining facilities in the San Francisco area to nonleaded gasolines was expected to create substantial excess supplies of naphtha in the near future, creating both an air pollution and a disposal problem unless facilities existed to convert this naphtha into products other than gasoline. Dow managers expected to be able to purchase the company's naphtha requirements from San Francisco area refineries and transport it by barge to the new production sites.

Dow planners had estimated that it would cost more than $500 million (in 1975 dollars) to construct the facilities over a five- to seven-year period. About 1,000 construction workers would be required to build the plants. Once completed, the plants would be expected to provide 1,000 new permanent basic manufacturing jobs, 600 of these being in Contra Costa County and 400 of them in Solano County. These jobs would have an estimated annual payroll of $15 million. The facilities would increase the tax base in Contra Costa County by about five percent and the tax base in Solano County would be increased by 14 percent.

The company's Pittsburg site was already zoned for heavy industrial use. The Solano County site chosen is a 2,700-acre parcel which in 1971 was included in the Solano County general plan for water-oriented heavy industrial development. The land itself is isolated, remote marginal agricultural land located in rolling hills with elevations up to 250 feet. Dry-farming practices are conducted in a three-year cycle. It produces grain one year; the second year it is used for sheep grazing on grain stubble; and it is allowed to lie fallow during the third year in this cycle. Value of the food and fibre products produced on the ranch is $70 per acre per year. This is considered to be the best agricultural use of this land. Before it was acquired by Dow it had been advertised nationally for three years as an industrial plant site.

Dow proposed to utilize about 800 acres of this site, leaving the remaining 1,900 acres in a green belt zone which would continue to be used for agricultural purposes.

The 13 units would include plants to produce styrene, ethylene, and propylene and there would be a benzene unit. From there, Dow planned to move downstream to ethylebenzene, cumene, phenol and acetone, propylene oxide, and high- and low-density polyethylene. There would be caustic chlorine, and a vinyl chloride unit that could well become a target of the environmentalists.

The materials to be produced in the Dow plants were basic in the sense that they would find their way into a wide variety of end products such as: soap, paper, insecticides, insulation, cleaning solvents, plywood, aluminum, steel, hospital equipment, furniture, and clothing, as well as auto bodies, boats, latex paint, kidney dialysis filters, Styrofoam plastic, brake fluid, and many others.

The Permit Process

Dow managers are old hands at coping with the environmental exigencies of new plant construction. Dow had installed new facilities of comparable size to the proposed Collinsville operation in the United States and abroad in recent years. The new plants were expected to be complex, but not a difficult challenge. The concern for environmental regulation held a high priority from the start. Dow claims to be in the forefront of industrial environmental concern, and from the first public statements managers expressed a commitment to maintain the quality of the environment in the Collinsville area.

The permit process began informally in the fall of 1974 with private discussions between corporate officials and governmental agencies about the feasibility of the proposed operations. The sequence of events that followed between Dow and governmental agencies is shown in exhibit 1.

It was determined that 65 permits would be required from 12 federal, state, and local agencies. These are listed in exhibit 2.

In February 1975, the company concluded that a plant at Collinsville would be feasible and managers publicly announced plans for construction. California law requires the designation of a "lead agency" to evaluate the impact of any project such as Dow's, and upon request the Governor's Office of Planning and Research designated Contra Costa County as a "party of special interest." Contra Costa was asked to participate in the environmental impact report (EIR) review process, to conduct its own hearings, make legal findings of adequacy, and to advise Solano County of its conclusions.

---------------------------- **EXHIBIT 1** ----------------------------

CHRONOLOGY OF GOVERNMENTAL AND PUBLIC CONSIDERATION
OF THE DOW PETROCHEMICAL PROJECT

Fall 1974	Dow officials met privately with local, regional, state, and federal government agencies to discuss plans for proposed project.
February 1975	Public announcement of plans.
August–December 1975	Environmental Impact Report completed and approved by Contra Costa and Solano Counties after extensive public hearings. Portion of Solano County site rezoned general manufacturing.
December 1975	Sierra Club, Friends of the Earth, and People for Open Space filed petition in Solano County Superior Court asking for a writ of mandate against Solano County for improper findings on EIR, canceling part of Williamson Act contract and rezoning of land.
January–April 1976	Applications for permits, easements, leases made to state agencies.
April 1976	Draft Environmental Statement published by U.S. Army Corps of Engineers for federal permits.
May 1976	Application for permit to Bay Area Pollution Control District for construction of styrene plant.
June 1976	Public hearing by Corps of Engineers. Secretary of State Resources Agency requested Corps to withhold approval of federal permits until state is satisfied with environmental impacts. State boards delay consideration of permit applications.
July 1976	Comments received on Draft Environmental Statement from interested persons.
August 1976	Denial of styrene permit by Bay Area Air Pollution Control Officer. Appeal to Hearing Board initiated by Dow. Hearings started September 16.
December 1976	Hearings for five state agencies on environmental effects of project convened by State Office of Planning and Research.
January 19, 1977	Dow withdraws from project.

---------------------------- **EXHIBIT 2** ----------------------------

DOW PETROCHEMICAL PROJECT
SUMMARY OF PERMITS REQUIRED

Federal	Purpose	Number Required	Total
U.S. Army Corps of Engineers	a) Dock and ship turning basin	1	1
	b) Water intake	1	1
	c) Water discharge	1	1
	d) Pipeline crossing	1	1
U.S. Coast Guard	a) Transport (operational) over dock	1	1
Subtotal (Federal)			5

State

Regional Water Board	a) NPDES for osmosis reject	1*	1*
	b) NPDES for water return on dredging spoils	1	1
	c) Certificate of conformance	1	1
	d) Evaporation ponds	1 ea. pond	2**
	e) Sanitary treatment (even if no discharge)	1	1
	f) Storm water run-off from land maintained in ag use	1	1
Water Resources Control Board	a) Appropriative water rights	1	1
Dept. of Water Resources	a) Dam safety	1	1
Fish and Game	a) Alteration of stream bed for dock, water intake, and pipelines	1 ea.	3
Reclamation Board	a) Alter levees	1	1
State Lands Commission	a) Lease for easements across state lands for dock, pipelines, and water intake	1	1
Bay Area Air Pollution Control District	a) Construction	1 each plant	13***
	b) Operation	1 each plant	13***
Subtotal (California)			40

Counties

Sacramento	a) Use permit for pipelines	1	1
Solano	a) Building	1 each plant	7
	b) Sanitary	1	1
	c) Potable water	1	1
	d) Grading	1	1
	e) Use permit for pipelines	1	1
Contra Costa	a) Building	1 each plant	6
	b) Grading	1	1
	c) Use permit for pipelines	1	1
Subtotal (Counties)			20
GRAND TOTAL			65

*Obtained September 26, 1975.
**Absolute minimum number of ponds is two.
***Absolute minimum since each plant has at least one vent.

Solano County, faced with the need for a massive EIR, and lacking expertise in such matters, went to J. B. Gilbert and Associates, a consulting firm in Sacramento that specialized in this type of work. Dow agreed to pay Gilbert's fee.

Environmentalists were later to refer consistently to the report as "Dow's EIR," not Solano County's.

After preparation of the report, Solano County began its consideration of the impact of Dow's project in September 1975. Copies of the report were sent to interested parties with requests for comments. Nicholas Arguimbau, attorney for the Sierra Club and the Environmental Defense Fund, recalls that they had to move rapidly. The Environmental Defense Fund did not receive its draft copy of the EIR until September 11. The County Planning Commission requested comments by September 18. On September 16, the EDF asked for a time extension, but hearings were held as planned, and on November 4, the County Commissioners approved the EIR.

In December, the Sierra Club, Friends of the Earth, and People for Open Space jointly filed suit against Solano County's Planning Commission, its Board of Supervisors, and the County itself. They asked that the permit process be halted, and they charged that the EIR did not adequately consider all of the environmental problems related to the proposed new plants.

Upon approval of the EIR by the County, Dow paid $230,000 in Williamson Act contract cancellation fees to the State of California, and the County rezoned 834 acres of Dow's site from agricultural to industrial. California's Williamson Act provides a ten-year tax break to farmers if they promise to keep their land in agriculture; however, the contract may be abrogated if back taxes and certain fees are paid to the state. Dow also negotiated agreements with the County regarding the maintenance of roads leading to the site during the construction period.

Following the Solano County approval, Dow managers filed applications for the state permits required (see exhibit 2), and began the federal environmental review process. This latter process is necessary for the federal permits indicated in exhibit 2. The federal process was conducted by the U.S. Army Corps of Engineers (the permit issuing agency) and required the approval of the U.S. Environmental Protection Agency. The federal Environmental Impact Statement (EIS) was completed and circulated by the Corps of Engineers in April 1976.

In May 1976 Dow made application to the Bay Area Air Pollution Control District for authorization to construct the first unit of the complex, a $50 million plant to convert ethylbenzene to styrene. To complete construction of all 13 units Dow needed 26 permits from the District. District regulations require that each unit must be treated as a separate plant and that a permit to construct and a permit to operate is required for each plant. Further, substantial construction must be underway within two years after each permit is granted. Each application requires a detailed description of the plant including storage tanks, all emission points and emission control equipment. The styrene plant has 14 emission points. Dow's engineering included consideration of each emission point and specification of effective control equipment.

The analysis of the application by the District's engineers resulted in their conclusion that all emissions were less than the District's requirements.

Dispersion calculations were then made to obtain values for ground-level concentrations of the emitted materials to determine whether these concentrations were deemed to be "significant."

The District's Regulations contain the following section:

> The Air Pollution Control Officer shall deny any authority to construct . . . any facility . . . which may cause the emission or creation of a *significant* quantity of any air contaminant which would interfere with the attainment or maintenance of any air quality standard . . . anywhere in the District.

The regulation does not define "significant quantity"; however, the Air Pollution Control Officer and his staff have adopted a criterion of "significance" in considering permit applications. The criterion is that a quantity of emission is a significant quantity if the dispersion calculations predict that it will result in a ground-level concentration that could be detected by air monitoring instrumentation.

In the case of combined sources, the District analyzes the several emission points and area sources individually and significance is achieved when the *sum* of the individual contributions exceeds the instrument sensitivity of detection.

These calculations showed that the Dow plant would emit significant quantities of hydrocarbon, NO_X, SO_2, and particulate.

Once the quantity of emissions has been determined, it remains to be determined whether the emissions will interfere with the attainment or maintenance of air quality standards. In the case where standards are exceeded or will be at the time of proposed source operation in the area impacted by a significant emission, a recommendation to deny the permit is made by the staff.

The staff determined that the Collinsville area in Solano County exceeds standards on several days per year for particulate, hydrocarbons, and oxidant. Thus, the permit was denied. Although the NO_X and SO_2 emissions were found to be significant quantities, the standards for these materials in the area were said not to be exceeded.

Dow says the styrene plant is a very clean plant and very low in emissions. The NO_X, SO_2, and particulate are due to the burning of fuel for the reactor. Eighty-three percent of the fuel is gas, 17 percent is oil or liquid process residue hydrocarbons. The emission values for fuel-burning were assigned values from the EPA compilation # AP-42. In some cases there are ranges given in AP-42, such as a range of 5 to 15 pounds of particulate per million standard cubic feet of gas burned. In such a case, the District assigns the highest number, that is, 15. The hydrocarbons are emitted from the burning of fuel, storage tanks, and process hardware. Average hydrocarbon emission is five pounds per hour. The District uses an instantaneous maximum emission of 13.5 pounds per hour, which can occur at a time of unloading a ship, which is about one day of each 45 days. This summing up of all worst possible conditions into the same time period is performed by the District to insure that the standard will not be exceeded under the worst possible conditions.

Dow managers felt the permit was denied by the Air Pollution Control Officer on the basis of "a very restrictive definition of significant quantity and of the federal and state ambient air quality standards."

The Air Pollution Control Officer told Dow that under present regulations there was no way he could grant a permit. He said the requirements of the EPA determined his decision, and the only remedy he could suggest was to persuade Congress to amend the Clean Air Act. Dow's response was to initiate an appeal of the permit denial with the Hearing Board of the Bay Area Air Pollution Control District.

Dow also disagreed with the conclusion of the San Francisco Air Pollution Control Officer that "detectability" has to take place inside the plant instead of at the plant boundary. Historically, Dow said, a plant's impact on ambient air quality has always been considered to take place at the plant boundary, where it impacts on air space to which the general public is exposed. Industrial hygiene standards (OSHA) were applied to the air environment within the plant. Dow believes that it can meet the detectability test being used by the Air Pollution Control Officer if it is applied at the boundary line.

The control officer, D. J. Callaghan, in an interview with *Chemical and Engineering News*, agreed that the styrene plant was a clean one. Callaghan said, holding his thumb and forefinger a few millimeters apart, "It was this close." However, in August he turned it down. "I was the only one to make a decision. Unfortunately, it was a negative decision. I had no other choice."

Early in 1975 the company planners had made application to several state agencies for permits, leases, and easements. At the time of Dow's troubles with the Air Pollution Control District, permits were pending before the Reclamation Board, Water Resources Control Board, and Department of Water Resources. Lease applications and easement requests had been made to the Fish and Game Department and State Lands Commission.

Several of these agencies were uncertain about their authority in interpreting the EIR as it related to the function of the agencies. Dow managers in fact claimed that the Secretary of the State Resources Agency had asked the Corps of Engineers to withhold decisions on all federal permits until the state was satisfied with concerns that it had about the project.

Thus, by the fall of 1976, Dow managers had achieved the approval of the project EIR by Solano County, and had arranged for the associated easement and road requirements. A total of four permits had been issued, and the company's land had been rezoned. Dow had struck out with Air Pollution Control (and was appealing its case), was moving slowly with state agencies, and federal permits were on the back burner. Managers calculated they would need 65 permits in total to finish the job, and the prospects were growing dimmer.

Pros and Cons

Public interest and involvement with the project had been growing steadily and by late 1976 the list of organizations involved in regulation, or lending support to one side or the other was quite impressive. *San Francisco Magazine* counted 81 such groups. They included both public and private organizations, ranging from the

U.S. Army Corps of Engineers to the Associated Students at the University of California, Davis, and included such disparate interests as the Associated General Contractors of California and Save Florida.

Dow drew major support from the counties of Solano and Contra Costa, the Contra Costa Taxpayers Association, The Bay Area Coalition of Labor and Business and organized labor in the form of the State Building and Construction Trades Council. These groups saw the benefit of jobs, trade, and an expanded tax base as paramount considerations.

On the other side of the issue were environmental forces led by the Sierra Club, Friends of the Earth, and People for Open Space. Their arguments focused on potential damage to the environment. While almost every possible environmental issue was discussed, several major problems occupied the center stage throughout "the process." These major issues together with the responses of Dow Chemical are as follows.

First, the opposition charged that the EIR was inadequate to assess the impact on the environment. The California Environmental Quality Act required the EIR to describe fully the expected impact of the project on "land, air, water, minerals, flora, fauna, ambient noise, and objects of historic or aesthetic significance." Dow defended the EIR as follows:

> The Environmental Impact Report that has been prepared for this project is one of the most thorough and extensive ever prepared for any major project conceived in California. It cost $750,000 and more than 30 consultants, all leading experts in their field, participated in its preparation.
>
> It was the subject of numerous public hearings and reviews in both Solano and Contra Costa counties. All state agencies and local government groups with an interest in the project commented extensively on the report, as did many public interest groups, school classes, and private citizens. Responses to all their questions and comments were prepared, reviewed and published before the reports were legally certified by both counties as an adequate assessment of the significant environmental, social and economic impacts of the project.
>
> This·process covered an 18 month period and was necessary before Dow could apply for the 70 different government permits that it must obtain before the project can be completed. Certain federal permits are also required and the entire state environmental review process must be duplicated at the federal level before the federal permits can be obtained. This federal review process is now underway.
>
> Environmental laws require that only the possible bad or adverse impacts of any project be reviewed and assessed. Environmental Impact Report writers must describe the worst possible situation that could conceivably happen, even if the situation is only a hypothetical one. They ignore any good impacts.
>
> The Environmental Impact Report on the Dow project weighs four pounds, and it covers every subject that the experience and imagination of man can conceive, from air, water and solid waste impacts to transportation, taxes, housing, agriculture, highways, schools, the economy, every area plant and animal species from birds to field mice.
>
> The plants Dow wants to build will have zero water pollution like our Pittsburg plant. They will have zero solid waste pollution. Air emissions will be well within any standard that is required.

Second, it was charged that the Dow plant would withdraw valuable agricultural land from farming uses. The Sierra Club claims that the Williamson Act contract was broken illegally, and that Solano County violated its general plan when it zoned 834 acres for industrial use. The Dow management responded:

> The plant site is presently used for dry farming. It produces barley and sheep. Historically it has provided a modest living for farm families. The land, by all standards, is marginal agricultural land.
>
> The Solano County general plan designated the area several years ago as one that it wanted to be used for industrial development.
>
> The land presently produces less than $70 worth of agricultural products per acre per year. These yields are less than one fourth of one percent of the average productivity of agricultural land in California. And the farming practices employed there are judged by all experts as being the best use that can be made of this land if it is used for agricultural purposes.
>
> Dow estimates that more than $50 million of products will be produced each year by its proposed new plants which will have both a direct and an indirect benefit for agriculture in California.

Third, there was concern that the entire area might be converted to an industrial complex if Dow were allowed to build. Opponents used the term "The Ruhr Valley of California" to describe their expectations for the area. In fact, Arco Chemical had announced plans to build a petrochemical plant roughly twice the size of Dow's proposed operation on an adjacent site. They had also been denied a permit by the APCD. National Steel and Pacific Gas and Electric also either owned or had optioned land nearby. Dow claimed:

> The Dow project does not depend upon other industrial development of the area. Our customers are already using the products we will produce. The only difference will be that we will produce them in California instead of on the Gulf Coast.
>
> What other companies do in the future will be determined by them and the decisions of Solano and Contra Costa County officials, as well as the multilayered and complex system of government agencies. They control the pace, style and type of development that occurs anywhere. Both counties, as well as the regional, state and federal government entities, have well trained, competent staffs.
>
> If other industries do locate in the area, we hope they will be required to meet the same high standards that are being required of Dow.

Fourth, opponents feared that since the plant would be located in the path of marine air blowing through the Carquinez Strait, this major source of fresh air for California's agriculturally rich Central Valley basin would be seriously polluted. Some experts believe that wind conditions and inversion heights make the basin a candidate for worse air pollution than the Los Angeles basin. It was claimed that because of these potential problems *any* addition of pollution to the atmosphere would be intolerable. Dow managers assessed the air pollution problem as follows:

> Dow's proposed plants will utilize the latest and best air control technology in the world. Many technological improvements have been made in recent years which are impractical or too costly to use in older plants but which can be designed into new plants today.
>
> If our plants cannot be designed to meet air standards, we will not be able to get permits to build them.

Will we be able to eliminate all air emissions? No one has been able to accomplish this. But we keep trying.

Fifth, the 55,000-acre Suisun Marsh is located a few miles downstream from Dow's proposed site. Some 202 species of birds and 26 mammal types live there. The marsh is also the wintering grounds for birds moving along the Pacific Flyway. The southern bald eagle and the peregrine falcon, both endangered species, inhabit the area. Critics warned that chemical spills from Dow manufacturing or shipping operations could devastate the marsh as well as threaten king salmon, striped bass, and sturgeon indigenous to the Sacramento river itself. Dow said:

> The marsh is a very tender and fragile wildlife resource and the possibility that our plants might have some impact on this area was the subject of much and careful thought before the Solano County site was selected. The marsh already has a number of industrial neighbors, located either adjacent to it or across the river. Many ships carrying chemicals and other products have been traversing the Sacramento River Channel in front of the marsh for years enroute to Stockton and Sacramento ports and to industrial locations in the Delta area. Dow ship traffic will be about three ships or barges per week. Damage to the marsh from Dow's operations if it occurred, would have to be from chemical spills caused by ship collisions in front of the marsh or upstream, or from the possibility of accidental spills at the Dow dock during loading and unloading operations. Recognizing this possibility, Dow developed one of the most sophisticated spill prevention and containment plans ever devised. It calls for three lines of defense to contain spills at the dock if they occur, and a system of mobile booms, skimmer boats and other facilities to protect environmentally sensitive points throughout the Delta, not just the marsh. The chemical materials Dow will be handling evaporate within six hours, should a spill occur. Studies of tides, current and winds and ship traffic in the Delta and Bay area enable us to determine where spilled materials will go under any conditions that may exist at the time of an accident. This knowledge will enable us to get ahead of the spill and protect sensitive areas.
>
> Dow has been shipping chemicals past the marsh for more than 38 years. The only spill that occurred during that time happened at our Pittsburg plant dock. It involved a spill of 50 gallons. It was quickly contained at the dock.

Sixth, neither the EIR nor the EIS specifically states the level of vinyl chloride emissions to be expected from the plant. Both lump all hydrocarbon emissions together. Opponents pointed out that the Texas Air Control Board estimates vinyl chloride emissions from Dow's Freeport Texas plant at 16.3 tons per day. Dow has contended that those figures are out of date and that emissions from the new plant would be very small.

Dow's statement about vinyl chloride was:

> Dow has been producing vinyl chloride for many years. There has never been one single case of cancer detected in a Dow employee that was related to work in a vinyl chloride plant. Dow has been monitoring the health of its employees since it established research laboratories in the 1930's to study the health effects associated with the use or production of chemical substances. The health of Dow employees who work every day in chemical plants throughout the world is significantly better than the national averages and the incidence of cancer is much lower than national averages.
>
> About 15 years ago Dow urged the government to set a safe exposure for workers in

vinyl chloride plants. Dow studies had indicated that a safe level—one that Dow used in its plants—was 50 parts per million. The government did set a standard; but it was 500 parts per million instead of 50. Dow continued to use its own 50 parts per million standards.

Last year, because of publicity about vinyl chloride plants and cancer caused by conditions that existed 30 years ago, the exposure standard was reduced to one part per million—50 times the known safe level of exposure.

Today all Dow plants, as well as vinyl chloride plants operated by other producers, comply with the one part per million standard. If they don't comply, the government shuts them down.

Seventh, ship and barge traffic up the Sacramento Channel would have increased because of the Dow plant (critics claimed the traffic would double). The EIR states that after completion of the plant there would be an "18-fold increase over the 1973 total tonnage of hazardous material transported on the Sacramento River." Opponents were concerned about the possibility of spills of dangerous material. Dow managers said this about their water operations:

An analysis of water shipments and accidents in the nation shows that the probability of an accident involving a Dow ship in the Delta is one every 40 years. These statistical odds, however, ignore technological advances that have been made in very recent years in the field of marine accident prevention and clean up techniques.

A study of the 65 marine accidents which have occurred in the Bay Area's waters from all shipping, including the Delta, during the last eight years indicated only three actually resulted in spills of materials into the water. None of these collisions involved spills of materials being transported by Dow.

Very elaborate facilities have been designed to prevent or contain accidental spills at the Dow dock.

Even the four pipelines which will be constructed below the Sacramento riverbed will be designed to minimize danger of rupture in the event of earthquakes.

The Hearings

As the arguments grew more heated, Dow managers became concerned about the possibility of ultimate failure for their project. At a meeting with Governor Edmund Brown, Jr., they complained of the delays and government red tape that were holding up the project. According to Bill Press, Director of the Governor's Office of Planning and Research, the Governor's only assurance at that meeting was that Dow would get a fair hearing. However, as a result of the meeting, Press agreed to set up a special hearing at which Dow managers and representatives of five interested state agencies would be present. It was hoped that this approach would provide an opportunity for Dow to respond to all of the relevant questions so that state agencies could get on with the issuance of permits, where appropriate. Contrary to Press's statements about the Governor's commitment, Dow managers have insisted that the Governor agreed to definite time limitations for state action, and to a specific format for the hearings.

The consolidated hearings were set for December 8 and 9, 1976. They were later extended to include December 17. The participants were to be Dow Chemical

Company, the State Reclamation Board, the State Water Resources Control Board, the State Lands Commission, and the Department of Water Resources, together with such witnesses and other interested parties as each might call.

Two significant events were to occur before the hearings convened. First, on November 5, Bill Press wrote to Ray Brubaker, Dow's Western Division Manager, enclosing a list of 76 separate questions to which various state agencies would like answers at the hearings. Two examples follow:

> Dow has applied for an Authority to Construct from the Bay Area Air Pollution Control District for a styrene plant, one of the thirteen plants of the proposed petrochemical complex. The APCD has denied this permit because emissions from this plant will interfere with the attainment and maintenance of ambient air quality standards for particulates, oxides, and hydrocarbons. Considering that the other twelve plants will produce additional emissions, how does Dow propose to meet these air quality requirements with the proposed facilities at the Collinsville and Pittsburg sites?
>
> For each chemical or mixture to be transported, what physical or chemical properties may affect spill dispersion and impact, toxicity to humans, toxicity to animals, toxicity to plants, toxicity to aquatic life, hazards to the public, and effectiveness of countermeasures designed to mitigate spills or releases? What other adverse effects on fish and wildlife, including water associated mammals and birds and their habitats, have been identified? Would any of the chemicals or chemical components transported be soluble in water, and if so, could they enter surface soils and have long lasting sub-lethal effects on aquatic vegetation, aquatic life or wildlife?

Second, on November 16, the State Water Resources Control Board wrote to the State Attorney General requesting legal clarification of the California Environmental Quality Act (CEQA). The Board asked, "What alternative procedural and substantive steps can responsible agencies take to ensure compliance with CEQA prior to taking final action on the project?"

The Attorney General's response was to come on December 7, just one day before the hearings were to commence. In the opinion of his staff:

> The lead agency principle does not exempt agencies from the requirement of CEQA. It only excuses them from the duty of preparing an EIR when another public agency has prepared an EIR on the project. The lead agency principle is designed to prevent duplication of paperwork. It is not to be used as a device to avoid the basic responsibilities under the act.

and:

> The need for the concurrence of all responsible agencies in the adequacy of an EIR reflects the independent obligation of all public agencies to comply with CEQA.

In summary, the opinion letter advised the state agencies that they were not required to accept the lead agency (Solano County) EIR, that each agency must satisfy itself independently of the environmental prudence of issuing permits, and if deemed appropriate, each agency should supplement or modify the EIR for its purpose. It also advised that state agencies could rely on the federal Environmental

Impact Statement for the project if they deemed that document adequate. The determination of adequacy would be left to the individual agencies.

One result of the Attorney General's determination was to broaden the focus of questions asked by the state agencies during the hearings. In addition, the opinions of a wide range of citizens were introduced into the testimony. Issues quite divergent from those raised in the questions conveyed by Press to Brubaker were introduced, although the stipulated subject matter was reviewed thoroughly. In the words of one Dow manager, "It looked like it was open season on Dow, and everybody was shooting."

The hearings proceeded for three days. The transcript covers 1,200 pages.

Following the hearings, on January 3, 1977, Bill Press wrote to Arthur M. Shelton, counsel for Dow, requesting further information required by state agencies. He indicated that responses when submitted ". . . will be used by state agencies to formally supplement the Dow EIR prepared by Solano County."

The material that Press conveyed with his letter contained 134 additional questions raised by state agencies. Of these, 29 were requests for additional material relevant to questions asked at the hearings—material that Dow's managers had agreed to provide. The balance of the questions covered essentially new subject matter. Included were questions from five state agencies not previously publicly identified as interested in the Dow project and from whom permits were not required. These agencies are:

> The State Air Resources Board
> The Department of Food and Agriculture
> The Department of Health
> The Solid Waste Management Board
> The Seismic Safety Commission

Then, on January 19, Dow made its announcement that it would withdraw the project, citing continued delays in the involved permitting process, and its need to act promptly to assure production facilities to meet future demand. According to Paul Oreffice, Dow's president, "In the final analysis, what killed us was the uncertainty."

However, at least one participant in the process felt that Dow's decision to withdraw was a satisfactory one. In its official newspaper, *New Man Apart*, Friends of the Earth headlined a story about the Dow project, "Can a quiet agricultural county on the Sacramento River find true happiness with a huge messy chemical plant?"

CASE QUESTIONS ─────────────────────────────

1. Should the Dow plant have been built? On balance, would the net gain from its existence outweigh costs to the environment and society?
2. What critical assumptions, if any, did the Dow planners make at the start of the project which later proved to be faulty?
3. The issues described in the pros and cons section of the case were taken

from public statements of environmentalists and Dow spokespersons. Discuss these points of view in terms of their potential to sway public opinion.

4. How would you propose to improve permit procedures in California, if your objective was to make it easier for industry to locate there and still preserve the environment?

References

For further reading about the events discussed here see, Earl V. Anderson, "Dow Halted by California Regulatory Tangle," *Chemical and Engineering News,* April 25, 1977, pp. 8–12; and Anne Jackson, "Industry vs. Ecology Showdown: The $500 million Dow plant," *California Journal,* February 1977, pp. 43–46. California newspapers, particularly those in San Francisco, Sacramento, and Los Angeles, carried accounts of the action as it occurred. For a story about a similar regulatory tangle that stopped another industrial project in California see, George Baker, "Who's To Blame for the Sohio Fiasco?" *California Journal,* May 1979, pp. 156–158.

DISCUSSION GUIDES ON CHAPTER CONTENT ────────

1. What is power? What types of power do large corporations have?

2. It is frequently said that large corporations exercise too much power. Is there any generally acceptable way to measure the power of a large company?

3. A number of writers assert that there is monolithic power in the combination of giant corporations and the government, and that this power overtly dominates consumers and individuals. Is this a myth or reality? Explain and justify your position.

4. Do you think that the majority of corporations in the United States use what power they have in a reasonably responsible way? Explain.

5. What is the issue of legitimacy? Is it important?

6. Discuss the power elite model as it applies to American business.

7. What is a pluralistic society? How does pluralism operate in American society?

MIND-STRETCHING QUESTIONS ────────────

1. The proxy ballot has been alleged to produce "automatic self-perpetuating oligarchies." If this is so, why has it not been replaced as a method of electing management? Can you propose some alternatives?

2. Is the large corporation losing or gaining power today? Explain.

10
THE GOVERNMENT- BUSINESS RELATIONSHIP: AN OVERVIEW

A) CHRYSLER CORPORATION BAILOUT*

In early August 1979 Chrysler Corporation orally petitioned the United States Government through the Treasury Department for $1 billion immediate cash aid. The top management of Chrysler said it had a cash flow crisis and that if it was not corrected the company would be forced into bankruptcy. While it was generally known in financial circles that Chrysler was in trouble this proposal of the nation's third largest automobile producer (sales in 1978 were $13.6 billion) came as a surprise to both the public and the government.

During the preceding 18 months the company had lost $466 million. In the second quarter of 1979 the loss was $207 million, the largest in automotive history, and the company anticipated that total losses for 1979 would be from $600 to $700 million.

Chrysler was loaded with a huge inventory of large automobiles which were not selling on the market. Its share of the market fell from 12 percent in 1977 to 10.7 percent in the summer of 1979, and total sales in the second quarter of 1979 were down 28 percent from the same period in 1978. During the 1979–1980 period of time Chrysler calculated that it must spend $1 billion in addition to normal outlays to meet federal automobile regulations. The company had hoped to be able to satisfy this capital need but its cash projections saw no way short of federal aid.

Chrysler chairman John J. Riccardo said that "We are not talking about bailout, we are not talking about handout, we are not talking welfare. We are talking about money we intend to repay."[1] He asked the government to give the company an "accelerated tax credit" of $500 million in 1979 and another $500 million in 1980. Under current tax law the losses of a company may offset profits for up to five years, which means, of course, reduced income taxes. Chrysler's proposal was to

*Prepared by George A. Steiner

62

give up future loss offsets in return for $1 billion in 1979 and 1980. The company made no promise that the government would eventually break even on this arrangement, but it did say that it expected to make a profit in 1981.

Treasury Secretary G. William Miller rejected the Chrysler proposal because he said it would amount to an interest-free, unsecured cash advance from taxpayers' funds and that would be contrary to "the principle of free enterprise." However, he said the Administration "recognizes that there is a public interest in sustaining [its] jobs and maintaining a strong and competitive national automotive industry." Therefore, he proposed and President Carter accepted a loan guarantee of from $500 to $750 million. Before making such a proposal to Congress, however, Secretary Miller said the company must prepare a plan to assure the continued viability of its operations. Such a plan, he said, should deal with both short- and long-term considerations and include substantial contributions and concessions from all those who have an interest in Chrysler's future, namely, management, employees, stockholders, creditors, suppliers, other business associates and governmental units.[2]

Chrysler's Actions To Improve Cash Position

Up to the writing of this case on September 1, 1979, Chrysler had taken a number of significant actions to improve its cash position. Among the important ones were the following:

It agreed "in principle" to sell its receivables—the right to collect payments from car buyers—for $730 million. Household Finance Corp., bought $500 million and the General Motors Acceptance Corp. picked up $230 million.

To reduce its exceptionally large inventory of $700 million in 435,000 unsold cars and trucks it offered cash rebates amounting to $400 per car.

It began selling some of its subsidiaries. For example, it announced it had agreed to sell for about $200 million in cash its wholly-owned Chrysler Realty Corp. and was seeking a buyer for its marine division (which made boats and marine engines).

Around 25,000 hourly workers were laid off and reductions in salary were announced for about 1,700 company executives.

Discussions were begun with the banks to refinance their loans in such a way as to expand borrowing capacity.

The company asked the United Auto Workers Union to accept a smaller wage increase from Chrysler than from General Motors Corp. and the Ford Motor Co., in its contract talks which were underway at the time. The UAW leadership indicated some willingness to do this and strongly endorsed Chrysler's proposal to the government.

In addition were many other programs including general cost reductions and success in speeding up official car purchases of Chrysler products by the State of Michigan.

Should The Government Help Chrysler?

The critical problem in this case is whether or not the federal government should step in to help Chrysler and, if so, precisely how it should help. A storm of controversy surrounded this case and the following arguments were advanced for and against government help.

Arguments Against Federal Aid

Thomas A. Murphy, chairman of the General Motors Corp., voiced the core argument of those opposed to the proposal. He said that such action "presents a basic challenge to the philosophy of America, the free enterprise system." He went on to say that if government bails out businesses that fail in the competitive race, "It removes and compromises that discipline in the marketplace." No company should be insulated from competition, he said. "Competition is inherent in our American system and competition is what got us where we are today," he added.[3]

An editorial in the *Wall Street Journal* of August 3, 1979, made the same point in saying: "To maintain a healthy economy government must simply let companies adapt to their changing fortune, cutting losses before they become unmanageable."

It was argued by others that management problems lay at the root of Chrysler's difficulties and that the government should not be asked to rescue inefficient managers from the consequences of their ineptitude. For instance it was pointed out that Chrysler had acquired failing companies in Europe that created severe cash drains, that the company had stuck too long with large "gas-guzzlers," and that the company delayed too long in launching a subcompact car to compete with GM's Vega and Ford's Pinto.[4]

In partial defense of such statements, Chrysler's president Lee A. Iacocca pointed out that Omni sales (Chrysler's subcompact car) would be very much higher were it possible to get more deliveries of engines from Volkswagen. Also, he said, Chrysler's problems would be solved with a one-percent increase in share of market.

Altogether, the basic case against government aid to Chrysler was an ideological one. Dean Phil C. Neal, of the University of Chicago Law School, put it succinctly this way in his testimony concerning the L-1011 loan guarantee:

> The whole objective of the competitive system is to maximize economic productivity by channeling resources into the most efficient hands. The failure of a firm, assuming that it cannot be made profitable through the structuring of ownership and management that will flow from reorganization proceedings, is a signal that it represents an inefficient or wasteful combination of resources.[5]

Arguments For Government Help

It was argued with considerable justification that bankruptcy of Chrysler would result in an immediate loss of about 360,000 jobs with rippling effects throughout the economy and a final unemployment tally of 500,000. It would, of course, result in millions if not billions of dollars of losses among thousands of businesses, and accelerate a national economic recession which was just beginning in the summer of 1979.

Some help from the government was justified, it was said, because bankruptcy of Chrysler could leave the federal Pension Benefit Guaranty Corp. with a responsibility of about $800 million in insured but unfunded pension obligations to Chrysler's employees. Help now, it was said, which might be virtually costless to the government might save the government many millions of dollars in the event of Chrysler's bankruptcy.

It was also pointed out that Chrysler's bankruptcy would leave only two strong United States automobile companies—Ford and General Motors. In the absence of Chrysler these two companies could have three quarters of the domestic automotive market, a dangerous concentration of power. This argument is countered with the observation that today there is plenty of foreign competition in the American automobile market and it is likely to continue. Furthermore, if Ford and General Motors did monopolize the market there are many things the government can do to restore competition.

It was argued that when the federal government gave a loan guarantee of $250 million to the Lockheed Aircraft Corporation in 1971 because of the financial difficulties of that company stemming from the L-1011 program, a precedent was set for distressed companies like Chrysler. Others pointed out, however, that circumstances surrounding this arrangement were very different from those facing Chrysler, not the least of which was the fact that the British government asked for the guarantee since it was financing Rolls Royce, the producer of the engines for the Lockheed L-1011, and it wanted to make sure its support would not be wasted with a bankrupt Lockheed. (The loan, made by banks but guaranteed by the government, was paid off in 1977 and the government pocketed a fee of $31 million.)[6]

If the L-1011 loan guarantee was not a precedent, it was said, then guaranteed loans to steel companies certainly were. In 1977 the steel industry was making large cuts in employment and closing plants as a result of a three-year decline in orders. Upon the recommendation of President Carter the Congress passed legislation to guarantee loans made by banks to the steel industry. The Economic Development Administration in the Department of Commerce was authorized to make loan guarantees of $550 million. To date it has guaranteed loans totaling $293 million, the latest and largest of which was to the Wheeling-Pittsburgh Steel Corporation for $100 million in August 1979. In addition, the Farmers Home Administration of the Department of Agriculture guaranteed another $50 million to this company.

Competing companies, and other people, condemned these low-cost loans as being a threat to the discipline of the private enterprise system. Lewis W. Foy, chairman of the Bethlehem Steel Corporation, said, for example, that managements asking for such loans were "unwilling to compete fairly under the free enterprise system which provides the opportunity to succeed or fail."[7]

Wheeling-Pittsburgh Steel Corporation wanted the loan guarantee primarily to get funds to build a new modern rail mill at its plant in Monessen, Pennsylvania. R. J. Slater, president of the CF&I Steel Corporation, a unit of the Crane Company, filed suit in Federal District Court in Denver asking that the loans be invalidated because, he said, the new mill would create excess capacity in this segment of the steel industry. Managers of the U.S. Steel Corporation and the Bethlehem Steel Corporation said that this new mill would put their older mills at a competitive disadvantage and the government should not do this.[8]

Ezra Solomon summarized such arguments for government support in these words of testimony given in connection with the L-1011 debates:

> The case for approving a loan guaranty seems very clear to me; by so doing, we avoid potentially large losses in employment, output, and exports, which society would suffer as a result of (the company) going into bankruptcy. Given existing employment conditions in the manufacturing sector of the economy and in the capital markets here and abroad, the adverse effects of such a business failure could be serious indeed. Certainly the cost to the government of offsetting such adverse effects, after the fact, would be many dozen times larger than the likely cost of extending a loan guaranty now. Indeed, given the various safeguards incorporated in the terms of the loan guaranty, the likely cost of positive action is close to zero.[9]

One observer commented that the old profit test of survival works beautifully in a simple society composed of small and perfectly competing companies. In today's extremely complex world that simple formula should, on occasion, be replaced by something in the nature of a societal cost/benefit analysis. Public opinion, this observer goes on to say, tends to be pragmatic rather than ideological. That is, people are more worried about jobs and income than the purity of competition. So, political processes have resulted in government protection from the rigors of competition in many areas—beet sugar growers, cattle ranchers, steel makers, textile producers, and so on. We are developing a sort of two-tier competition. The classical type still exists among very small businesses. It also exists among product divisions of large corporations. For the largest corporations, however, there is a drift towards protecting them from competitive forces, for a while at least, if their failure may do great damage in the economy. That is a fact of life. Is it in the long-run interests of the nation? That I do not know, he said.

Other Considerations

While Thomas Murphy strongly objected to the government guaranteeing loans for Chrysler he, and others taking his position, blame unnecessary, costly, and sometimes arbitrary government controls for a large part of Chrysler's trouble. He said, ". . . I think something should be done about the government standards. I think we should address the whole problem of regulation, sort it out and make sure it gives all Americans, all of the competitors, a fair shake."[10]

William Randolph Hearst, Jr., likewise is opposed to the loan guarantee on ideological grounds but insists in strong language that we should ask and probe such questions as these:

> Shouldn't we be concerned whether [Chrysler] . . . workers have, through their unions, priced themselves out of the market?
> Shouldn't we be concerned that our politicians, responding to the wishes (sometimes

whims) of the environmentalists, have turned the automobile into an impractical machine, too costly from a consumer's standpoint? Shouldn't we be concerned that our corporate tax laws which take away 50 percent of the profits of a large outfit like Chrysler, have stifled the ability of many companies, particularly those bordering nonprofitability, to re-invest in new plants and equipment? Shouldn't we be concerned that we have triple-taxation on American-made cars—the corporate tax, plus the tax on dividends, plus the sales tax—to such a degree that new investment is discouraged?[11]

Herbert Stein, a former member of the Council of Economic Advisers under Presidents Nixon and Ford, raises questions of ambiguous government philosophy and blame in these words:

> The plight of Chrysler Corp. has revealed to some commentators the merits of the free enterprise system. They have discovered that the system implies losses as well as profits and that it would be wrong—unfair, inefficient and inconsistent with the system—to "bail out" a corporation that makes losses.
> Fine. But where were these commentators when the profits of the oil companies were reported? How many explained to their audiences that the system implies profits as well as losses, and that it would be unfair, inefficient and inconsistent with the system to tax away the oil company profits? None.
> But, I can hear them say, the oil company profits were windfall profits, Yes, and Chrysler losses are windfall losses. If the price of gasoline were still 50 cents a gallon, people would still be buying Plymouth Furys and Chrysler would still be making money.
> A philosophy in which the government says to the private sector that your losses are your own but your profits are ours could not survive if consistently followed to its logical conclusion. Fortunately, we follow nothing consistently to its logical conclusion.[12]

The United Automobile Workers were reported to want the government to buy $1 billion of Chrysler's stock to help the company and to gain a voice in management.[13] John Kenneth Galbraith made a similar recommendation and added a few other hooks to government aid, as follows:

> . . . it does seem reasonable, especially as one reflects on the impressive sum involved, that those providing this largesse seek some small concessions. Thus if, as taxpayers, we are to invest one billion dollars in Chrysler, could we not be accorded an appropriate equity or ownership position? This is thought a reasonable claim by people who are putting up capital. Also, as Chrysler becomes a publicly funded business, may we not properly ask that its executives confine their compensation to [say] the general range of pay thought acceptable for the President of the United States. Compensation is now rather higher, although not, one judges, as a reward for good profit performance. And most important of all, in this high noon of the great conservative revolt, could we not ask that all corporations and all corporate executives that approve, or acquiesce by their silence in this expansive new public activity, refrain most scrupulously from any more of this criticism of big government.[14]

CASE QUESTIONS

1. What is your position with respect to whether the federal government should or should not give Chrysler a loan guarantee?
2. If you approve a loan guarantee what safeguards would you suggest to

make sure that such action does not weaken the competitive discipline of the existing market mechanism or lay a strong precedent for government nationalization of productive facilities?

3. Do you think the Administration was right in denying accelerated tax credits to Chrysler and instead offering loan guarantees?

4. Should the government modify its emission regulations and mileage standards in order to reduce capital investment requirements by Chrysler to meet these standards?

5. In the case of the guaranteed loans to steel companies do you think it is proper for the government to assure low-cost loans to one company to buy capital equipment that gives it a competitive advantage over other companies? How would you reconcile government's interest in assuring jobs for workers through guaranteed loans and the possibility that by doing so one company may gain a competitive advantage?

6. What is your assessment of Galbraith's proposals?

Notes

1. *Time,* August 20, 1979, p. 39.
2. "Statement by the Secretary of the Treasury Regarding Possible U.S. Financial Assistance to the Chrysler Corporation." An announcement made at the conclusion of the meeting between Chrysler Corporation and the Treasury Department. Undated.
3. Quoted by Reginald Stuart, "GM Chief Opposes U.S. Aid to Chrysler: It Challenges American Philosophy," *Los Angeles Herald Examiner,* August 3, 1979.
4. "Is Chrysler The Prototype?" *Business Week,* August 20, 1979.
5. U.S. Congress, Senate, *Emergency Loan Guarantee Legislation, Hearings Before the Committee on Banking, Housing and Urban Affairs, On S. 1567, S. 1641, Etc.,* 92nd Cong., 1st Sess, 1971, p. 385.
6. For a short account of the L-1011 loan guarantee circumstances see George A. Steiner, "The L-1011 Federal Loan Guarantee," in George A. Steiner, *Casebook in Business and Society* (New York: Random House, Inc., 1975).
7. Agis Salpukas, "Wheeling Steel Gets U.S. Aid," *New York Times,* August 29, 1979.
8. *Ibid.*
9. U.S. Congress, *Emergency Loan Guarantee, op. cit.,* p. 1189.
10. *Ibid.*
11. William Randolph Hearst, Jr., "Editor's Report: A Cautious Approach to Chrysler," *Los Angeles Herald Examiner,* August 19, 1979.
12. Herbert Stein, "Help Wanted: President, Must Have . . ." *Wall Street Journal,* Tuesday, August 14, 1979.

13.   "'Sick Man of Detroit': Analysts Say 20 Years of Mistakes Led to Plight," *Los Angeles Times,* August 10, 1979.
14.   Letter to the Editor, *Wall Street Journal,* August 14, 1979.

DISCUSSION GUIDES ON CHAPTER CONTENT

1.   Briefly describe the major constitutional provisions that permit the federal government to regulate business.

2.   It is often said that the federal government and business are partners. What does this mean to you? Is it a good or bad thing?

3.   What are the basic ways in which government influences business?

4.   Discuss the various reasons underlying government's regulation of the private sector. Why do you think that in recent years regulations increasingly have been concerned with broad socio-political questions rather than conventional marketplace flaws?

5.   Do you agree with the finding of a poll that "the growth of government in the U.S. now poses a threat to the freedom and opportunity for individual initiative of the citizenry"? Explain why or why not.

6.   What are the principal flaws in the behavior of business and government?

7.   Discuss the nature of the second managerial revolution that is now taking place with respect to the transfer of much managerial decision-making powers to public servants in the federal government.

MIND-STRETCHING QUESTION

1.   Does the United States today have the "right" balance between government and business? If you think it does, describe some of the principal characteristics. If you disagree, explain why and suggest ways to assure the right balance.

11

NEW PATTERNS IN GOVERNMENT REGULATION OF BUSINESS

A) THE SALES TAX ON WORMS

Most people are aware that the tax collectors in our governments use their awesome powers with little regard for the personal feelings or conditions of the taxpayer. Seldom, however, has the tax collector demonstrated his diligence with lesser reward than in the case of Jody Gerard, a 12-year old boy who lives in Eddyville, New York. Jody digs fishing worms in his backyard and sells them for 35 cents a dozen.

Someone alerted the tax department in Albany, New York, that Jody did not keep records nor did he pay the seven percent local and state sales taxes. Immediately the State of New York dispatched two investigators to Eddyville. The tax laws were duly enforced and Jody was forced to pay 64 cents in taxes due and 50 cents for a bank check.

"We're not embarrassed," a department official proclaimed later. "We're proud. Our taxpayer-service people were faced with a dilemma and reacted very sensitively to it. We sent somebody there personally, not to collect the tax but to alleviate their fears and give the boy a minilesson on the sales tax and the obligations of businessmen. The boy ended up being very pleased."[1]

CASE QUESTION

What is your reaction to this case?

Notes

1. *New York Times,* August 29, 1979.

B) FIRESTONE'S RADIAL RECALL*

The success of a corporation nowadays depends not only on how it makes and markets its products, but also on how it is perceived by the public. Members of Congress, government agencies, consumer groups, and the press are all scrutinizing business with an intensity and zeal rarely displayed in the past. Some of the scrutineers are bound to be hostile toward corporations—which makes it all the more important that businessmen exert every effort to demonstrate that their motives and actions meet the highest standards. In that regard, the response of Firestone Tire & Rubber Co. to its current, widely publicized radial-tire crisis may well become a classic, to be pored over by business-school students for many years to come.

Firestone stands accused of selling defective tires—the 500 series of steel-belted radials. According to the federal authorities, these tires are prone to blowouts, tread separations, and other dangerous deformities, and have been the target of thousands of consumer complaints. Records supplied to congressional investigators by Firestone and other sources indicate that there have been hundreds of accidents involving 500-series radials, and that these accidents have caused at least thirty-four deaths. No other radial-tire line has been associated with nearly that number.

The National Highway Traffic Safety Administration, which has the authority to order product recalls, has recommended recalling the 500 radials. Although the tire no longer is being produced, there are an estimated 13 million still on the road, out of the 23.5 million made from 1972 until production ceased early this year. The Traffic Safety Administration, an arm of the Department of Transportation, investigated the tire for seven months before announcing that it had made an "initial determination" of a safety-related defect.

The agency's findings were clouded somewhat by the fact that it was unable to specify the nature of the defect. Instead, it inferred the existence of one from analysis of the evidence. The agency studied 6,000 consumer reports dealing with more than 14,000 separate tire failures. It felt that the 500 radial was effectively damned both by the volume and by the nature of the complaints—which had been sent to its own offices, to Congress, to consumer organizations, and to Firestone. The agency based its decision as well on the so-called adjustment rate of the 500 radial. The adjustment rate is calculated by dividing the number of tires sold into the number that are returned—for full or partial refunds—by dissatisfied customers. Adjustments might be made for anything from a wobbly ride to a high-speed blowout. Firestone has testified that the 500 had an adjustment rate of 7.4 percent, more than twice the estimated average for other radial tires.

To the layman, it may seem surprising that the government can recall a product without pinpointing the defect. But courtroom precedent has established that this is a legitimate procedure, provided the government can demonstrate a pattern of excessive failures. The definition of "excessive" is, of course, subject to debate, but the Traffic Safety Administration plainly believes that the 500 radial fits the pat-

*Arthur M. Louis, "Lessons From the Firestone Fracas," *Fortune,* August 28, 1978.

tern. At this writing, the agency seems certain to issue a recall order. Firestone, however, can be expected to fight such an order in the courts.

Firestone's management has contended all along that the company has been unjustly accused. It did recall 400,000 of its 500-series radials last year—the largest tire recall in history—at the Traffic Safety Administration's suggestion. But that was because of what Firestone describes as a temporary production problem at a single plant in Illinois. Other production problems caused the company to recall a total of 10,245 more 500 radials on three earlier occasions. Nonetheless, Firestone contends that there is nothing fundamentally wrong with the tire, and it has strenuously opposed a complete recall. According to Firestone, practically all the tire failures can be blamed on consumer neglect and abuse. It claims that consumers damage their tires by overloading them, banging them against the curb, failing to keep them adequately inflated, and driving at excessive speeds.

Controversy over the 500 radial has been raging in the public forums for months, and the Firestone name has been besmirched in courtrooms and a congressional hearing, as well as in the press and on the air. As one might expect, the unfavorable publicity has caused defections from the ranks of Firestone customers. The company is having trouble selling its seven current radial lines, although none of them has been found defective. Despite extra-heavy advertising and promotion, and the creation of a special warranty, Firestone's share of the multibillion-dollar radial-tire market has slipped by about a half percent. A company officer says the drain on sales already has amounted to scores of millions of dollars.

The company stands to lose a great deal more if it is forced to recall the 500 line. Under the terms of the recall, a customer would be entitled to a new tire free of charge, regardless of how far he had driven on the used tire. By law, the recall order can apply only to tires sold during a three-year period before the order is issued. Perhaps as many as two million out of the 13 million 500-brand radials on the road would be exempted, but that still would leave 11 million tires to be replaced, at a production cost of at least $275 million. In addition, Firestone might have to replace private-brand tires—similar to the 500—that were made for Montgomery Ward and Shell Oil. If other variants, made for General Motors, were also recalled, the potential bill could easily exceed $300 million. Firestone had revenues of $4.4 billion, and net income of $110.2 million, in the fiscal year ending last October, and it lost $37 million in the first half of the current fiscal year.

Firestone also is coping with a spate of lawsuits, charging everything from bent fenders to loss of life and limb. Since production began, the company has been hit with some 250 suits seedking millions of dollars in damages because of alleged failures of the 500 radials. Nine of the cases resulted in courtroom verdicts against Firestone, while the company has won twenty-two and settled sixty-four out of court for less than the plaintiffs demanded. The largest settlement by far—approximately $1.4 million—was made in the case of a Nevada family. Both parents were killed, and a child was left a paraplegic as the result of an auto accident in which the right rear tire—a 500 radial—blew out. Firestone felt it had a strong case, but decided not to take its chances with a jury.

The purpose of this article is not to judge whether the 500 radial is in fact defective. What does seem clear, however, is that Firestone, in its attempts to ward off disagreeable consequences and defend its honor, has often been its own worst enemy. At times, it has almost gone out of its way to provoke suspicion and doubt. One would expect a company convinced of its rectitude to cooperate fully with the government. But Firestone has repeatedly tried to thwart investigation of its tire, and has publicly impugned the motives of the investigators as well. In the process, it has simply prolonged and intensified its ordeal.

Firestone has demonstrated a penchant for blunders, some of them susceptible to the worst interpretation. Early last spring, at a time when the investigation hadn't yet become common knowledge, Firestone held a major clearance sale of 500's in the Southeast. New tires were sold in Miami and Birmingham at half the list price. Firestone explains that it was phasing the tire out, that clearance sales are a routine procedure when stocks get down to certain levels, and that it had planned for months to clear out this line. But the company should have anticipated that the government's investigation would eventually get lots of publicity, and that the sale would then appear—whether justly or not—as a desperate effort to unload damaged goods.

The Firestone 500 radial began attracting baleful attention from consumer advocates back in 1976, when the Center for Auto Safety, a Washington-based organization formerly associated with Ralph Nader, received a large number of complaints—mainly about tread separations and blowouts. During 1977, the center studied the tire complaints in its files, and found that half of them were leveled against Firestone, with the great bulk of these involving the 500 radial. Last November, Clarence M. Ditlow III, director of the center, wrote a letter about the findings to Mario A. Di Federico, the president of Firestone, and suggested—impudently, no doubt—that the company should shift half of its advertising budget into quality control.

Ditlow also turned his data over to the Traffic Safety Administration, which began its own investigation. Firestone contends that the agency bears a grudge against the company. In 1975, the agency ordered a recall of one million Firestone tires—bias-plies rather than radials—which it felt did not meet safety and durability standards. But it had to back down in the face of a company lawsuit, after the Justice Department advised that the case against Firestone was too weak.

Firestone also suggests that the Traffic Safety Administration is part of a Naderite conspiracy. Joan Claybrook, who heads the agency, is a former associate of Ralph Nader. So is Lowell Dodge, special counsel of a House subcommittee—headed by Representative John E. Moss, a California Democrat—which joined the investigation of Firestone last spring. Firestone finds something sinister in the common backgrounds of Claybrook, Dodge, and the other Nader alumnus in the case, Clarence Ditlow. As John F. Floberg, Firestone's vice president and general counsel, recently put it: "They scratch each other's backs. They get together and decide to play Ping-Pong or badminton with somebody." Firestone, he suggests, is the ball—or the shuttlecock—in the present game.

It is Floberg who has taken the most aggressive role in Firestone's response to the radial-tire crisis. He represented the company almost single-handedly at the House subcommittee hearings, while Richard A. Riley, the chairman and chief executive, has limited his participation in the public debate to a few reluctant interviews, including one with Fortune. The general outlines of the strategy had to be approved by Riley, but a source elsewhere in the industry says that Firestone's tactics bear the stamp of Floberg, a combative World War II veteran who spent seven years as assistant secretary of the Navy and an AEC commissioner before joining Firestone in 1960.

One of Firestone's legal tactics was an attempt to suppress the results of a survey of tire owners conducted by the Traffic Safety Administration. The agency says it was alarmed by the reports about Firestone's radials, and initiated the survey to determine whether Firestone was the only make that was proving particularly troublesome. It mailed 87,000 survey cards to people who had bought new cars equipped with radial tires. The respondents were asked to indicate the brands of their tires, and to tell whether they had experienced blowouts or other problems.

Only 5,400 people—6.2 percent of those surveyed—bothered to respond, but within this group, Firestone seemed to make the worst showing by far. The company got wind of the results, and learned that the agency was preparing to release them. It went into the U.S. District Court in Cleveland and asked for a restraining order, preventing the Traffic Safety Administration from making the results public. Firestone argued that the survey was statistically unsound, because of the small response and for other reasons as well, and claimed that the publicity would damage the company's business. The order was granted last March.

Firestone's effort at censorship backfired. People who had been unaware of the radial-tire crisis read about the court's action, and began asking what the company had to hide. In particular, the episode aroused the suspicions of Congressman Moss, an ardent consumerist and chairman of the subcommittee on oversight and investigations of the House Committee on Interstate and Foreign Commerce. After hearing of the judge's decision, he summoned his legal aides, and announced grimly, "We'll have to hold hearings." The hearings, which stretched over four days during the spring and summer, received heavy coverage in the press and on TV, and produced still more bad publicity for Firestone.

Ironically, the results of the survey reached the public anyhow. The Center for Auto Safety requested them, along with other data, under the Freedom of Information Act. Despite the restraining order, the results were sent to the consumer group, which passed them along to the press. The incident seemed to support Firestone's charges that the Traffic Safety Administration was out to nail the company. It was explained, however, that a staff lawyer had released the material "inadvertently." At the very least, the incident demonstrated that Firestone has no monopoly on blunders.

It seems clear that Firestone should never have hauled the Traffic Safety Administration into court. The company should have waited until the agency released the survey, then countered with a public statement of its own, attacking the statistical methods. Firestone might have scored some debating points this way. Or then again, the public might have dismissed the explanation as self-serving, since most people are hopelessly befuddled by disputes among statisticians. But in either case Firestone would have suffered less damage.

Firestone has tried to thwart the Traffic Safety Administration's investigation in other ways as well. Last December, the agency sent the company a long list of questions concerning steel-belted radial tires. It asked for copies of any and all complaints about failures of Firestone radials, for a list of all lawsuits against Firestone arising from these failures, and for a detailed account of any changes in the methods used to manufacture radials. The agency asked for prompt responses, but in an increasingly bitter exchange of letters and telegrams, Firestone kept insisting that it could not supply all the information requested without spending many months researching and compiling.

The agency ran out of patience, and last April it sent Firestone a "special order"—a list of the questions that had not been answered, together with additional questions that had been raised during the investigation and questions about production prior to 1975. There were twenty-seven items in all, and the agency demanded a full and prompt response, under penalty of prosecution.

In a long and defiant reply, drafted by a Cleveland law firm, Firestone objected to practically all the questions. It continued to insist that they would require too much time and effort, and it questioned whether the Traffic Safety Administration had the authority to demand the information. The company argued that the agency could require answers only to "specific questions," and that some of the questions weren't specific. It also argued that Firestone was being asked to analyze documents and compile new ones, when the agency had the authority only to ask the company to make existing documents available for inspection. Firestone upbraided the agency for asking it to send copies of certain documents when the company, under the law, only had to make the documents available at headquarters. And it objected to a request for information about tires produced more than three years ago, on the ground that such tires are exempt from agency control.

The agency received the reply with something less than joy. It took Firestone to court in Washington in an effort to force compliance with its "special order." The matter is now before U.S. District Judge Thomas A. Flannery. But whatever the judgment may be, the company inevitably has raised public doubts about its good faith by refusing to cooperate fully with the Traffic Safety Administration, and by choosing instead to split legal hairs. Firestone, of course, doesn't see it that way." I think we've been completely aboveboard," says Chairman Riley.

When John Floberg appeared before the House subcommittee, he found himself in hostile surroundings. Chairman Moss and most of the other subcommittee members were antagonistic toward the company. What's more, Floberg had been preceded to the stand by seven witnesses—two police officers, two consumers, a Firestone dealer, a writer, and Clarence Ditlow—all of whom had testified against the 500 radial. Still, the hearings offered Firestone a broad forum, and a chance to redeem itself in the public eye.

The company muffed the chance. Floberg's prepared statement was eloquent at times. But his adversaries on the subcommittee had done their homework, and they managed to trip him up. He lapsed into obfuscations and tortured explanations. The situation called for a heavy dose of candor, but Floberg came across strictly as a lawyer fighting a tough case.

At one point, Floberg stated that the 500 was one of two steel-belted radials that had been rated above all others in a Consumer Reports survey. But Lowell Dodge, the subcommittee counsel, pointed out that the ratings, which appeared in the October 1973, issue, had been made according to tread wear, not safety.

A while later, Floberg tried to make the point that the industry encouraged consumers to take proper care of their radial tires. He cited a television ad that Firestone had run on the subject. But, as he conceded, this was not a very potent example, since the advertisement had been forced on Firestone by the Federal Trade Commission, in partial settlement of a lawsuit. The FTC had been upset because earlier ads had stressed the safety of the company's tires *without* mentioning the need for proper maintenance. The FTC also fined the company $50,000.

An adversary, Representative Albert Gore Jr., Democrat of Tennessee, wondered about the seemingly high adjustment rate on 500-brand radials. Floberg tried to show that the rate—7.4 percent—might not be out of line. He mentioned that the tire had been Firestone's most expensive, and that buyers might therefore be "more likely to seek adjustment when they are unhappy with it." He added that the industry guards its adjustment rates "very jealously" and suggested that the 500 might compare favorably with other top-priced tires. But the subcommittee had demanded adjustment data from the other major tire makers, and none of them indicated a rate even half that of the 500's on competitive steel-belted lines for the years 1975–1977. At Goodyear, Firestone's chief competitor, the highest adjustment rate was 2.9 percent.

Last month, the Traffic Safety Administration made its "initial determination" that the 500 radial had a safety-related defect. It recommended that Firestone recall the tires immediately, although it refrained from issuing an order until after a public hearing earlier this month. But whatever happens from here on, Firestone has long since lost the radial-tire war. It has vividly demonstrated the wrong way of dealing with the government and the public.

CASE QUESTIONS

1. Do you believe that Firestone's managers reacted appropriately to federal governmental regulators? Explain your position in detail.

2. If you believe that Firestone's managers did not react appropriately, explain in detail a posture that you believe would have been much better for Firestone and all parties concerned in this case.

C) LIFT CONTROLS ON TRUCKING?

The Case For:*

Q. Mr. Shenefield, why do you favor legislation loosening government controls over the trucking industry?

A. First of all, I have a basic bias in favor of the free-enterprise system. Wherever possible, competition should prevail. Only where there is a clear, natural monopoly should the government intervene and regulate an industry.

The trucking industry is not even close to being a monopoly. At last count, it consisted of more than 16,000 firms. It's a wholly deconcentrated, diverse industry, which, if freed of government controls, would be highly competitive. Its continued regulation is unnecessary.

Q. Without government controls, isn't it likely that many of the 16,000-plus firms would merge and that the industry would thus become more concentrated and less competitive?

A. That argument is made by many truckers, but it is a complete phony. There would have to be an awful lot of mergers to get from 16,000 firms down to a level that would concern economists and antitrust officials.

If there are competitive problems growing out of mergers, the antitrust laws ought to be able to prevent them, just as they do in any other industry.

Q. Wouldn't truck rates soar without controls?

A. I can't think of a single reason why that should happen. In the absence of regulation, truckers would be free to move their own rates up or down. If they tried to move them too far up, other truckers would come in and offer lower prices. The natural force of competition would adjust rates to costs, just as it does in any other industry, and rates should decline.

We've already seen that happen in the 1950s, when shipments of fresh and frozen dressed poultry and frozen fruits and vegetables were declared exempt from federal regulation. Trucking rates for these products dropped substantially—between 20 and 30 percent.

Q. Even if rates decline, wouldn't the abolition of rate bureaus, where truckers collectively decide what to charge, increase shipping costs? Shippers would have to hire more people to keep track of the hundreds of different rates—

A. If that theory is true, then why are shippers so much in favor of deregulation?

In any other industry, rate-bureau price setting would be a felony. It's price fixing. Competitors get together to fix prices, with immunity from the antitrust laws. They have no incentive to keep prices low. Without that immunity, rates would be lower—and shipping costs would be, too.

The Council on Wage and Price Stability has estimated that the cost of regulating the trucking industry is about five billion dollars a year. The Interstate Commerce Commission has a bureaucracy of 2,000 people, of whom 900 are engaged in

*John H. Shenefield, "Pro and Con—Lift Controls on Trucking?" *U.S. News and World Report,* August 13, 1979.

reviewing rates and operating rights. Another 700 monitor compliance with ICC rules. There is a vast underground of Washington lawyers who make their living dealing in arcane ICC rules.

That adds up to an enormous social cost. And for what reason? So that competition is limited and prices are kept up! It doesn't make any sense. To combat inflation, we ought to do away with these unnecessary costs.

Q. Wouldn't service to small towns be cut back as carriers turned to more profitable routes?

A. No, quite the contrary. Small-town service would probably improve. Right now, the ICC hasn't got the faintest idea about the quality of service on individual routes. The Commission can't tell you whether the route from, let's say, Peoria to Dubuque is being served by one truck line or several, or how good the service is. Once a trucker has ICC approval to carry goods over a certain route, the trucker can serve or not serve without the commission ever knowing.

So why are truckers serving these cities now, if no one is forcing them to? They are doing it because it is profitable. That profit will continue even without regulation.

Q. Wouldn't some trucking companies be likely to shift their operations to serve the more profitable big cities?

A. Without regulation, truckers would certainly focus on where they can make a profit. If they can make a profit by serving the small towns, they'll serve the small towns. But if there isn't a profit there, then you have to ask: Why should the government force truckers to serve small towns at the expense of big-city customers who end up paying more than their share to subsidize service to small towns?

There is a perfectly appropriate, economically sensible way to handle this problem without a vast, expensive bureaucracy regulating the entire industry. If the government wants to make a trucker serve a small town as a matter of social policy, the government should directly subsidize that route.

Q. Without government controls, wouldn't there be a danger of chaos in the industry—and perhaps the economy?

A. No. We don't regulate food stores, but there isn't a danger of chaos in grocery stores. Nor is there a danger of chaos in any other industry which is freely competitive. *Chaos* is another word for competition. We can't predict what's going to happen. But that's what the free-enterprise system is all about.

Q. Couldn't unscrupulous, fly-by-night operators take advantage of shippers?

A. That's a very narrow kind of problem. It doesn't make sense to regulate every facet of the industry—entry, exit and prices—to deal with that very small problem.

If it does become a problem, the way to deal with it is by setting up a certification process on financial responsibility.

Q. What about safety on the highways, with thousands of independent truckers flooding the roads—perhaps including many who are operating vehicles that are unsafe?

A. Again, if safety is a problem, let's deal with that by itself.

There is no need to regulate the entire industry just because of safety concerns.

The Case Against:*

Q. Mr. Whitlock, why do you oppose legislation relaxing government controls over trucking?

A. Trucking is the one segment of the transportation industry that works. There is no need for radical change.

Federal regulation has brought stability to the trucking industry. It permits us to serve all our customers at reasonable rates and without discrimination, no matter how large or small they are and no matter where they are located.

Under deregulation, there's no question that a large shipper, such as Sears, Roebuck, would have the economic clout to get a lower rate than some small manufacturing firm in a small town. Deregulation would also mean that the larger cities will get the better service.

Q. Wouldn't trucking service to small towns be improved with deregulation?

A. Of course not. Just as truckers would be allowed to start serving new markets, they would also be able to abandon some of the cities they now serve.

Some 39,000 towns in America are completely dependent on trucks for transportation service. Take away the requirement to serve, and ther's no question that carriers will abandon many of these small towns in favor of those where shipments are bigger.

This is already happening with airline deregulation. Every day, there are new complaints about the loss of air service to small towns. The same thing would happen under trucking deregulation.

Q. Wouldn't deregulation increase competition?

A. No, just the opposite. Deregulation would increase concentration. Today, there are 16,874 companies in the trucking industry. More than two thirds of these gross $500,000 or less. Under deregulation, many of these companies would have to merge to survive. Others would simply die. In the end, there would be fewer companies, less competition and higher rates.

Q. Aren't there certain routes now where one or two trucking companies have a clear monopoly and where deregulation would increase competition?

A. No one company has a clear monopoly. There may be some areas where two companies dominate the market, but that's probably all that demand warrants. You could always add another 18 companies, but with that many companies, shippers wouldn't get good daily service.

Q. Truckers are now permitted to establish rates collectively. Wouldn't the end of that practice, as envisioned under deregulation, result in lower rates?

A. No. Collective rate-making helps keep rates low. Without it, each firm would have to file a separate rate for every commodity and route that it takes. There would be trillions of different rates. And even if these new rates were lower than what is now being charged, shippers wouldn't save a penny. They would have to hire many more people in their traffic departments to keep up with all the different rates. They could no longer go to just one place—the rate bureau—to find out the cost of shipping goods from one point to another.

*Bennett Whitlock Jr., *Ibid.*

Q. Hasn't regulation allowed trucking companies to earn excessive profits?

A. Not at all. According to the Interstate Commerce Commission, the rate of return on equity for the top eight trucking companies is 27.7 percent.

I admit that sounds high, but the ICC accounting procedures are different from those used by most large industrial firms. If you apply general accounting practices to the trucking industry, you will find that our return is only 15.3 percent, compared to approximately 14 percent for the top 500 U.S. companies. In my view, that's not excessive.

Q. Would deregulation lower costs by doing away with restrictions on the commodities and routes that a carrier can take?

A. These restrictions have very little to do with trucking rates. Even so, we would like to do away with them. We're not in favor of commodity limitations that say, for example, that someone who carries steel coffins can't carry copper coffins. That doesn't make sense. But surely that can be corrected by the ICC. Legislation isn't necessary.

Q. Given the nation's energy problems, is it now time to end the rule that bars many truckers from hauling loads on return trips?

A. If anything, deregulation would increase fuel consumption, not decrease it.

Deregulation would have no effect on empty back hauls, because most of them are unavoidable. Only 3 percent of them can be attributed to regulation. Deregulation wouldn't cure the fact that for every four trucks going to Florida, only one comes back full. It's simply that Florida is a larger consuming area than a producing area.

Nor would deregulation solve the problem of an automobile transporter. He carries only automobiles from the assembly plant to a dealer. There's no freight he can put on that equipment to take back. The same thing is true for many of the tank trucks designed to carry chemicals. They can't carry milk on a return trip.

Q. How would deregulation result in more fuel consumption?

A. In the first four or five years, many entrepreneurs would try to get into the industry. Unlike most other industries, all it takes to get started is a simple down payment for a rig. Many more trucks would be on the road, but the amount of freight shipped would not increase. Truckers would end up carrying smaller loads and wasting fuel.

Q. Hasn't regulation smoothed the way for high wage settlements between the Teamsters Union and trucking firms? Companies know they will be able to pass increased labor costs on to shippers and consumers—

A. I don't agree. I don't think the wages we are paying the Teamsters or their annual increases are excessive. In fact, the settlement negotiated this spring was below some of the other contracts that have won approval from President Carter's inflation advisers.

CASE QUESTIONS

1. If you were a congressional representative which of these arguments would you accept in a vote on relaxing government controls on the trucking industry?

2. If you were for relaxing controls which ones would you relax and which ones would you keep?

3. Visit a local trucking firm or independent trucker and find out how they would react to any relaxation of controls.

4. Visit a local firm that ships by truck and inquire about how the management views relaxing controls over trucking.

5. If the Congress has passed legislation relaxing federal controls over trucking following the writing of this case in August 1979, report on what the Congress did and how local truckers and shippers have reacted to the legislation.

References

For two recent and brief analyses of trucking deregulation see Charles G. Burck, "Truckers Roll Toward Deregulation," *Fortune,* December 18, 1978; and *Business Week,* "Trucking Deregulation is Moving Fast," November 27, 1978.

For more thorough analyses see Thomas Gale Moore, *Freight Transportation Regulation,* (Washington, D.C.: American Enterprise Institute, 1972); and Ann F. Friedlaender, *The Dilemma of Freight Transport Regulation* (Washington, D.C.: The Brookings Institution, 1969).

DISCUSSION GUIDES ON CHAPTER CONTENT ───────

1. Discuss how government regulations are altering the cost structure of industries.

2. What are the important implications of the new pattern of functional regulations as contrasted with traditional industrial regulation?

3. Would you say that industries are still capable, under current conditions, of capturing or dominating the agencies that regulate them? Explain.

4. What are the salient characteristics of the newer regulations in terms of their purposes, policies, and methods?

5. Discuss the various criticisms made against independent regulatory commissions, such as their lack of accountability, misallocation of resources, and others.

6. What are "nonsense" regulations? Explain, using examples.

7. How are technological advances affecting the nature and thrust of government regulation, especially in the area of environmental pollution control?

8. Define "legal pollution." Could excessive regulation foster disrespect for the law?

9. Distinguish between economic, legal, and political rationalities. Explain how they could, and do, come into conflict with each other.

MIND-STRETCHING QUESTIONS ───────

1. In what specific way do you think government regulation of business could be made more effective?

2. Is it reasonable to expect a mutually satisfactory relationship between business and government, or is an adversary approach inherent in the situation?

FIELD RESEARCH: GOVERNMENT REGULATION OF SMALL BUSINESS

Small businesses, especially those just starting, generally face difficult economic problems that tax the ingenuity of the entrepreneur-owner to survive. When costs of complying with government regulations are added to economic problems such as finding customers, meeting competition, financing inventories, and so on, problems of making a profit and surviving are multiplied for the typical small business.

Visit a small business in your community and prepare a report on the nature and costs of government regulations to which the person in the business must comply. Ask the person in business how much of the cost objectively can be considered proper, how much of doubtful justification, and how much clearly unjustified.

12
CHANGING MANAGERIAL IDEOLOGIES

A) PRESIDENTIAL SUCCESSION AT MAGNUM INDUSTRIES

Methods and rituals for choosing leaders have been a perennial social problem over the course of recorded history. As events in connection with the Watergate scandal in Washington remind us, neither philosophers nor statesmen have yet devised a perfectly reliable system. Leadership status may be based upon wisdom, age, wealth, heredity, conquest, election, charisma, or other criteria, but there is no proven method of insuring that leadership status and the ability to lead will coincide. This is as valid an observation regarding the leadership of the modern corporation as it is with other large human organizations. Consider the following case-in-point.

Magnum Industries, a giant conglomerate with headquarters in Seattle, Washington, ranks within the top 50 companies on the *Fortune* 500. The company has large operations in pharmaceuticals, electronic gear, ship-building, aerospace components, and chemicals. Because of its far-flung impact the firm has been under heavy crossfire from government agencies, minority groups, consumer advocates, and local politicians in the Seattle headquarters area where a large wire-milling operation has produced water effluents that anger environmentalists. With an aging president, the corporation is also in the midst of a succession process visible only to a few insiders in the highest executive levels.

One morning, shortly after the annual stockholders' meeting, President Harold Clements, 64, an acid and slightly reclusive veteran of 41 years with Magnum Industries (11 of them as President), walked down the carpeted hallway of the corporate inner sanctum to the office of Robert Beckett, his vice-president of finance. Nodding to Beckett's secretary in the alcove, Clements stepped through the door and found Beckett seated behind his long mahogany desk working on a report for the next board meeting.

As Beckett looked up, Clements eyed him with some assurance. The two had a good deal in common. Beckett, at 46, was an aggressive and nakedly competitive graduate of the University of Chicago. Ever since his iron-fisted handling of the Wire Milling Division had stifled a trend toward permissive management and led to a string of record profit years, Beckett had been marked as a rising star in the Magnum constellation. Although Clements knew that many suspected the Vice-President of pursuing his ambitions in unscrupulous ways, nothing of an unsavory nature had ever surfaced. Clements also knew that widely shared opinion held that he admired Beckett, and he had done nothing to dispel such a notion.

At age 64, Clements would face mandatory retirement in less than one year and the members of the board of directors, a congenial lot including many of his personal friends, let it be known that he had a free hand to choose his successor. Although Clements made no effort to conceal his liking for Beckett, he had considered both Beckett and his executive vice-president, Edward Lippencott. For the past year, both men had waged a subtle campaign to succeed Clements and he had found their political intrigues both amusing and revealing.

Lippencott, 51, had been with the company for 21 years, coming to the position of executive vice-president through the production route, as had Beckett. In addition to his superior performance as head of Magnum's Ship Construction Division, and later as executive vice-president, Lippencott had devoted much time to community affairs, and the walls of his office were burdened with Chamber of Commerce plaques, outstanding citizen awards, and other acknowledgments of community participation which inevitably come to the outgoing in business. Additionally, Lippencott had taken a two-year leave of absence in the mid-1960s to serve a term on the City Council of Seattle. Both as a city official and a corporation executive he had become known as a man sympathetic to the viewpoints of minority, consumer, and environmental groups. Although Lippencott, a graduate of the Harvard Business School, was a superior manager with a fine performance record, his reputation as a spokesman for some kind of new social consciousness had made the greatest impression on President Clements.

In truth, Clement's consideration of Lippencott as a successor was less than whole-hearted, even though he knew that Lippencott would appeal to many of the board's members and stockholders as much as Beckett would. The Executive Vice-President's lobbying efforts had discreetly built up support for his candidacy over the past year; but in the final analysis he feared that Lippencott might be transformed into a crusader when he had the power of the presidency behind his actions. Although Clements knew that the powers of large corporations were being questioned increasingly, he doubted the permanence of concepts such as "corporate social responsibility." As a sometime student of history, Clements categorized the antibusiness upheavals of the 1960s and early 1970s as a new reassertion of the deeply ingrained suspicion of big business manifest in the earlier Populist and Progressive movements. He felt that this new movement would, like its predecessors, fade away. The job of the American capitalist would remain unchanged. Clements knew that Beckett embodied more of this hard-headed wisdom than Lippencott. Indeed, he personified it in singleminded fashion.

Now, President Clements answered Beckett's quick greeting and spoke himself. "Bob," he said, "I plan to resign within the coming year and I want you to prepare yourself for the assumption of new duties. As you know, the Board of Directors will go along with my decision." "Yes, sir," said the smiling Beckett.

CASE QUESTIONS ━━━━━━━━━━━━━━━━━━━━━━━━━━━━

1. Do you agree with President Clements' decision?
2. Do you believe that the selection process at Magnum Industries is typical

of large corporations in the United States? If so, is this relatively simple method of selecting chief executive officers adequate?

3. Would you suggest any changes in the process or increased democratization? If so, what reforms might be instituted?

4. Can you think of any situations where methods of selecting leaders have altered because of increasing social pressures on institutions? Is American history revealing in this respect? Explain.

5. Is there a relationship between succession processes (methods of acquiring power) and later developments in the exercise of power?

References

Surprisingly little has been written recently on the process of selecting presidents of large companies. This is probably due to the fact that each situation tends to be unique. There has been a good bit of writing, however, about the requirements of top managers of large corporations which tends to establish a frame of reference for the selection process. See for instance Isadore Barmash, *The Chief Executives,* (Philadelphia: J. B. Lippincott Company, 1978), especially Chapter 15, "The Passing of the Imperial Chief Executive; and William H. Newman, *Managers for the Year 2000,* (Englewood Cliffs, New Jersey: Prentice-Hall, Inc., 1978). For a survey of major factors in reaching top management levels among 1,700 executives in 750 companies, see John A. Sussman, "Making It To The Top: A Career Profile of the Senior Executive." *Management Review,* July 1979.

DISCUSSION GUIDES ON CHAPTER CONTENT ────────

1. What is business ideology? What is its function?

2. Are business ideologies nothing more than public relations statements, or do they really perform some useful purposes? Explain.

3. Contrast the classical business ideology with the new managerial creed. What are the basic differences between the two?

4. Identify major gaps in the business ideology and explain why they have not been filled.

5. Are there any major inconsistencies and/or conflicts that you have detected among the business ideologies?

MIND-STRETCHING QUESTIONS ────────

1. Many business people in the latter part of the nineteenth century embraced the doctrine of Social Darwinism and, in their economic activities, they often exploited both people and society. Should they be judged on the basis of values and ideologies that existed at the time or according to our present-day values and modern ideologies?

2. In the light of the findings of studies by Lodge and O'Toole, what do you think are the chances of the new ideology of communitarianism becoming widely accepted in the business world?

13
THE SOCIAL RESPONSIBILITIES OF BUSINESS

A) CORPORATE AMERICA CONFRONTS THE APARTHEID SYSTEM*

Introduction

The apartheid policy in South Africa has aroused protests from activists against United States corporations that do business in that nation. Protestors are demanding the withdrawal of United States firms from South Africa in order to exert pressure on the government there to end apartheid. These protestors feel that constructive efforts on the part of American firms to improve the employment conditions of a minority of blacks in South Africa cannot break down social and political apartheid. In addition, student activities are demanding that colleges and universities in the United States divest their stock in companies with South African interests. These activists think that divestiture on the part of colleges and universities can create pressure on American firms to withdraw. Due to international pressure, the South African government has appointed a labor reform commission to improve labor practices for blacks, and this has aroused great resentment from white labor unions. All these issues will be addressed in this case.

Historical Background of South Africa

Before 1652, South Africa was inhabited by Bushmen, Hottentots, Strandlopers, and Bantu (Africans). The Bantu were hunters and pastoralists, while the other groups were nomadic fishermen and hunters. The Dutch settled at the Cape in 1652, became farmers (Boers), and imported slaves from the East Indies. In 1795 Holland was defeated by French troops, which were in turn defeated by the British. Thus, Britain first occupied the Cape in that year. During an armistice in the Napoleonic wars, the Cape was returned to Holland for a short period of time, but

*This case was prepared by Marjorie Chan under the direction of John F. Steiner.

was reoccupied by Britain in 1806. Britain's possession of the Cape was sanctioned by the Congress of Vienna in 1815.[1]

While the early Dutch settlers practiced racial segregation and white supremacy, the British missionaries and administrators had a comparatively liberal attitude towards blacks. In 1833 the British abolished slavery. In order to avoid British interference with the practice of racial inequality, the Boers went into the interior of South Africa and established the independent Republics of the Orange Free State and the Transvaal. Due to the discovery of diamonds and gold in the Boer Republics in 1867 and 1886 respectively, the British became very interested in the Boer territories. The British entered the Boer Republics, and conflict between the Boers and the British culminated in the South African War of 1899–1902, which resulted in the defeat of the Dutch Republics by the British. During the reconstruction period of 1902 to 1910, both the Boers and the British worked towards the political union of South Africa. In 1910, the Union of South Africa was formed.

In order to conciliate the Boers, the British allowed racial inequality to continue in the former Republics. Later, the right to vote was taken away from the nonwhites in the Cape as well. By the Natives Land Act of 1913, nonwhites were not permitted to own land outside of the Native Reserves. In 1948, the Nationalist Party, consisting of almost all Afrikaners, won a landslide election, and it has stayed in power and practiced apartheid ever since. In 1961 South Africa became an independent republic, and it withdrew from the British Commonwealth due to criticism of apartheid.

The Apartheid Policy

Apartheid means racial segregation enforced in practice by various discriminatory laws. Racial inequality is manifest in both "grand" apartheid and "petty" apartheid. "Grand" apartheid denotes separate development whereby nonwhites do not obtain citizenship and land ownership rights in over 87 percent of industrialized white South Africa. Nonwhites are to reside in homelands or Bantustans on 13 percent of the barren land in outlying areas of the country. The program for separate development involves the resettlement of blacks to their homelands from the black areas of the South African urban districts occupied by whites. As the urban areas are industrialized, and the African tribal homelands are not, many black Africans illegally migrate to the black areas of the urban white territory. In order to control the influx of these illegal blacks, "pass laws" are enforced whereby every black South African over 16 years of age has to carry a passbook that provides information such as the bearer's name, tribe, and employer. The employer's signature must also be in the passbook. This passbook must be presented to a police officer on demand when the bearer is in a white area. Blacks found to be in a white area illegally may be fined or thrown in jail. The "pass laws" are disliked by blacks. Bishop Desmond Tutu, for example, head of the South African Council of Churches, has called them, ". . . among the most humiliating of the dehumanizing laws and regulations applied to this country."[2]

"Petty" apartheid denotes that whites and nonwhites are to have separate housing, schools, hospitals, job opportunities, public transportation, recreational facilities, public lavatories, and so on. Furthermore, blacks are not permitted to vote.

The apartheid policy is enforced by a brutal police force, and many blacks have been killed in uprisings against white minority rule. The Sharpeville Massacre in 1960 resulted in the deaths of 69 blacks who participated in a pass-burning ceremony organized by the Pan-Africanist Congress in opposition to apartheid. As a result of this incident, both the Pan-Africanist Congress and the African National Congress were banned. In 1976, demonstrations in Soweto, a large black township outside Johannesburg, led to the killing of over 700 blacks by police. In 1977, Steve Biko, banned leader of a "black consciousness" movement, died of head injuries allegedly inflicted on him by brutal interrogators during his detention. All 17 organizations associated with the "black consciousness" movement were banned.

Efforts of United States Firms to Ameliorate Apartheid

Due to pressure from church groups, student activists, unions, and blacks, United States firms have tried to perform a constructive role in South Africa so as to influence apartheid policy indirectly. Two notable examples are the Polaroid Experiment and the Sullivan code of conduct originally proposed by Reverend Leon Sullivan, a black director of General Motors. These efforts will be discussed here briefly.

The Polaroid Case

On Oct. 7, 1970, in the United States, a group of Polaroid employees with the title of Polaroid Workers Revolutionary Movement (PWRM) rallied against Polaroid's sales to South Africa. This was the first major indication of American blacks' resentment of the repression of blacks in South Africa. (At that time, Polaroid sold its products in South Africa through an independent distributor, Frank and Hirsch, and its sales there amounted to less than one half of one percent of its worldwide business.)

PWRM accused the company of exploiting cheap black labor in South Africa and selling its film and cameras to be used in implementing the passbook system. The activists demanded withdrawal of Polaroid from South Africa and the contribution of profits from the South African operation to support black revolutionary attempts in that country. On October 27, mass demonstrations organized by the PRWM took place in Boston and activists called for a worldwide boycott of Polaroid products.

In response, Polaroid set up a committee of 14 employees to look into the engagement-disengagement issue. The committee unanimously denounced apartheid and Polaroid became the first United States company to announce publicly its opposition to the South African government.

One of the recommendations proposed by this committee was to send a biracial team of two black and two white employees to South Africa to learn directly from

South African blacks their opinions with respect to whether or not Polaroid should pull out. This was done, and after talking with many people the four-member team concluded that Polaroid should stay. The team recommended undertaking an experimental program to improve conditions for blacks. This experiment consisted of the following measures.

1. The company will take steps with its distributor and suppliers in South Africa to increase remuneration of nonwhite employees.
2. Polaroid's business associates will be obliged to develop training programs for nonwhites so they can be promotable to responsible positions in their companies.
3. A percentage of profits from the South African operation will be allocated for the education of blacks.
4. Polaroid is looking into the possibility of "creating a black-managed company in one or more of the free black African nations."[3]

On December 30, 1971, Polaroid released a report that revealed the accomplishments of the Polaroid Experiment. It revealed, for example, that: "The average monthly salary including bonus for black employees has increased 22 percent. Individual increases have ranged from 6 percent to 33 percent."[4] Furthermore, Polaroid appointed eight black employees to supervisory positions, and provided training for nonwhite employees and educational expenses for their children. Polaroid contributed a total of $75,000 in educational grants to three black educational organizations in South Africa.

In November 1977 Polaroid terminated its business relationship with Frank and Hirsch, its independent distributor in South Africa, when this concern violated its 1971 agreement by selling Polaroid products to the South African government.

General Motors Takes Action

General Motors has been operating its South African auto assembly plant at Port Elizabeth since 1926. It has publicly denounced apartheid, and it engages in constructive involvement in South Africa by pursuing a progressive company policy that improves the working conditions of nonwhites. A notable example of General Motors' constructive engagement in South Africa is its endorsement of the Sullivan principles, which aim to improve employment conditions for nonwhites. These principles were drafted in 1977 as a result of meetings between Reverend Leon Sullivan, a black director of GM, a civil-rights activist who is pastor of the Zion Baptist Church of Philadelphia, and top executives of major United States corporations. Because the six principles were proposed originally by Reverend Sullivan in 1975, they are named after him and are as follows.

1. Nonsegregation of the races in all eating, comfort, and work facilities.
2. Equal and fair employment practices for all employees.
3. Equal pay for all employees doing equal or comparable work for the same period of time.
4. Initiation of and development of training programs that will prepare, in substantial

numbers, blacks and other nonwhites for supervisory, administrative, clerical, and technical jobs.

5. Increasing the number of blacks and other nonwhites in management and supervisory positions.

6. Improving the quality of employees' lives outside the work environment in such areas as housing, transportation, schooling, recreation, and health facilities.[5]

As of June 1979, *Business Week* reported widespread adoption of these principles.

> So far, 120 U.S. companies have signed the Sullivan code. These companies employ about 100,000 workers, but that figure includes only 50,000 of the 5.7 million "economically active" blacks in South Africa. Nevertheless, the code represents the first cohesive attempt by American companies to combat apartheid. In a survey of code performance published in April, Arthur D. Little Inc., gave 66 companies a nod of approval and 16 a slightly lower grade. The remainder were more or less ungraded.[6]

GM has decided to stay in South Africa because it believes that its presence can influence South African government policy constructively. GM has been progressive in its treatment of blacks. For example, it has narrowed pay scales between whites and nonwhites, increased the number of blacks in higher-level positions, built comparable facilities for nonwhites and whites, provided housing assistance, developed training programs for nonwhites, and offered educational assistance to nonwhite employees and their children. Furthermore, GM believes that its withdrawal from South Africa would lead to great financial losses for the company without visible gains to blacks. GM hires around 4,000 nonwhite employees, and its withdrawal from South Africa would lead to unemployment of these workers and those of its suppliers. The company also believes that if it withdrew it would be forced to sell its properties at highly distressed prices.

Critiques of the Sullivan Principles

Thaddeus H. Spratlan, a professor and researcher on the social performance of business at the University of Washington, criticizes the basic assumptions of the Sullivan principles. He makes the following arguments:

> "A first false assumption is that blacks in South Africa want only jobs and improved working conditions." They want most of all an end to apartheid. Therefore, the use of economic sanctions, disinvestment and the denial of bank loans to the South African government can be a more effective strategy to overcome apartheid.
> "A second false assumption is that reforms of South African institutions are possible within the framework of apartheid." Improvement in working conditions cannot crack down social and political apartheid which denies the rights of nonwhites to vote and to own land in urban white South Africa.
> "A third false assumption of the Sullivan statement is that through jobs something meaningful can be done about the status of blacks and other nonwhites." The gains to nonwhites as a result of the enforcement of the Sullivan principles might be minimal in a land that legalizes apartheid.
> "A fourth false assumption is that helping a few blacks to improve will help all

blacks move toward their ultimate goal of liberation." This is false because it creates an illusion of change while providing material comfort only for a few. It also diverts attention from the main issues: the proper sharing in power by the nonwhites of South Africa.[7]

Spratlan capsulizes his disdain for the Sullivan principles when he writes that, "At this stage in the progress of social responsibility and in the struggle against apartheid in South Africa, more than next to nothing is required to oppose apartheid."[8]

Timothy Smith, director of the Interfaith Council on Corporate Responsibility (ICCR), also criticizes the Sullivan principles, as follows:

Even the South African press raised questions about the character of the principles. The March 4 *Financial Mail* stated, 'Two main points must be made about the manifesto. The first is that it is more significant for what it leaves out than for what it says. The second is that signing statements of principle, however worthy, on one side of the Atlantic is one thing; putting them into practice on the other is another.'[9]

Various church groups also believe "that the progressive example of United States corporations cannot bring about systemic social change."[10] Since even the South African government is willing to endorse the Sullivan principles, Smith raises the concern that their effects might be minimal. "If these principles were in any way a threat to the system of apartheid," he says, "it is unlikely that the architects of apartheid would endorse them."[11]

Should United States Companies Get Out?

United States direct foreign investment in South Africa is 16 percent of total direct foreign investment in that country. The United States has increased three-fold its direct investment in South Africa in a period of 10 years, from $490 million in 1966 to $1.67 billion in 1976. There are around 400 U.S. companies operating in South Africa and they employ approximately 65,000 blacks, who constitute about 1 percent of the total labor force in South Africa.[12]

The Argument Against Withdrawal

Due to the inhuman treatment of blacks in South Africa, activists call for the withdrawal of United States firms from that country in order to exert pressure on the apartheid regime to change its racial policies. Yet there are strong opponents to the withdrawal of United States firms from South Africa, and some of their arguments will be given here.

George Kennan, former diplomat, advises against an isolation policy with respect to South Africa with the following argument:

South Africa, separated by thousands of miles from the remainder of the Western world, already suffers from an excess of isolation, . . . Apartheid is to some extent the reflection of this isolation. The reactionary and racist tendencies within South African society positively thrive on it . . . Why any opponent of that system should wish to intensify the very condition it feeds upon is difficult to imagine.[13]

George Ball, undersecretary of state for Presidents Kennedy and Johnson, puts forward this argument.

In dealing with the Communist nations, liberal opinion in the United States has adopted as its working hypothesis that social and political change can best be promoted by opening the windows and assuring maximum intercourse with the outside world. I fail to understand the logic of some of my liberal friends . . . who, while passionately promoting such a policy in our dealings with the Iron Curtain countries, insist that we pursue a diametrically opposite course with respect to South Africa.[14]

Those who favor the continued presence of United States firms in South Africa think that the prime role of corporations is not to make social change, but to engage in business in a country. This view is supported by Roger Williams, a journalist, in these words:

Aside from the illogic of forcing American companies out of South Africa, is there reason to be satisfied with what they are doing there? I think the answer is yes—provided we don't misconstrue the nature or overestimate the importance of their involvement. Especially in an alien society, private enterprise is not, and cannot be made to be, an aggressive, steadfast agent for social change. A corporation is formed not to effect change but to sell goods. It can be pressured into treating its employees more equitably. But it can't be expected to openly challenge the laws and, as some would demand, the precepts of current South African society. Those who insist otherwise are trying to get a businessman to do a diplomat's—or a soldier's—job.[15]

There are others who argue that increased foreign investment can be an effective strategy to end racial discrimination. This view is expressed by Harry Oppenheimer, chairman of South Africa's Anglo American Corporation group. He says:

So long as the advanced sector of the economy is growing, it is bound to draw more and more blacks away from the rural areas to live in or near the large white cities where the major industrial development is taking place. The faster the modern sector of the economy grows, therefore, the greater the proportion of the black population that will live and work outside the homelands.

The apartheid policy really only becomes plausible to the extent that a shortage of investment capital makes it impossible to provide jobs in the advanced sector for the numbers who would wish to enter it. Thus, a high level of investment in the advanced sector, not a low level, is best calculated to end racial separation and discrimination.[16]

John Connally, former Secretary of the Treasury and Governor of Texas, supports Oppenheimer's view this way:

I think we should encourage investment and so help expand economic activity in South Africa. That would mean more jobs for the blacks and the brown people. We could encourage additional change, but in a diplomatic way. We should encourage American businessmen to inaugurate training programs; to set an example of what we would like to see in our own country.[17]

Increased foreign investment is also advocated by Gatsha Buthelezi, the most popular leader of South African blacks, as follows:

> . . . Black and white alike, our need is for *peaceful* change, and foreign investment is one of the best agents of that change.
>
> As industry expands, propelled by domestic and foreign investment, a severe shortage of qualified men is increasingly appearing, and black people are of necessity being advanced to more responsible positions. The government has not only accepted this but made it a matter of policy. So I'd say that further improvement in black labor conditions is irreversible unless something happens to cause the economy to slow down—such as a withdrawal of foreign investment. As the process continues, the role of blacks in South African industrial management will become critical, which will give us more and more economic and political leverage. Our demands are thus increasingly likely to be met, as long as we maintain the pressure at other points.[18]

Black workers also oppose withdrawal of American firms. Freddy Sauls, an organizer for nonwhite workers in the Port Elizabeth auto industry, expresses the concerns of blacks this way:

> It's all very well for people to urge disinvestment who sit in safe comfort in some nice office 8,000 miles away. But if the American auto plants here closed down, I'd have thousands of men looking for work and literally wondering where the next meal would come from.[19]

Due to government regulations in South Africa, disinvestment involves great losses to corporations. Herman Nickel of *Fortune* states:

> For while South African foreign-exchange regulations allow the free repatriation of profits, this does not apply to capital. There is thus no way of packing up the plant and shipping it home. If an American corporation found a South African buyer, the proceeds would first have to be invested for at least seven years in low-yield South African government securities—a solution as unattractive politically as it is financially. The alternative of selling out to another foreign enterprise would merely give the buyer the competitive break of being able to pick up a plant at a knockdown price—and without any obvious gain for South Africa's blacks.[20]

Because European direct foreign investment in South Africa constitutes 57 percent of total direct foreign investment in that nation, United States withdrawal from South Africa would not lead to European disengagement as well.[21] When United States corporations withdraw, their business would be taken over only by the Europeans or the Japanese, who might not be as sympathetic to the plight of blacks. Some firms have improved the working conditions of nonwhites by paying them wages comparable to whites, upgrading their skills, and offering them on-the-job training so that they are promotable. Furthermore, these firms provide educational expenses for nonwhite employees' children, offer low-interest loans to these employees so that they can build their own homes or provide housing facilities for themselves.

The Argument for United States Withdrawal

Cotter *et al.* express the views of those who oppose United States engagement in South Africa this way.

> . . . (1) Even if American firms paid equal pay for equal work and made other improvements, they would still be supporting apartheid because of their direct and indirect support of the white minority government; and (2) employee benefit improvements would not affect the majority of nonwhites and could not crack the apartheid system that so limits and circumscribes the fundamental human rights of nonwhites.[22]

Furthermore, Timothy Smith points out that U.S. technology has been used through direct foreign investment by the South African military, police, and the government, the very institutions that repress blacks with the enforcement of apartheid. He adds:

> Citibank has loaned $300 million directly to the South African government; IBM still provides computers to that government for any purpose, however repressive; Caltex and Mobil are major suppliers of oil to the South African military, and through South Africa they are the oil lifeline to Rhodesia; Union Carbide assists apartheid by investing in and on the borders of Bantustans; Caltex is in the midst of a $134 million expansion that acts as an economic vote of confidence in white South Africa's future. The list goes on.[23]

Smith further contends that the benefits accrued to a minority of blacks through higher wages and improved conditions offered by United States firms operating in South Africa are insignificant when compared to the contributions these firms make to the "maintenance of apartheid" in terms of "the transfer of technology, the taxes paid to South Africa, . . . and the provision of strategic products to the racist government."[24]

Spratlan considers that the constructive engagement of United States firms is a less effective strategy than their disengagement in order to end apartheid. "Economic action such as the denial of loans, credits, and investments," he writes, "would do more to hasten the end of black subjugation than affirmative action in jobs."[25]

Oliver Tambo of the African National Congress represents the view of those black leaders who favor United States disengagement. Says Tambo: "We demand total isolation of the racist regime—no investment and withdrawal of existing investment."[26]

Finally, the General Assembly of the United Nations has approved resolutions that call for action against economic and military collaboration with South Africa. In other words, the United Nations officially favors isolation of the apartheid regime.

Labor Reforms in South Africa

While the Sullivan code and the European Community code of conduct exhort United States and European multinational corporations respectively to improve labor conditions for blacks in South Africa, the South African government has also attempted to improve labor practices by appointing a multiracial citizens commission chaired by Professor Nicholas E. Wiehahn, an industrial relations expert, to engage in labor reforms. The Wiehahn commission calls for the recognition of black labor unions with the right to strike and the permission to engage in collective bargaining, the abolition of the job reservation statute which denies blacks opportunities for many jobs, equal pay for whites and nonwhites with comparable skills, and the integration of various company facilities. The South African government accepts the following recommendations of the Wiehahn report.

1. The name of the Department of Labor will be changed to the Department of Manpower Development, which is "indicative of the new and more encompassing role which the department will have to play in the new dispensation."
2. A National Manpower Commission will be appointed on a permanent basis to advise the government on labor legislation and policy with respect to fair and equitable labor practices for blacks.
3. The National Manpower Commission will also be assigned by the South African government the duty to implement the Wiehahn commission's recommendation that "the concept of freedom of association should be extended to all workers in the South African economy."
4. The job reservation statute will be abolished so that jobs reserved solely for whites under this discriminatory law will be opened to all races.
5. A new industrial court will be established to settle labor disputes.[27]

The proposals of the Wiehahn Commission aroused great opposition from white labor unions. Wessel Bornman, general secretary of the South African Confederation of Labor with 200,000 white members, voiced his opposition in these words: "One wonders how long it will take before other legislation that is close to the hearts of whites also disappears."[28]

Arrie Paulus, union leader of the white mineworkers, has stated that the white employees would be "left at the mercy of the employers who will definitely replace them with cheaper black labor," if the Wiehahn proposals are legalized by Parliament.[29]

There is also criticism of these proposals because they do not apply to two million black immigrant workers. Also, white unions do not have the obligation to take in black members, and employers are not required to abandon discriminatory practices. "The principle underlying the (Wiehahn) proposals is commendable," says Dr. Nthato Motlana, a black leader of the township of Soweto, "but there has been no suggestion that discrimination in industry should be outlawed."[30] With discriminatory practices still permitted in industry, Motlana laments that "all the fine intentions" of the Wiehahn proposals "will mean nothing."[31]

Demands of Student Activists for Divestiture

Student activists have been clamoring for divestiture by universities of stock in American companies that do business in South Africa. The proponents of divestiture think this will lead to the withdrawal of American firms from South Africa, which will in turn create pressure on the South African government to reform its apartheid policy.

Some universities decided to divest all their investments in companies that have business dealings with South Africa, including Hampshire College, the University of Massachusetts, Antioch College, Ohio University, and the University of Wisconsin. Total divestiture was the greatest for the University of Wisconsin, where it amounted to $11.1 million at a loss of around $420,000.[32] Other universities take the position of Derek Bok, president of Harvard, who thinks divestment is plausible only if the following propositions are valid:

1. The withdrawal of American companies will help materially in overcoming apartheid. (Otherwise there is no adequate purpose to justify the drastic step of divestment.)
2. Corporate withdrawal will invariably contribute more to the defeat of apartheid than an effort on the part of American companies to improve the wages, employment opportunities, and social conditions of nonwhite workers. (If not, the proper course is to vote our shares in appropriate cases for improvements in employment and social policies.)
3. Selling Harvard's stock has a strong probability of persuading American firms to leave South Africa. (If not, one cannot justify the heavy costs and other disadvantages of divestment.)
4. Divestment is a substantially more effective way of inducing companies to withdraw than continuing to vote our shares and communicate with management in other ways. (Unless this is true, we should proceed by voting our shares rather than by selling them.)[33]

Bok considers it highly improbable that the aforementioned propositions are correct. He also says that university resources are to be used to further academic purposes and not to fight injustices. University trustees who divest run the risk of being legally liable for any resultant financial losses. Bok supports this point by referring to cases whereby the Attorney General of Oregon and legal counsel to various universities have taken the position that trustees who incur financial losses due to divestment are legally liable for their action.

Bok does indicate that Harvard has denounced apartheid by pursuing the following strategy:

. . . We have refused to purchase certificates of deposit in banks that are making loans to the South African government, and we are considering shareholder resolutions on a case-by-case basis to decide whether to vote for withdrawal or to support efforts to improve the employment and social conditions of nonwhite workers . . .[34]

Like Harvard, some other colleges and universities also oppose divestiture, but agree to examine their investments on a case-by-case basis. Some others divest only from banks that make loans to the South African government. Trustees of colleges and universities who oppose divestiture have stated that, "their holdings in companies like IBM, Ford, Mobil, and General Motors equal less than one percent of the value of corporations that, in turn, do less than one percent of their total business in South Africa."[35] They also support their position with the argument set forth by former United States U.N. Ambassador Andrew Young and Percy Qoboza, a newspaper editor in Johannesburg, "that the active presence of American companies can work against apartheid."[36]

Those who strongly advocate divestiture quote Senator Dick Clark of Iowa. "The net effect of American investment," argues Clark, "has been to strengthen the economic and military self-sufficiency of South Africa's apartheid regime."[37]

Student activists say that "the size of college holdings is of secondary importance—that divestiture is a symbolic action that will wield influence because of the role of the university in American society."[38]

Meanwhile, the Regents of the University of California and the Trustees of Stanford University have voted in a stock proxy against General Motors' sales to the South African military and police. Stanford and UC have a total investment of $13.8 million in GM, and Governor Brown, a regent of the University of California, considers that the vote "was just the beginning of a heightened social responsibility on the part of not only the University of California but all publicly held trust funds."[39]

CASE QUESTIONS

1. Do you favor withdrawal of United States-based corporations from South Africa, or their constructive engagement in that country? Why or why not?

2. Do you agree with the argument presented by Derek Bok, President of Harvard, against divestiture by universities of stock in American companies that do business in South Africa? Why or why not?

3. Do you agree with the critique of the Sullivan principles presented by Thaddeus H. Spratlan, a professor at the University of Washington? Why or why not?

4. Roger Williams, a journalist, supports those who favor the continued presence of American firms in South Africa in these words:

A corporation is formed not to effect change but to sell goods. It can be pressured into treating its employees more equitably. But it can't be expected to openly challenge the laws and, as some would demand, the precepts of current South African society. Those who insist otherwise are trying to get a businessman to do a diplomat's—or a soldier's—job.

What is your opinion of this quotation?

5. One of the reasons that American firms refuse to withdraw from South Africa is that this action will involve great financial losses. Do you think that business firms should carry out their social responsibilities regardless of the financial costs involved?

6. Precisely what social responsibilities do you believe United States-based companies should assume in South Africa?

7. What do you think would happen in South Africa if all United States-based companies decided to leave?

Notes

1. *Background Paper on South Africa* (London: Amnesty International, Sept., 1971).
2. Jack Foisie, "'Black Visas': South Africa Draws Line in Passbooks," *Los Angeles Times,* July 7, 1979, p. 8.
3. "An Experiment in South Africa," *Los Angeles Times,* January 13, 1971, p. 8.
4. "A Report on South Africa," Polaroid Corporation, December 30, 1971.
5. "General Motors in South Africa," *General Motors Public Interest Report,* 1976, p. 50.
6. "Why Pretoria is Giving Black Workers a Break," *Business Week,* June 18, 1979, p. 130.
7. Thaddeus H. Spratlan, "Sullivan's Follies," *Business and Society Review,* No. 26 (Summer 1978), p. 74.
8. *Ibid.,* pp. 74–75.
9. Timothy Smith, "Whitewash for Apartheid from Twelve U.S. Firms," *Business and Society Review,* No. 22 (Summer 1977), p. 60.
10. *Ibid.,* p. 60.
11. *Ibid.,* p. 60.
12. Lindsey Phillips, "South Africa's Future: No Easy Walk to Freedom," *Working Papers For a New Society,* March-April, 1979, p. 34.
13. Ernst Conine, "It Takes More Than Good Intentions to Overcome an Evil Like Apartheid," *Los Angeles Times,* Jan. 17, 1971.
14. *Ibid.*
15. Roger M. Williams, "American Business Should Stay in South Africa," *Saturday Review,* Vol. 5, No. 25 (Sept. 30, 1978), p. 20.
16. "Investment not Violence," *Business Week,* Oct. 9, 1978, p. 27. Emphasis in original.
17. "'Significant Changes,'" *Ibid.,* p. 26.
18. John Train, "South Africa: U.S., Don't Go Home," *Forbes,* Nov. 27, 1978, pp. 33–34.
19. Herman Nickel, "The Case for Doing Business in South Africa," *Fortune,* Vol. 97, No. 12 (June 19, 1978), p. 63.
20. *Ibid.,* p. 61.
21. Phillips, *loc. cit.*
22. William R. Cotter, Robert Denerstein, and Nancy McKeon, "The Proxy Contests Over Southern Africa," *Business and Society Review/Innovation,* No. 5 (Spring 1973), p. 65.
23. Smith, *loc. cit.*

24. *Ibid.*
25. Spratlan, *op. cit.,* p. 74.
26. Quoted in Derek Bok, "Reflections on Divestment of Stock: An Open Letter to the Harvard Community," Supplement to the *Harvard University Gazette,* April 6, 1979, p. 3.
27. Statement submitted by the Minister for Labor from the Parliamentary Office in Capetown, South Africa, May 1, 1979.
28. Peter Webb and Helen Gibson, "South Africa's Break for Blacks," *Newsweek,* Vol. 93, No. 20 (May 14, 1979), p. 72.
29. *Ibid.,* p. 72.
30. "South Africa Labor Reforms: Pretoria's Modest Proposals," *Time,* Vol. 113, No. 20 (May 14, 1979), p. 47.
31. *Ibid.,* p. 47.
32. Marc Fisher, "Showdown Over South Africa," *Change,* Vol. 11, No. 1 (Feb., 1979), p. 28.
33. Bok, *op. cit.,* p. 5.
34. *Ibid.,* p. 2.
35. Fisher, *op. cit.,* p. 29.
36. *Ibid.,* p. 29.
37. *Ibid.,* p. 29.
38. *Ibid.,* p. 29.
39. Jim Cramer, "Regents Send GM a Message," *Herald Examiner,* May 19, 1979.

B) WILLIAM ROBERTSON

William Robertson, a senior vice-president for the Chicago Steel Corporation, wrote an article for a national magazine deploring the fact that his company, together with other corporations in the Chicago area, had not done enough to avoid polluting Lake Michigan. Furthermore, Robertson declared, they ought to take the lead in really getting everyone involved to clean up the lake. He mapped out a clean-up program costing hundreds of millions of dollars.

Some of the customers of the corporation became annoyed at this blast, because they felt the net result would be demands by the government to undertake costly antipollution programs that the customers could not afford. The more disgruntled customers actually canceled orders.

The top management of the corporation felt that Robertson had gone much too far. They felt they had done much to avoid polluting the lake and that this publicity denigrated what they had done. Moreover, it promised not only to get them involved in very costly programs but to embroil the company in all sorts of unnecessary political and social battles. As a result, the chairman and chief executive officer asked Robertson never again to comment publicly without clearing his statement in advance with him.

Robertson resigned, saying that he refused to give up his responsibilities as a citizen. This action was considered too drastic by the top management, who suggested that Robertson manage for a year or so a new plant in France, which the corporation had recently acquired under his leadership. Robertson refused the position, saying that his conscience would not permit him to evade the issue in this fashion.

Robertson's friends viewed the matter in different ways. One executive said: "I have devoted my life to this corporation and its well-being is a matter of major significance to me. If I have to give up a few things to support the company, that is a small price to pay. My compensation is high and covers many things I may not like." Another said: "As long as Bill works for the company, it seems to me he ought to accept the company position and not stick a knife in its back." Another took a more philosophical position, saying: "No one has forced Bill to take his job. But, so long as he has the job, he cannot, as a major officer of the company, separate himself from it. He enjoys free speech under the Constitution, but the Constitution does not protect his job. The company has a right to defend itself from public statements of its officers if it wishes to do so."

CASE QUESTIONS

1. To what extent should a corporation protect its image? Should an executive be asked to follow a prescribed company position on a public issue, even if it deprives him of his right to speak out as he sees fit?

2. Comment on the moral issues raised in viewpoints expressed by Robertson's friends.

3. Suggest some methods that top managers of companies might use when dealing with protests both within and outside the company concerning company policies. (For a survey of managerial opinion on this point see David W. Ewing, "Who Wants Corporate Democracy?" *Harvard Business Review,* September-October 1971. See also other references to case XX.)

C) SMOKEY CIGARETTE COMPANY

You are the president of the Smokey Cigarette Company. A delegation of community leaders has just left your office after declaring in the strongest language possible that you have a deep social responsibility to stop advertising your products because advertising does in fact induce young people to start smoking and also maintains demand among those who are now smoking. You know the FTC has stopped all cigarette advertising over TV. You feel that the Surgeon General's Report on the relationship between cigarette smoking and cancer does present convincing evidence of the connection. Yet you still have some doubts. You know there is a close correlation between cigarette advertising and sales by brand. If you stopped advertising, sales would drop, and there would be a serious impact on earnings and stock prices. Furthermore, many farmers and your own employees are dependent on your company.

CASE QUESTION ────────────────────────────────

1. What do you think your social responsibilities are in this case?

D) DOLLARS FOR DECIBELS

The noise caused by human activity has been a problem for centuries. In the year 50 B.C., for example, Caesar banned chariot traffic at night in the streets of Rome to lower the noise level. Today because of the complexity of interests in society it is harder to deal with noise pollution. Airport noise is a particularly stubborn problem.

The township of Greater Westchester is located adjacent to the busy Los Angeles International Airport, and noise from jets taking off and landing in the vicinity has been an annoyance for years. The noise of a jet aircraft, of course, is enormous. A three- or four-engine turbofan aircraft three miles downrange from take-off or landing produces approximately 110 decibels on the ground. The noise is progressively louder as the plane nears the runway. For purposes of comparison, it is commonly accepted that prolonged exposure to 80 decibels, which is about the level of rush-hour surface traffic in a major city, may result in hearing loss.

In the past the City of Los Angeles has purchased property for suitable compensation from homeowners whose peace might have been disturbed because of location under an approach pattern to a runway. Still, losses can be substantial. In 1961, for instance, property assessments were reduced as much as 20 percent near L.A. International.

In 1967 L.A. International opened two new runways, Runway 24L and Runway 24R, which cut through populated areas. Take-offs and landings averaged 322 a day for 24L and 26 a day for 24R during peak periods. Property owners were indignant, claiming that not only was there physical damage to property taking place but that individuals were suffering severe nervous and psychological disruptions as a result of the intermittent blasts from the jet engines of commercial airliners. Property values naturally plummeted.

In 1968, 825 Westchester families in the vicinity of the new runways began seeking damages from the city. Most settled out of court, but in January 1975, six and a half years later, the case finally went to trial in Superior Court with 64 families remaining.

City appraisers estimated the homeowners' property to be worth $565,000 and appraisers hired by the complainants estimated its value to be $1,025,000. After five months of trial a jury awarded the Westchester residents $751,300 to cover fair market values of between $42,750 to $80,000 for their homes. Judge Bernard S. Jefferson also agreed to hear 51 personal injury claims for problems ranging from hearing loss to heart conditions. These claims, according to Jerrold A. Fadem, attorney for the property owners, would be $1 a day per person since the opening of the runways—or $1,462,920 at the time of the property settlement in 1975.

CASE QUESTIONS

1. What is an external cost? What are the full costs of airline and airfreight operations?

2. In your opinion is judicial remedy in cases such as this an efficient way of allocating total costs efficiently? If not, can you think of a better way?

3. In this case, who should be paying the costs of lowered property values and damage to residents' health: airlines, airplane manufacturers, airport authorities or city governments, property owners themselves, other government agencies, or a combination of two or more of these groups?

Reference

See Howard J. Sherman and E. K. Hunt, "Pollution in Radical Perspective," *Business and Society Review/Innovation,* No. 3 (Autumn 1972), pp. 48–53; and Gordon McKay Stevenson, Jr., *The Politics of Airport Noise* (Belmont, California: Duxbury Press, 1972), esp. Chapter 5.

DISCUSSION GUIDES ON CHAPTER CONTENT

1. What is meant by the "social responsibility of business"? Which of the many definitions in the text do you think is most useful?

2. "It is often said that the old classical managerial responsibility was to maximize profit in the short run. The idea that managers had to balance the interests of constituents was accepted because this was needed to maximize profits in the long run. So also is the idea of social responsibility accepted, since it is necessary to assure long-range profit maximization." Do you agree? Explain.

3. Argue the case against the assumption of social responsibilities by business.

4. Argue the case for the assumption of social responsibilities by business.

5. What is the concept of voluntarism? Of what significance is it in this argument?

6. Give an assessment of how top managers view their social responsibilities and how this view compares with that of managers at lower levels.

7. What are the pros and cons of institutional investors using their portfolios to influence companies in which they own stock to take social actions the investors consider desirable?

8. What are "social costs of business"? Is it possible to determine what social costs a business should bear?

9. Discuss some of the models of business social responsibilities and comment on their relative merits.

10. The text sets forth major criteria for determining the social responsibilities of business. Are they adequate? Should others be added?

MIND-STRETCHING QUESTIONS ———————————

1. Is it right for society to expect business to help further national goals even though the result might be that a corporation earns less money in the process?

2. Do you think the question of social responsibilities for business will have much to do with the preservation of individual political and economic freedom in the future?

3. "One of the greatest problems that the United States must face today and in the near future is this: Shall private enterprise function in a comparatively free market within a broad framework of law? Or shall business be considered an instrument to be used by the state to achieve social objectives that people generally feel have the highest priority?" What are your thoughts on these questions?

14
MAKING SOCIAL RESPONSIBILITIES OPERATIONAL IN BUSINESS

A) THE MIDDLE MANAGER AND COMPANY POLICIES FOR SOCIAL RESPONSIBILITIES

Michael Goodman is the general manager of the Metal Stamping Division of the Atlantic Manufacturing Company. His division is the largest in the company and is responsible for 65 percent of the corporate net profits. He is sitting at his desk—angry, frustrated, and puzzled. A delegation of employees has just left his office threatening a strike if his production line is not slowed down. Yesterday he became embroiled in a losing battle with the government's pollution supervisor because his air emissions were above allowable levels. Over the past six months, he has watched the productivity of his plant decline because central headquarters has forced him to employ increasing numbers of hard-core unemployed who, without requisite skills for their jobs, cannot meet productivity standards.

What bothers Goodman most is being forced, on the one hand, to take action that will reduce productivity and profits, while, on the other, being judged strictly on the returns on investment of his division. To make matters worse, he cannot seem to impress the president of the company with the fact that his speeches about all the great things the company should do to meet its social obligations are putting great pressure on Goodman to do things that will reduce his ability to achieve his profit goals. For instance, in a speech to the local League of Women Voters last week, the president said: "Our company is and will continue to be in the forefront of those that stand as good citizens in the community. We recognize our obligations to help those with whom we are associated, inside as well as outside our company, to lead the good life." Goodman thinks there is a direct connection between such rhetoric and the increasing demands made upon him to do things which reduce his profits. The president disagrees with Goodman and points out that if the environment of a business, internally and externally, is vibrant and healthy the profits of the company will expand.

CASE QUESTIONS

1. Identify some of the basic problems in this case. How do you account for the dichotomy between presidential rhetoric and Goodman's problems in implementing social programs?

2. You are hired as a consultant by this company to make recommendations for specific policies and plans to put the president's fundamental social aims into operation. What do you recommend?

B) CGI'S SOCIAL AUDIT

Conglomerate Growth International is one of the largest companies in the United States, with sales of around $2 billion. During the past 10 years, the company has been moderately successful, with earnings at or slightly above the average for most industries in which the company has important interests. In some of its product divisions, however, earnings have not been too satisfactory, and the company is having difficulties in meeting competition.

At the present time the company is engaged in the following lines of business. Its aircraft division, which is responsible for approximately one quarter of its total sales, makes small executive aircraft, wing assemblies for Boeing and McDonnell Douglas commercial aircraft, and helicopters for the U.S. Army. The Architectural and Construction Division has contracts around the world in port development, dam construction, and oil pipelines. The company also has wide-ranging interests in other areas, including paper and pulp mills, electronic assembly in Hong Kong and Taiwan, glass containers, and food containers.

Not long ago, the president of the company became concerned about social responsibilities and asked his principal managers to give him a report on what individuals in CGI were doing in this area. He was astonished to learn of the many activities in which his managers were engaged on their own. He felt that not only should such activities be encouraged, but that they ought to be accompanied by similar efforts on the part of the company.

Each year principal officers of the company from all over the world gather to review the performance and long-range plans of each of the affiliated companies and divisions and to discuss major company problems. The president felt that it would be useful if this year he asked a professor from a local university to talk with his managers about the subject of social responsibilities for companies. Following this talk, the president and managers decided that the company should make an audit of its social affairs.

CASE QUESTIONS

1. What is a business "social audit"?
2. Why do larger companies make social audits?
3. What type of social audit would you suggest to the president of CGI?

4. Should the social audit be made mandatory? (See John J. Corson and George A. Steiner, *Measuring Business' Social Performance: The Corporate Social Audit.* New York: Committee for Economic Development, 1974; Raymond A. Bauer and Dan H. Fenn, Jr., *The Corporate Social Audit.* New York: Russell Sage Foundation, 1972.)

DISCUSSION GUIDES ON CHAPTER CONTENT

1. What is meant by institutionalization of social values in the decision-making process of a business?

2. Explain whether you think it is easy or difficult to inject social values into the decision-making process of a typical large company? a very small company?

3. Discuss the various phases in the conceptual model for managing social responsiveness and compare them with some of the other operational models mentioned in the text.

4. Are structural and managerial changes necessary in managing social responsibilities?

5. What types of social audits have been made?

6. In your judgment does the idea of a social audit adequately assure appropriate corporate accountability?

7. "The whole thrust of business social audits will not get very far until there are creditable measures of the social performance of business, and they will not be developed very soon." Comment on this quotation.

8. Evaluate the model for a social audit suggested in the text.

MIND-STRETCHING QUESTIONS

1. Draw up a set of social policies for the Product Development Department of Inland Steel Corporation. Defend your proposal.

2. Where and in what ways can business increase short-term profits while at the same time helping society resolve some of its pressing problems?

3. The Chairman of the Board of General Motors Corporation asks your advice in answering this question: On which urban problems can I act to ease society's burdens and at the same time demonstrably increase the corporation's long-run profits? What is your response?

4. Even assuming that someday the social audit will be mandatory for business, do you think it will be as precise and uniform as today's financial audit?

5. What do you think the social audit of General Electric Company will look like in the year 1990?

IV
SELECTED POLICY AREAS WITH SOCIETY-WIDE IMPLICATIONS

15
POLLUTION PROBLEMS AND PUBLIC POLICY

A) "LOVE CAN BE DANGEROUS TO YOUR HEALTH"*

So read the headline of an advertisement trumpeting the leadership of the *Niagara Gazette* in exposing the danger of poisonous wastes in the Love Canal.[1] In 1976 the *Gazette* had run a few articles about chemical odors from the canal area, but the story faded. A year later, however, it was picked up by Mike Brown, a young *Gazette* reporter who wrote over 100 stories between 1977 and 1979.

The story attracted nationwide media coverage, most of it critical of Hooker Chemical Corporation, the company that had dumped toxic wastes into the Love Canal. Story after story detailed the deadly health consequences of chemical seepage from the canal and made the company seem about as socially responsible as a pillaging army. Hooker, on the other hand, feels that background information about the dumpsite which ameliorates its blame has not been publicized sufficiently.

This case focuses on the Love Canal dumpsite. Hooker, now a subsidiary of Occidental Petroleum, had in fact dumped thousands of tons of toxic chemical residues into 20 Niagara Falls area dumpsites over a 45-year period. The facts about other sites may well inspire different conclusions, but the problems of Love Canal are generic to all toxic waste disposal sites.

The Pre-Scandal History of the Love Canal

The Love Canal dumpsite was an environmental time-bomb that went off. In order to evaluate the culpability of Hooker and other owners of the dumpsite in what *Business Week* called "one of the nation's worst environmental disasters," it is necessary to know the history of the area.[2]

The story begins around the turn of the century when the Niagara Falls area became very attractive to industry. Companies located there because of huge potential for electric power from the falls, because access to transportation was easy, and because water for industrial processes was abundant. There were also enormous deposits of salt nearby.

Hooker, which built its first chemical plant in the area in 1905, was one of the companies lured by these assets. Today the company has 3,100 employees in Niagara Falls engaged in the manufacture of chlorine, caustic soda, plastics, pesticides,

*Prepared by John F. Steiner

fertilizer, and other chemicals. It is one of the economic mainstays of the city, a fact that has led critics to charge local government with avoiding firm action against Hooker.

In 1894, a few years before Hooker arrived, an ambitious businessman, Col. William T. Love, planned to build a "Model City" north of Niagara Falls. Because long electric power transmission lines were an undeveloped technology in those days, Love proposed to generate power for his Model City by building a canal between the upper and lower Niagara Rivers. This power canal would utilize the 300-foot drop in water level between the two channels to generate electricity for industries in Model City. Work started on the canal but the site was abandoned after economic depression made financing difficult and the invention of alternating current transmission lines brought a cheaper method for getting electricity to distant points. Only about one-half mile had been built. The canal lay abandoned for 30 years, used by local residents as a swimming hole in summer and a skating rink in winter.

The fun stopped in 1942, when Hooker got permission to use the Love Canal as a dumpsite for toxic chemical residues. The site was ideal. It lay in an undeveloped, sparsely populated area, and because of its impermeable clay walls it would retain liquid material dumped into it. Tests confirmed that the walls had a water penetration rate of only one-third inch in 25 years.

Hooker trucked in liquid, solid, and semisolid chemical wastes in steel and fiber drums. Workers dumped them into the trench. Sometimes men were splashed when the drums broke and they went to a nearby house to get hosed down. From there Hooker sent them to the hospital. The drums were not expected to contain their toxic contents over years of interment, but were used simply for convenience in hauling. Rows of drums were laid down in section after section of the original trench and then covered with several feet of claylike material. Hooker also claims to have placed a soil cap over the top of the dumpsite, but no confirming records have been located. In 1947 Hooker purchased a 16-acre area, including Love Canal, from Niagara Power and Development Company.

No complete records of the wastes dumped in the canal were kept at the time, and Hooker relied on reconstruction of past operations and the memories of old-time employees to determine its contents. To date, over 300 separate chemicals have been identified and the site contains an estimated 21,800 tons of wastes, including 200 tons of wastes from the production of 2,4,5-trichlorophenol, an organic pesticide and industrial intermediate containing traces of 2,3,7,8-tetrachlorodibenzo-*para*-dioxin, one of the most toxic poisons known. Estimates are that up to 100 pounds of dioxin could be present in the canal and, according to *Chemical Week*, in early 1979 dioxin had been detected just outside the Love Canal pit.[3] Dioxin is so toxic that just three ounces in the New York City water supply could kill everyone in the city.

Property Acquired by the Local School Board

In 1953 the Niagara Falls Board of Education was attracted to the Love Canal property, now standing idle, and wanted to build a school near the canal. Hooker representatives appeared before the school board in a public meeting and argued that utilizing the canal area was not a good idea—especially for a school. Initially, the school board backed off, but then inexplicably changed its mind and began condemnation proceedings to obtain adjacent parcels of land. Hooker again warned the school board of the potential dangers of the toxic wastes on at least one more occasion. This had no effect and in 1953 Hooker sold the land to the school board for $1.00. All members of the school board at that time are dead, so the reasons for their improvident decision remain unknown.

In deeding over the land in 1953, Hooker stipulated that all risk and liability for claims in the future passed on to the school board. Part of the deed reads as follows:

> Prior to the delivery of this instrument of conveyance, the grantee herein has been advised by the grantor that the premises above described have been filled, in whole or in part, to the present grade level thereof with waste products resulting from the manufacturing of chemicals by the grantor at its plant in the City of Niagara Falls, New York, and the grantee assumes all risk and liability incident to the use thereof. It is, therefore, understood and agreed that, as a part of the consideration for this conveyance and as a condition thereof, no claim, suit, action or demand of any nature whatsoever shall ever be made by the grantee, its successors or assigns, against the grantor, its successors or assigns, for injury to a person or persons, including death resulting therefrom, or loss of or damage to property caused by, in connection with or by reason of the presence of said industrial wastes.[4]

Oblivious to the danger, the school board constructed the 99th Street School on land that had not been part of the dumpsite, next to the canal. Previously unused sections of the canal were filled with municipal refuse and a playground was built. The school board also deeded part of the land to the City of Niagara Falls to build a park (which was never built) and part to a private developer. When Hooker learned of the impending sale to the developer, company representatives again went to a school board meeting to discourage the sale. A follow-up letter detailing possible problems was sent. Again, the school board ignored Hooker. Each subsequent deed, however, contained the same protection against liability for Hooker found in the 1953 deed.

By 1964, developers had built over 150 houses on streets lining Love Canal and by 1976, 50 more homes had been added for a total of more than 200. Over the years these residents shared unnerving experiences in the area. Flowers failed to bloom in the spring. In the summertime spontaneous fires from rising chemical gases occurred, but the residents called Hooker, and the company would send out a bulldozer to spread ash over the flames. When heavy winter rains and melted snow swelled the underground water table, rotted drums popped to the surface in back yards and on the school's playing field. Chemical odors were omnipresent, but strongest in warm weather. Children and animals suffered chemical burns and skin rashes, but county officials responded to complaints by saying no danger existed. Worse, there seemed to be an unusually high incidence of miscarriages, birth defects, and nervous disorders in the area. At the time, families assumed these were just private tragedies.

The real time-bomb was about to go off. On at least one occasion, and probably others, tons of soil had been removed from the top of the dumpsite by developers constructing the homes and streets. This violated the integrity of the clay cap in wholesale fashion. At that point, water got into the canal and mixed with the toxic brew inside. Hooker Executive Vice-President Bruce D. Davis describes how the Love Canal was unleashed on the innocent homeowners.

> We believe that surface water resulting from heavy rain and melting snow entered the Canal, which gradually filled up just like a bathtub, and then overflowed. The water mixed with chemical wastes, producing a liquid called leachate, which seeped into some basements of houses built on adjacent properties.[5]

In 1976, local authorities and newspapers received new complaints from area residents about mysterious odors and sickness. The leachate from the Love Canal had moved through the ground and entered nearby basements through cracks in cement walls, pooling on basement floors. Strong chemical odors were noted by homeowners as the air in their basements became saturated with chemical fumes. Tainted water pooling in back yards was iridescent from chemical contamination. Residents noticed that children who played near the canal became mysteriously ill. People with seemingly minor ailments suddenly died.

Of the 300 or so chemicals present in the soil and homes at Love Canal, approximately 100 have been identified precisely. David Axelrod, State Health Commissioner of New York, estimates that 10 percent of these are mutagens, teratogens, and carcinogens. If so, many of the health problems around the location could be explained. Freelance writer Dorothy Gallagher has described reporter Mike Brown's door-to-door medical sleuthing in the Love Canal residential area.

> One woman opened her door seated in a wheelchair. 'I don't know *what's* wrong with me,' she told Mike. She simply had become progressively weaker over a period of time, until one day she had fallen down and been unable to get up. Her doctors were at a loss to name the source of the problem. Mike asked the woman if she had spent a lot of time in her basement. The answer was yes. She had operated a beauty parlor in her basement, and often had spent up to 12 hours a day there. Mike strongly suspected that the woman was suffering from benzene poisoning, one of the chemicals discovered leaking into basements along Love Canal.
>
> There was Jean Guagliano's daughter, who was four months old when the family moved to Love Canal. At the age of three, Lisa developed kidney problems and began to hemorrhage. Since then she has had frequent bladder and kidney infections, surgery, and at the age of eight she cannot control her bladder. Renal damage can be an effect of exposure to carbon tetrachloride, one of the many chemicals identified at Love Canal.[6]

Residents complained of a wide range of health problems. For example, there were an unusually large number of birth defects, including mental retardation, deafness, deformed teeth and ears, cleft palate, and heart, kidney, and hip abnormalities. A report by the New York State Health Department in August 1978 showed abnormalities in 5 of 24 children born to families around Love Canal between 1958 and 1975. The Department's report also documented a high miscarriage rate and a greater-than-expected incidence of liver disease. Other problems included hyperactivity in children, epilepsy, rectal bleeding, nervous breakdown, and possible latent illnesses. Some residents thought the suicide rate for the area was unusually high. Doctors hypothesized that the sudden deaths from apparently minor illnesses resulted from release of deadly chemicals stored in body fat. When sickness came the body metabolized some fatty reserves, removing the poisons from storage and putting them into the system. These problems were manifest in two rings of residences abutting the canal.

Alerted by residents and reporters to the problems, the State Health Department went house to house in the canal zone in May 1978 taking blood samples and medical histories. In early August, Commissioner Robert Whalen closed the 99th Street School, citing "great and imminent peril" to students. He also recommended evacuation of pregnant women and children under two years old from the first two rings of houses. This recommendation was later extended to six blocks. That fall, in an unprecedented move, President Carter declared the Love Canal a disaster area. This qualified families for federal assistance and was the first time a disaster proclamation had been made for a ground pollution episode. By November 1978, 237 families had moved out. The State of New York purchased their homes for approximately $10 million. Today, the deserted houses are surrounded by an eight-foot-high chain link fence. Some families just outside the disaster area have been forced to remain near Love Canal because the state will not buy their houses. Mailman Chester Gawel, who delivers their mail, wears a gas mask as he walks his appointed rounds.

Hooker Joins in the Cleanup Efforts

After complaints by Love Canal residents the City of Niagara Falls in 1977 engaged an engineering consulting firm to study the canal site and recommend remedial action. Hooker employees supplied the consultants with technical information and help. Later, a second study was done and its cost was shared equally by the city, the Board of Education, and Hooker. According to Hooker executive Bruce Davis:

> The company's technical and economic response to this situation reflected not only our recognition of the problem that was developing, or could develop, but also our very real concern for the safety, comfort and well-being of the residents of the Love Canal area, both in terms of their personal protection as well as that of their homes and property.[7]

The second report recommended remedial work costing an estimated $850,000 and Hooker offered to pay one third. Work on this project started in October 1978. Completed within a year were a tile leachate collection system on both sides of Love Canal, an activated carbon treatment facility to decontaminate water from the leachate collection system, and a new clay cap over the southern third of the canal to keep rainwater and melting snow from seeping into its poisoned vault. An extensive soil and sump sampling program has been carried out to map leachate migration from the site, and groundwater movement under the canal is being studied in three deep wells placed nearby.[8]

The company in 1979 was faced with over $2 billion in potential awards to plaintiffs in lawsuits. Because of its environmental problems Hooker has already suffered financially. Net sales rose from $1.6 billion in 1977 to $1.7 billion in 1978, yet earnings were $42 million less in 1978. Second-quarter earnings for Hooker in 1979 were 38 percent less than for the corresponding period in 1978. The company says this was "due principally to additional provisions for special environmental costs associated with past practices."[9]

Public Relations Problems for Hooker

In the meantime, Hooker came under fire for its disposal practices at other dumpsites. Several other sites in the Niagara Falls area were suspected of releasing toxic chemicals. For example, in the summer of 1978, divers employed by the city were sent on a routine inspection dive to the bottom of the shore shaft of the municipal water treatment plant, which treats Niagara River water for a population of 100,000. They brought up sludge samples containing various chemicals of the same kind as those made by Hooker. Subsequently, divers trying to clean out the sediments in the short shaft had to change gloves repeatedly as high concentrations of chemicals in the sludge ate through them.

Although the company pointed out that the city's treated water has been found safe for drinking and contains lower levels of some dangerous chemicals, such as chlorinated organics, than most other industrial cities, suspicion immediately focused on a Hooker dumpsite adjacent to the City Water Treatment Plant. The two are separated only by a street. Hooker drilled more than 70 monitoring wells to check for possible migration of chemicals in the groundwater but valid findings were slow in coming because it takes several months for groundwater wells to stabilize. So far, the city's water supply remains safe.

Early in 1979, Michigan sued Hooker, demanding that it pay to clean up hundreds of thousands of gallons of chemical wastes dumped near Montague, Michigan. Leachate from the dump, located in the woods behind a Hooker plant, had entered the groundwater aquafer and was migrating. This problem only came to light when Hooker's parent, Occidental Petroleum, tried to take over the Mead Corp., a large Ohio paper products firm. Mead, in resisting the takeover bid, hired consultants who probed Hooker's disposal sites trying to show that Occidental had liabilities it failed to disclose to the Securities and Exchange Commission while pursuing the takeover. These liabilities, Mead argued, were material to stockholders thinking of selling to Occidental. (The takeover bid subsequently failed.)[10]

Hooker Defends its Actions at Love Canal

In its defense, Hooker, in Congressional testimony and in other public statements, made several points.

First, the company said its disposal practices in the 1940s and 1950s were no better or worse than others in the industry. The Love Canal, in particular, would have retained its basic integrity as a prison for wastes if its clay cover had not been disturbed by developers. Because Hooker dumpsites have been investigated and publicized more than those of other companies, Hooker has taken an unwarranted publicity beating.

Other large, diversified chemical companies such as Du Pont, FMC, Monsanto, PPG Chemicals, and Velsicol also are guilty of leaving toxic wastes in dumpsites that have released their contents into the environment. The EPA, which first established standards for solid waste dumpsites only in 1979, has identified more than 400 cases of damage to health and the environment due to improper management of hazardous wastes. The hazardous waste disposal problem is actually part of a much larger problem of solid waste disposal in nearly 20,000 American dumpsites. Harmful leachate plumes may come from ordinary municipal refuse piles containing old batteries, metals, household chemicals and poisons, human and animal viruses, and other menacing substances.

Second, Hooker claimed to have accepted its social and moral responsibility for environmental damage, even though it has questionable legal responsibility for Love Canal. A Hooker publication states: "Hooker is making every effort to cooperate with responsible Federal, State and local agencies to provide historical information about the site and to participate in joint studies of the problem aimed at working out remedial measures."[11] At the 1979 annual shareholders' meeting of Occidental Petroleum in Beverly Hills, California, Oxy chairman Dr. Armond Hammer:

> . . . assured those attending the meeting the Occidental feels a moral responsibility regarding the Love Canal matter regardless of the legal issues involved. He said that, even though the disposal of chemical wastes at Love Canal happened long before Occidental acquired Hooker Chemical Corporation, 'We shall carry out our moral responsibility with cooperative efforts to rectify the problems and do all we can to help.'[12]

In 1979, Hooker had more than 140 employees doing environmental health and safety work and claimed to have spent "in excess of $40 million" for environmental protection.[13] Indeed, Hooker claims to be an industry leader in cleaning up chemical waste disposal sites because of its experiences with the Love Canal and other dumpsites. It claims to have developed advanced expertise in hydrological study and groundwater analysis that makes it a leader in understanding ground pollution clean-up problems.

Finally, in its defense, Hooker has urged society to adopt a more balanced and fair perspective. Society has encouraged industrial development with its attendant risks and the entire country benefits from the gains in the quality of life associated with products containing Hooker chemicals. Problems such as Love Canal are tragic, but the great benefits of using household cleaners, pesticides, herbicides, insecticides, and fertilizers must be remembered also. Chemical waste disposal problems are only one kind of environmental trade-off in the industrial revolution. There have been many others.

No Light at the End of the Tunnel for Hooker

Early in 1980, Hooker was still undertaking exploratory studies and monitoring waste disposal sites around Niagara Falls to determine the extent of the escape of poisons. Lawsuits over property damage and health damage are still being heard in the courts, and the House of Representatives is exploring the idea of legislation to impose on chemical companies the costs of cleaning up toxic wastes. According to Representative Albert Gore, Jr., (D-Tenn.) of the House committee probing Hooker's problems, the bill was inspired by hard feelings in Congress about Hooker's actions. The press continues to research Hooker's past sins also.

Whatever the nature of the final reality to be shaped by these forces, the real losers will still be the people who lived beside the Love Canal. No financial statement, Congressional reprimand, or press revelation can fully restore their lives and health. A hidden blessing, if there is one, is that the Love Canal has become a symbol for focusing national attention on problems of toxic waste disposal.[14]

CASE QUESTIONS

1. Has Hooker met its social and moral responsibilities to a) the residents of the Love Canal area, b) the school board, c) local and state authorities, and d) the natural environment? Explain your views.

2. Should Hooker have done more in the past to keep track of events at the Love Canal?

3. Do some research on the problem of solid waste pollution. How typical or atypical an incident is the Love Canal?

Notes

1. The ad appeared in many places, for example, in *U.S. News & World Report,* August 6, 1979, p. 11.
2. *Business Week,* May 7, 1979, p. 44.
3. *Chemical Week,* January 3, 1979, p. 16.
4. Recorded on July 6, 1953.
5. "Statement by Bruce D. Davis," before the United States House of Representatives Subcommittee on Oversight and Investigations of the Committee on Interstate and Foreign Commerce, Washington, D.C., April 10, 1979, p. 9.
6. In "The Tragedy of Love Canal," *Redbook Magazine,* Vol. 152, No. 6 (April 1979), p. 67. Emphasis in the original.
7. Davis, *op. cit.,* p. 10.
8. "Love Canal," Draft Report of the New York State Interagency Task Force on Hazardous Wastes, March 1979, pp. II-76-77.
9. Occidental Petroleum Corporation, "Six Months Results," 1979, p. 2.
10. Bob Secter, "Poison Waste Dumps Peril Water Supply," *Los Angeles Times,* September 6, 1979.
11. "A Hard Look at the Love Canal," Hooker Fact Line No. 1.
12. "Annual Shareholders' Meeting 1979," Occidental Petroleum Corporation, 1979, p. 27.
13. This claim was made in "A Hard Look at the Love Canal," *op. cit.*
14. For further information see, Michael H. Brown, "Love Canal, U.S.A.," *New York Times Magazine,* January 21, 1979, pp. 23-44; Donald Janson, "New

Environment Chief Vows Firm Jersey Rules," *New York Times,* August 27, 1979, B1; Bruce McWilliams, "Special Report, Love Canal," *Oxy Today,* Number 13, 1979, p. 5; and "Toxic Waste Disposal a Growing Problem," *Science,* Vol. 204, No. 4395 (May 1979), pp. 819–823.

DISCUSSION GUIDES ON CHAPTER CONTENT

1. What is environmentalism? What are the major ideas promoted by the environmentalists? What are the factors militating against the environmental movement in recent times?

2. Do you think the "issue-attention cycle" identified by Downs has been working in the United States? Explain.

3. Our society is a complex of systems within a system. In the light of this, the establishment of pollution standards may conflict with other systems. Illustrate a few conflicts.

4. Describe briefly the functions of the Council on Environmental Quality (CEQ) and the Environmental Protection Agency (EPA).

5. What are Environmental Impact Statements? Of what consequence are environmental impact studies to business? to society?

6. Identify the Clean Air Act. Appraise its significance.

7. What are the major types of environmental pollution today, and why be concerned about them?

8. Who should bear the costs of pollution control?

MIND-STRETCHING QUESTION

1. Many people think it is time that an international agreement be made to assure cooperative action on the part of all nations of the world to reduce the pollution of the oceans. What major problems exist in trying to do this? How would you suggest trying to get needed cooperation?

16
POLLUTION POLICY ISSUES

A) THE SNAIL DARTER VERSUS PROGRESS IN TENNESSEE

In 1967 Congress authorized the Tennessee Valley Authority (TVA) to build a dam on the Little Tennessee River. The dam, known as the Tellico Dam, would flood 16,500 acres of farmland to create a 33-mile-long reservoir upstream from the river's mouth. The dam was part of a larger overall development project designed to generate electricity, control flooding, and promote economic development in the area by construction of recreational and residential facilities along the new shoreline.

After 1967 Congress appropriated money each year for the project but environmentalists and local residents whose property would be flooded combined forces in powerful stop-the-dam efforts. Opponents of the dam called it pork-barrel politics, said it was damaging to the environment, and produced figures purporting to show that it was not really a net boost to the local economy. Their efforts came to an initial halt when the Environmental Defense Fund lost a suit it had brought against the TVA in a U.S. District Court in Tennessee.

Then the coincidence of two unrelated events breathed new life into the anti-dam forces. In the summer of 1973 a Tennessee ichthyologist, Dr. David Etnier, Jr., discovered a previously unknown species of perch in the cold, clear waters of the Little Tennessee. The fish became known as the snail darter. The snail darter is a tan, minnowlike fish about two or three inches in length. Subsequent study determined that a population of 10,000 to 15,000 snail darters inhabited 17 miles of streambed and gravel shoals above the rising edifice of Tellico Dam. Spawning took place at Coytee Springs, about 15 miles above its gates.

Discovery of the snail darter was not particularly noteworthy. There are over 120 species of darters in North American waters and over 90 are in Tennessee, including the stargazing darter, Blenny darter, Ouachita darter, and the banded sculpin. New species are discovered at the rate of about one a year. The fish has no commercial value in the local economy.

At nearly the same time as the mundane discovery of the snail darter, Congress passed the Endangered Species Act of 1973 by overwhelming margins in both houses. The act called for the Secretary of the Interior to list and protect species of animals, birds, fish, and plants determined to be threatened with extinction.

In January 1975, opponents of the Tellico Dam petitioned to have the snail darter classified as an endangered species and that November, with the dam 75 percent completed, Secretary of the Interior Thomas Kleppe publicly proclaimed such status for the fish. Kleppe also made those areas of the river inhabited by the darter a "critical habitat," or one necessary for the species' survival and, therefore, also protected. The justification for this action was that flooding the reservoir would submerge the darter's habitat under many feet of water and destroy the ecological niche by altering temperature, current, water quality, exposure to sunlight, and other factors.

In response to the Secretary's action, TVA officials speeded up construction of the dam. They were convinced that the 1973 law was not intended to stop on-going projects started before its passage and that the further toward completion the dam was, the harder it would be for opponents to stop it.

Environmentalists finally were able to obtain a court injunction bringing construction to a halt in 1977 when the dam was 95 percent complete and over $113 billion had been spent on it. The TVA appealed the injunction and in June 1978 the Supreme Court affirmed the lower court in a 6 to 3 decision. In the majority opinion written by Chief Justice Warren Burger the Court said that when Congress passed the Endangered Species Act it clearly intended no exceptions and barred all actions that would threaten endangered species. A dissent by Associate Justice Lewis Powell argued that Congress could not possibly have intended to throw away millions of dollars and sacrifice the potential benefits of the project simply because an obscure new species of fish had been discovered six years after starting construction of the dam. The majority opinion stated, however, that the legislative history of the Endangered Species Act showed Congress intended to view the value of threatened species as "incalculable." Hence, destruction of a species could not be offset by any economic benefits of a public works project.

Following the high court's decision in *TVA* v. *Hill*, Congress amended the Endangered Species Act to set up a cabinet-level Endangered Species Committee in Washington, D.C., and empowered it to exempt government-financed projects from the law protecting endangered species even if extinction of a species resulted from the committee's action. Exemptions were to be granted *only* if no feasible alternative existed and the economic benefits of a project outweighed alternative courses of action. Despite a special provision in the amendment that the Tellico Dam situation be given special consideration by the committee and despite the fact that the TVA made efforts to transplant the snail darter into nearly identical Tennessee streams (where the fish did reproduce successfully), the Endangered Species Committee on January 23, 1979, refused to grant an exemption to TVA authorities.

Now, the dam gates cannot be closed and the flickering shape of the snail darter is still seen among the sand shoals of the Little Tennessee, living in the shadow of an ironic monument to conservation.

CASE QUESTIONS

1. Should the snail darter be protected at great financial expense and at the cost of foregoing economic benefits? Were alternative solutions possible in this case? If so, what were they?

2. Is the Endangered Species Act a well-written regulation? Why or why not?

3. What are some of the arguments for and against protecting endangered species? Should a distinction be made between minor species such as darters and more important species such as the grizzly bear and bald eagle?

References

James J. Kilpatrick, "Lessons to Be Learned From a Bad Law," *Nation's Business* (August 1978), pp. 11–12.

Ian C. T. Nisbet, "Endangered Species and Emerging Values," *Technology Review* (December 1978), pp. 8–9.

The Conservation Foundation, "Humans Attach Many Values to Wildlife Species," *Conservation Foundation Letter* (May 1978).

Lawrence Haworth, "Rights, Wrongs, and Animals," *Ethics,* Vol. 88, No. 2 (January 1978), pp. 95–106.

B) COST/BENEFIT DECISION AT BLUEBIRD SMELTER*

Bluebird Smelter is owned by a large, national mining company and located in Bluebird, a town of 12,000 in western Montana. The smelter, which has been operating profitably for 35 years with 125 employees, processes copper ore arriving by railroad. Its most distinguishing feature is a tall, brick stack, visible for miles and used as a landmark by nearby residents, which emits a visible plume and often leaves a faint, smudgy pall over Bison Valley, the geological basin in which Bluebird is located.

Bucolic Bison Valley has about 25,000 residents and attracts retirees from big city life and wealthy weekenders who build retreats or buy small farms in the area. The economy of Bison Valley has been primarily agricultural but tourism is an important—if small—component, as is Bluebird Smelter.

Bluebird Smelter is the only major industrial pollution source in the valley. Fugitive and stack emissions from the smelter include sulfur dioxide (SO_2), sulfuric acid, inorganic arsenic, particulates from copper and iron dust, asbestos, nitrogen oxides, aromatic hydrocarbons, and traces of other potentially injurious chemicals. On sunny days when the air is still and during periods of temperature inversion over the valley the action of the sun on smelter emissions contributes to photochemical smog similar to that in urban areas. Auto emissions and agricultural activities are also sources of photochemical oxidants, but smelter emissions are far more important.

Because of its conspicuous presence, dramatized by the tall stack, visible plume, and a lingering odor from SO_2 emissions, a small, local environmental group called the Earth Riders made the plant a target in the mid-1960s. Lawsuits and political pressures by the Earth Riders led to installation in 1972 of costly pollution control

*Prepared by John F. Steiner

equipment at the smelter that reduced emissions by 75 percent from an uncontrolled state. This brought improved air quality, but visible pollution, adverse health effects, and crop damage continued.

Later in the 1970s Bluebird Smelter was granted a series of variances from federal and state air quality standards when the company let it be known that further pollution control expenses would force closure of the plant. From the 75 percent control level, costs escalated rapidly and further controls—say to the 90 percent level—would cost more in total than the original 75 percent reduction. Bluebird Smelter could not afford it. The massive expenditures required would push the plant into long-term financial loss.

Many townspeople told reporters from big-city papers that they wanted jobs and were willing to tolerate a little dirty air. Local observers thought that closure of the smelter would throw Bison Valley into an economic recession. Despite opposition and organized protest by the Earth Riders, the Bluebird City Council passed five resolutions asking for deviation from air quality standards for the smelter and sent them to state and federal agencies. When several Earth Riders chained and locked themselves to railroad tracks leading to the smelter, demanding that ore shipments cease and the plant close down, the mayor of Bluebird, a veterinarian, placed a placard in his office window offering "Free Rabies Shots to Earth Riders. No Appointment Necessary."

In 1980 a state public health official conducted an epidemiological study of the region because it offered the unique opportunity to observe the health effects of a single, major source of industrial pollution. Using standard mortality tables the official determined that there had been 25 "excess" deaths in Bison Valley over the five-year period between 1974 and 1979. These were deaths from emphysema, lung cancer, tuberculosis, pneumonia, and ischemic heart disease over and above those naturally occurring in a population not exposed to similar industrial pollution. Such results were not surprising given the existing SO_2 and particulate levels. The unique element in the situation was that the cause was a single source rather than a collection of sources mixing together as in most industrial and urban areas. What could not be determined, of course, was which deaths were the "excess" ones. The extra five fatalities averaged each year were part of a group of several hundred deaths, most of which were statistically "expected."

Also, a group of economists from a prestigious research institute in another city picked the Bluebird Smelter as a test case for a research project on the health effects of pollution. The figures they produced led to debate among the various local groups involved in the controversy. The researchers looked at the operation of Bluebird Smelter in terms of costs and benefits to the community and to society. The following table shows their basic calculations.

The Earth Riders seized upon the study, arguing that if total costs of smelter operation exceeded benefits, then a clear-cut case had been made for closing the plant. It was already operating at a loss; in this case a net social loss of $730,000. Thus, in the eyes of the environmentalists Bluebird Smelter was in social bankruptcy.

The smelter's managers and members of the Bluebird City Council, on the other

---

TABLE 16.1

ANNUAL BENEFITS AND COSTS OF BLUEBIRD SMELTER

Benefits	Value
Payroll for 125 employees at an average of $15,000 each	$1,875,000
Benefits paid to workers and families at an average of $1,000 each	125,000
Income, other than wages and salaries, generated in the valley by the company	4,600,000
Local taxes and fees paid by the company	100,000
Social services to community and charitable contributions	20,000
Total	$6,720,000

Costs	
Excess deaths of 5 persons at $1 million each*	$5,000,000
Other health and illness costs to exposed population	450,000
Crop and property damage from pollutants	1,000,000
Reduction of aesthetic value and quality of life	500,000
Lost revenues and taxes from tourism	500,000
Total	$7,450,000

*Calculated on the basis of recent court decisions compensating victims of wrongful death in product liability cases in Western states. The figure reflects average compensation.

hand, ridiculed the study for making unrealistic and overly simplistic assumptions. They questioned whether the costs were meaningful, citing estimates of the value of a human life that were much lower than $1 million, made by other economists. They argued that health risks posed by the smelter were less than those of smoking cigarettes, drinking, or riding motorcycles and that benefits to the community were great. They even suggested that important costs had been left out of the calculations such as sociological and psychological costs to workers who would be laid off if the plant closed.

The debate raged and the smelter continued to operate.

CASE QUESTIONS

1. Do you believe that the costs to society of smelter operation outweigh the benefits?
2. Do you believe that the cost figures in the researcher's calculations, par-

ticularly those representing human life, are accurate? What are some alternative ways to calculate the value of human life? Could the social benefits exceed social costs using different values?

3. Are any important benefits or costs not included in the analysis of the smelter's operation? What are they?

4. Is the cost/benefit method of decision making an appropriate tool for deciding whether or not to close the smelter?

5. List and explain several alternative solutions to this controversy. Which is best and why?

References

Michael D. Bayles, "The Price of Life," *Ethics,* Vol. 89, No. 1 (October 1978), pp. 20–34.

Baruch Fischhoff *et al.,* "Weighing the Risks," *Environment,* May 1979, pp. 17–38.

William Lowrance, *Of Acceptable Risk* (Los Altos, California: William Kaufmann, Inc., 1976).

Walter Oi, "Safety at Any Price?" *Regulation,* November-December 1977, pp. 16–23.

Steven E. Rhoads, "How Much Should We Spend to Save a Life?" *The Public Interest,* Spring 1978, pp. 74–92.

Max Singer, "How to Reduce Risks Rationally," *The Public Interest,* Spring 1978, pp. 16–23.

C) DO WE NEED A NEW BILL OF RIGHTS?

"For years you have accepted this principle that where there are two or more parties at interest sharing the same resource or parcel of land, but for different purposes, there had to be some sort of accommodation that preserved the rights of each. So the farmer, the rancher, the pipeline company, the producer, and the community downstream all co-existed, maybe not altogether peacefully, but co-existed, on the basis that each had rights to be respected by others.

"Move the scene to a prized recreation area of great scenic beauty and scientific interest. Is there any difference, really, between the right of the farmer and the rancher to go about their business secure from harm resulting from oil operations, and the right of the motel owner, the marine operator, the marine biologist, the commercial fisherman to be secure from the same hazards? What of the right of the tourist to expect a clean beach; the right of the sports fisherman to expect fish where fish normally are to be found; the right of the marine biologist to make his observations in a habitat undisturbed by pollutants? Is there any difference, in principle, in responsibility for operations that on one hand leave a dead steer on the range and, on the other, a dead bird on a beach?"

CASE QUESTIONS ────────────────────────────

1. What is your reaction to this quotation?

2. If you think we need a bill of rights covering the environment, what would you put in it and how would you implement it? (See Hans F. Sennholz, "Controlling Pollution," *The Freeman,* February 1973, pp. 67–77.)

Notes

*From a speech given by Russell E. Train, then Under Secretary of the Interior, at the Fiftieth Anniversary Meeting of the American Petroleum Institute, Jesse H. Jones Hall, Rice Hotel, Houston, Texas, November 11, 1969. Reprinted by permission.

DISCUSSION GUIDES ON CHAPTER CONTENT ————————

1. Discuss the cost-benefit tradeoff between environmental quality and the exacerbation of economic problems like inflation and unemployment.

2. Would you say that business can be depended upon to initiate responsible antipollution measures, now that the importance of environmental protection is widely known? What do you think are the dangers of relying on such voluntary participation in antipollution programs by business in general?

3. What are equitable arrangements for sharing and distributing the costs of pollution control, considering that society has to meet them somehow?

4. What major tools are available to help decision makers be more rational in establishing pollution standards? Do you think the tools are as powerful as they should be?

5. Discuss some of the ways in which organizations have attempted to adapt their internal structures to provide for increased attention to environmental matters.

6. Why do the authors think that high environmental standards, regardless of cost, are no longer receiving unconditional support from lawmakers as they were in the 1970s? What is your assessment of future trends in this regard?

MIND-STRETCHING QUESTION ————————————

1. Considering that more and more scientific studies would provide society with specific data on the effects of various kinds of pollution, what is your evaluation of the nature of pollution control costs and programs in the next two decades? Would you say that a more realistic appreciation of cost-benefit tradeoffs will take place, or will there be a demand for even tighter standards of pollution control?

17
CONSUMERISM

A) CHEVMOBILE FROM GENERAL MOTORS*

In November 1976, Chicagoan Joseph Siwek took his new 1977 Oldsmobile Delta 88 to a mechanic for servicing. The mechanic discovered a Chevrolet engine under the hood and Siwek complained—first to Hames Oldsmobile, his dealer, and subsequently to the Chicago Commission of Consumer Sales, Weights and Measures. What followed was a flood of publicity about the substitution of Chevrolet engines of varying displacement in certain models of 1977 Pontiacs, Oldsmobiles, and Buicks. Consumers were outraged. The attorneys general of 44 states banded together to sue GM for damages in a class action. Throughout, General Motors maintained it did no wrong.

Why Switch Engines?

The interchange of parts is common in the auto industry. A number of corporate twins like the Dodge Omni and Plymouth Horizon share virtually all mechanical components. Some cars, like the Dodge Monaco and Plymouth Fury, are built on the same or parallel assembly lines and constructed identically until the very end of the line where distinguishing chrome and trim treatments and name tags are added to give each superficial differences in appearance. The diesel engine in the Cadillac Seville is made by Oldsmobile and the automatic transmissions in AMC cars are made by Chrysler. All four American auto manufacturers shuffle parts as do foreign makers. The automakers say that when parts are interchangeable widespread sharing keeps prices down for the customer.

GM offered two additional reasons for the switch to Chevrolet engines in a total of 128,000 cars, or 3.7 percent of its 1977 model production. First, it cited the need to meet government emissions, safety, and fuel economy standards. At the time, three sets of emissions standards had to be met—49 state, California, and altitude standards. Because certain engines were certified for particular standards, switches were often designed to help the company avoid the cost of certifying all engines for use in all standard areas. Thus, Pontiac Grand Prix automobiles came with Oldsmobile engines when they were sold in California or high altitude counties in which the customer wanted a 350-cubic-inch displacement (CID) V8. The Grand Prix was sold with Pontiac engines everywhere else.

Second, in 1976 and 1977, Oldsmobile was a red-hot division at General Motors in terms of sales. Many customers, not yet worried about the price of gas, were

*Prepared by John F. Steiner

opting to pay extra for Oldsmobile's 403 CID V8, which was offered on the Olds Cutlass, Vista-Cruiser, Delta 88, Custom Cruiser, Ninety-Eight, and Toronado. The 403 CID V8, Olds's largest engine, was an option replacing smaller displacement engines on all models but the Toronado, where it was standard. Customer preference for this option led to a shortage of engine blocks for 350 CID V8s by Oldsmobile, Pontiac, and Buick. The 403 CID and 350 CID V8s were built from the same block, but in manufacturing the cylinder holes for the former were bored larger.

The three other divisions turned to Chevrolet to supply 350 CID V8s because of the latter's capacity to turn them out at the beginning of the 1977 model year. Other Chevrolet engines were also used. For example, Chevy's four-cylinder 140 CID engine, produced at its Tonawanda, New York, engine plant, was used as standard equipment in the 1977 Olds Starfire. Chevy's 305 CID V8, built at Tonawanda and by GM of Canada at St. Catharines, Ontario, was optional equipment on both the Olds Starfire and Olds Omega. Buick engines were also used in Oldsmobiles. Buick's 231 CID V6 engine was standard equipment on six-cylinder Omegas and Delta 88s.

According to GM, this was a practice that benefited the consumer. E. M. Estes, president of GM, made the following statements to the press on March 9, 1977:

> There is no question that component and engine interchangeability have increased in recent years and will be extended in the future. The need to meet government standards on safety, emissions and fuel economy, make such a course of action a necessity . . .
>
> We, along with every other major manufacturer, produce no car which is unique in every one of its functional characteristics. To do so would result in a product beyond the financial means of the vast majority of people.
>
> In sharing of components across a number of product lines, each is selected to meet the product requirements of the particular vehicle and to provide the customer with a car that meets all of the standards of a General Motors vehicle and is in no way compromised. It is a fine product we can be proud of. Not only does our component interchange result in a product which meets our own standards, but each car meets all government requirements . . . . And General Motors warrants and stands behind every engine and car it manufactures.[1]

Customers were charged $190 extra for the 350 CID V8, whether it was made by Chevrolet or Oldsmobile.

Consumers Complain About the Engines

General Motors insisted it had not committed fraud. If the customer had wanted a 350 CID V8 with four-barrel carburetion and 170 horsepower, said the company, he or she had gotten that. Car buyers, consumer groups, and consumer protection agencies disagreed. There were some discrepancies between Chevrolet and Oldsmobile engines worth thinking about.

For one thing, although the engines virtually were identical in performance, small differences existed in the sizes of parts such as fan-belts and oil filters. Owners experienced service delays because of this. It was time-consuming for Oldsmobile, Pontiac, and Buick service departments to get Chevrolet parts. Customers were not, however, sent to Chevrolet garages.

Second, General Motors' advertising strategy over many years had been to build product differentiation in the public's mind between its model lines. Thus, Pontiacs, Oldsmobiles, and Buicks, in that order, have been promoted as increasingly more prestigious than Chevrolets. On top of this overall corporate strategy, Oldsmobile had attempted since 1949 to develop product differentiation for its "Rocket" engines by hawking them as better engines than other virtually identical GM engines. Hence, some customers felt humiliated to have paid for an Oldsmobile and in fact purchased a Chevmobile. They did not feel they had gotten the status for which they had paid a premium price. This raised knotty marketing issues. Even if the Chevy engines had virtually identical performance (and some experts felt they were mechanically superior), were they subjectively the same in the consumer's mind? If not, did they have the same monetary value to the customer? Was the car a utilitarian object or an ego expression for its buyer?

Third, there was a difference of about one mile per gallon in the fuel economy of some of the Olds models with Chevy engines. Environmental Protection Agency (EPA) figures showed, for example, that Mr. Siwek's Delta 88 with the Chevy engine got 15 MPG in the city, 20 MPG on the highway and 17 combined. With the Olds "Rocket" engine the Delta 88 got 16 MPG in the city, 22 MPG on the highway and 18 combined. Although public attitudes in 1977 were not as fuel-thrifty as they would become two years later, fuel economy was still an important selling point in the auto industry.

In addition, the tenor of the times created problems for GM. The company was accused of excessive secrecy, misleading advertising, and fraud. Adverse publicity filled the national media as editors, writers, and cartoonists chortled over "Bevrolets, Chontiacs or Chevrobiles as yet unregistered trademarks."[2] Robert A. Wilson, editor-in-chief of *Automotive Industries*, a trade publication, sermonized that: "There is nothing basically wrong with a family of engines approach. But GM is nonetheless blameworthy in its handling of this important change in philosophy and we feel they are probably going to pay for it."[3] *Consumer Reports* ran a cynically worded feature story on the problem entitled, "The Great Engine Switch and Other Magic Tricks Performed by the One-and-Only Auto Industry."[4] The engine switch cropped up as a topic on talk shows and GM customers across the country began popping their heads under hoods to see what engine they would find.

General Motors Moves Toward Restitution

General Motors' first response to the storm of indignation caused by the engine matter was to simply explain the practice and show that it was in the cost-conscious consumer's best interest. On March 23, GM's five car divisions—Chevrolet, Pontiac, Oldsmobile, Buick, and Cadillac—sent large showroom posters to their dealers across the country identifying for customers the GM engines used in 1977 car models. The posters also showed EPA mileage estimates for available model/engine combinations. Letters were sent to dealers stressing that car buyers were to be made aware of which engine was installed in the vehicle they purchased.

This action was not sufficient, however, to stop a growing number of suits against GM. In mid-March, Illinois Attorney General William J. Scott filed a class-action lawsuit against the company charging that it had deceived consumers by switching engines. The suit called for a $50,000 civil penalty to be paid by GM and each of its Illinois Oldsmobile dealers. Scott invited the attorneys general of other states to join in the suit, and 44 ultimately did.

Jane M. Byrne, then Chicago commissioner of Consumer Sales, Weights and Measures, to whom Siwek had first complained, also announced that she was filing an action against GM and Hames Oldsmobile, the dealership that had sold Siwek his ill-starred car. Byrne, who had received over 250 complaints, was upset because Hames sold Oldsmobiles with Chevy 350 V8s at a cost of $127 over the regularly equipped models, a charge the dealer denied. She also felt that there would be monetary losses to customers because of the EPA ratings differences.

Anthony L. Hames, of Hames Olds, said that the letter from Oldsmobile about the engine switch arrived too late to alert him to some of the substitutions, as in the case of Mr. Siwek's Delta 88. GM President Elliott M. Estes, however, stated publicly that Oldsmobile had notified its dealers one week in advance of the arrival of 1977 models that Chevrolet engines would be used. But according to Hames:

> Mr. Siwek's car was in production in Kansas City when we received this letter and assumed the regular engine had been placed in it. It wasn't until Mr. Siwek brought the car in for repair that we learned a Chevrolet engine, which is interchangeable, was in the car.
> Our mechanics did not send him to a Chevrolet dealer, but obtained the part for him. In the meantime, we offered him another Delta 88 with an Oldsmobile engine. It was one of our personal cars with less mileage than his.[5]

On April 25, 1977, GM made a unique attempt to quiet public controversy and lessen its legal liability. In an offer without parallel in auto industry history, it offered remedial options to owners of the 1977 car models affected. To assure customer satisfaction, GM said it would permit one of two choices for buyers.

First, the buyer could return the car to the dealer for credit toward purchase of another new 1977 car with another engine. This credit would be the original purchase price (excluding registration, licensing, or sales tax), less eight cents a mile from time of delivery, and less the cost of repairing any damage or restoring the car to its original condition if optional equipment had been added by the customer after purchase. The customer was not required to pay any sales tax, registration fee, or title transfer fee incurred solely because of the exchange of the car unless the new car selected was more expensive than the one returned for credit. In that case the owner was responsible for additional fees and taxes, if any.

Or, second, the owner could keep the car and GM, at no charge, would provide a "Special Mechanical Performance Insurance Policy" covering the entire power train (engine, transmission, and rear axle) for 36 months, or 36,000 miles from the date of original delivery, whichever occurred first. This policy was available only to original owners and could not be transferred to later owners.

The overall offer got mixed reviews. Although it resulted in settlements with the attorneys general in New York and Texas, most of the state law officers rejected what became known as the "eight cent offer." They found many flaws. First, some owners who swapped cars might still wind up with Chevy engines. Second, there was no way for traders to negotiate a fair price for their second cars, since they were captive buyers for the dealers. They lacked bargaining power and might have to pay the full, inflated sticker price. Third, the cost of repairing damage or unusual wear on the vehicle would have to be negotiated by the buyer, who would lack bargaining power in this also. Finally, car buyers who had added luggage racks, CB radios, or other options might have to go to considerable expense to restore the car to "original" condition.

The National Automobile Dealers Association (NADA) labeled the GM plan unilateral and said it was unfair because GM had not protected dealers against liability. It said dealers should also be able to return the cars to GM rather than sell them. Other unresolved issues had not been worked out. NADA President Reed T. Draper sent a letter to GM saying that: "This expanding controversy has reached the point where each dealer must have competent and accurate legal representation."[6] Reed also cited a clause in the franchise agreement of dealers that might exclude forced participation in the plan. Nevertheless, they did participate.

In February and March of 1978, letters were mailed to Pontiac and Buick owners. GM reported that of 14,465 offers received by Buick owners, approximately 13,020, or about 90 percent, accepted. In the case of Pontiac owners, about 93 percent of 8,700 owners accepted. At GM's annual stockholders' meeting in Detroit on May 20, Chairman Thomas Murphy reported that owners of the affected cars "by a nine-to-one majority," were choosing to accept the three-year insurance policy rather than the exchange offer.[7] He said GM had received replies from 24,000 of 87,000 owners affected by the offer. (The offer, of course, could not be extended to Oldsmobile owners in those states in which the attorneys general had joined in the suit against GM because settlement had not yet been made.) Murphy also revealed that sales of cars with substitute engines continued to be strong in the marketplace. "Nine out of ten of those who already own them are keeping them," he proudly declared, "and more people are buying them every day."[8] GM had continued selling the hybrid autos, but prominently displayed posters in showrooms that emphasized the use of interchangeable engines.

While the "recall" continued, GM was negotiating with the attorneys general for a settlement of their suit, a process that began when Ohio's attorney general, William J. Brown, wrote to GM on behalf of the entire group in mid-July 1977. Finally, in December 1977, GM announced a new offer, subject to court approval, that reflected agreement between the company and the attorneys general. In it, GM would offer a payment of $200 and a "Special Mechanical Performance Certificate," or warranty, to affected car owners. This new warranty was also for three years or 36,000 miles, but unlike the previous one, it was transferable to each subsequent owner of the cars.

On July 18, 1979, Federal Judge Frank J. McGarr ruled in Chicago that this settlement offer was "fair and reasonable," and cleared the way for it to be extended to approximately 67,000 eligible Olds owners in all 50 states. This court decision was necessary because attorneys general in several states had refused to accept GM's latest offer, holding out for bigger cash awards to owners.

GM and Its Critics Assess Blame Differently

It was estimated that the total cost to GM of the cash awards plus dealer-performed maintenance under the extended warranty would be more than $40 million. According to *Time* this was ". . . hardly a severe financial penalty to GM, which has earned as much as $1 billion profit in a single quarter."[9]

A cynical editorial in *The Nation* alleged that the whole tempest in a teapot was "the kind of pinprick that hardly bothers a giant."[10] *The Nation* pointed out that GM's sales are 15 times larger than the gross national product of Zaire and its profits approximate the GNPs of Ireland and Israel. The story concluded with the observation that "the willingness of this behemoth to switch engines on its customers tells so much about the difficulty, if not impossibility, of bringing these titans of the economy to heel."[11] Lawyers at GM may, however, feel differently. Between 1977 and 1979 the company was hit with a tremendous barrage of 350 lawsuits from government agencies, individuals, and state attorneys general, including 77 class actions. In September 1979, almost two years after the cars in question went on sale, 152 suits were still pending in the courts. These legal problems imposed considerable expense on GM, although the company has never said how much.

To the end, GM insists it did nothing wrong and continues to emphasize that the interchanging of parts is common industry practice and will continue. However, on September 11, 1979, the company acknowledged it was under federal investigation for substituting transmissions from the tiny, 2,100-pound Chevy Chevette in vehicles as large as the 3,765-pound Chevy Caprice. A spokesman for Ralph Nader's Center for Auto Safety, a Washington consumer group, said that over a thousand complaints of breakdowns of the lighter-duty transmissions had been received.[12]

If the engine case did not cause GM to rethink its parts-bin philosophy, it did provide a dramatic illustration of the power of a coalition of state legal officers arrayed against a large corporation. This may be an important precedent and have implications for future consumer-corporation showdowns.

Notes

1. General Motors Corporation News Release, March 9, 1977, pp. 1–2.
2. *The Nation,* May 7, 1977, p. 549.
3. *Automotive Industries,* July 1, 1977, p. 3.
4. April 1978, pp. 190–191.
5. "FTC May Probe GM Engine Swap," *Automotive News,* March 14, 1977, p. 50.
6. "GM Engine Plan Branded Unfair," *Automotive News,* May 9, 1977, p. 1.
7. General Motors Corporation News Release, May 20, 1977, p. 2.
8. *Ibid.,* p. 2.
9. "End of the Great Engine Flap," *Time,* January 2, 1978, p. 66.
10. *The Nation, op. cit.,* p. 549.

11. *Ibid.,* p. 549.
12. "GM Admits It's Target of Probe on Faulty Transmissions, $400 Average Repair Bills," *Los Angeles Times,* September 11, 1979.

QUESTIONS

1. In your opinion, is it misleading to the consumer when auto makers use parts interchangeably in two or more models?
2. Did General Motors trick its customers or commit fraudulent action in this case? Why or why not?
3. The switched engines were virtually identical. However, do you feel General Motors was selling Pontiacs, Oldsmobiles, and Buicks as utilitarian objects or as objects of ego satisfaction and prestige? Did the cars have the same value with Chevy engines in them?
4. Were GM's remedial options sufficient compensation for purchasers?
5. Should GM have done anything that it did not do?

DISCUSSION GUIDES ON CHAPTER CONTENT

1. What are the major motivating forces behind the current wave of consumerism in the United States?
2. What are "consumer advocates"? What is your view of Ralph Nader and his organization?
3. Identify a few types of legislative action that the federal government has recently taken to protect consumers. Do you favor them?
4. Do you think that businesspeople in your area have responded properly and satisfactorily to consumer complaints? Explain.
5. Do you approve of the FTC's regulation of advertising? Be specific in your evaluation.
6. Argue the pros and cons of the FTC's regulation of cigarette advertising.
7. Classical economists say that producers react to consumer wants, but Galbraith says that business forces consumers to buy what business wants to sell them. Who is right in your judgment?
8. Manufacturers probably can build many products to last a lifetime. Why don't they?
9. How does manufacturer liability to consumers differ today from, say, 25 years ago?

MIND-STRETCHING QUESTIONS

1. The President of Motorola (maker of TV sets) asks your advice about what policies his company ought to adopt in response to consumer complaints. What would you advise him to do?
2. Where does the government's obligation to protect its citizens end and interference with free enterprise begin? Just how far should the government go in protecting the consumer?

18
MAJOR
URBAN BUSINESS
SOCIAL PROGRAMS

A) UNITED STEELWORKERS OF AMERICA v. BRIAN F. WEBER*

In 1979 Brian Weber was an $18,000-a-year white laboratory analyst employed by Kaiser Aluminum and Chemical Corp. at its Gramercy, Louisiana, plant. The plant is located on the east bank of the Mississippi River, less than 50 miles above New Orleans.

Weber, 32, emerged from the anonymous ranks of millions of blue-collar workers to become a short-lived national celebrity when a case in which he claimed reverse discrimination against himself went to the Supreme Court. The central question in the case was whether his employer, Kaiser, had the right to pick blacks over whites with more seniority in a voluntary affirmative-action training program for skilled craft workers. Here are the facts.

Kaiser's Gramercy plant first began hiring workers in 1956, and the company claims that hiring practices were not overtly discriminatory. Some blacks were always on the payroll in the 1950s, but the number did not exceed 10 percent in an area that is 40 percent black.

The reasons for this low percentage were subtle. For one thing, most blacks lived on the west side of the Mississippi, opposite the plant. For another, Kaiser demanded a high school diploma and because of the relatively poor quality of black schools in the area this requirement eliminated more blacks than whites. Then there was the widely agreed-upon fact that a person needed political pull to get a job at the Gramercy plant in its early years, and blacks found such political influence a commodity in short supply prior to enactment and enforcement of the Voting Rights Act of 1965. Finally, many qualified blacks never applied to Kaiser simply because they felt their applications would not be taken seriously.

After Kaiser undertook various government-mandated affirmative action programs in the 1960s, blacks constituted 18 percent of the total workforce at Gramercy. However, less than two percent of 275 skilled crafts workers employed at

*Prepared by John F. Steiner

the plant were black. The reason was that blacks had additional problems becoming skilled craft workers. Kaiser had a requirement of five years' experience, a rule that eliminated most local workers, both black and white, from craft worker ranks. Training schools and craft unions, the two major proving grounds available to those with no experience, discriminated against blacks and practiced white nepotism.

To raise this very low percentage of black crafts workers at the Gramercy plant, Kaiser, as part of a 1974 collective-bargaining agreement with the United Steel-workers of America (AFL-CIO), agreed to set up a training program for skilled crafts workers and established a quota system in which 50 percent of the trainees chosen would be black and 50 percent white. Had workers been chosen solely on the basis of seniority fewer blacks would have qualified. Two seniority lists were set up, one black and one white, and names were chosen alternately from each list until the 13 positions in the program were filled.

Brian Weber, a former union activist, was one person on the white seniority list not chosen. Two of the blacks chosen, to his consternation, were lower in over-all seniority at the plant than he was. Galvanized into action by this perceived injustice, Weber wrote to the New Orleans office of the Equal Employment Oppor-tunity Commission to get a copy of the Civil Rights Act of 1964. After reading the act he concluded that it required all workers to be treated equally, regardless of race. He filed a complaint with the EEOC and subsequently brought a class-action suit on behalf of white employees at the Gramercy plant. A Federal District Court, which was later upheld by a divided Court of Appeals for the Fifth Circuit, held that the training program selection procedure was discriminatory. All employment preferences based on race, said the courts, violated the law. Weber had won an early victory.

However, the United Steelworkers and Kaiser appealed the decision to the Supreme Court, and the high tribunal agreed to hear the case, scheduling oral argu-ments for March 28, 1978. The courtroom was packed that day and over 100 spec-tators were turned away because the case had become a cynosure in the debate about reverse job discrimination.

Michael R. Fontham, Weber's attorney, told the Justices that it was illegal for a company to give preferential treatment to minority workers to correct racial imbalance in the workforce. Title VII of the Civil Rights Act of 1964, he argued, clearly forbids this kind of "reverse discrimination" or any other discrimination. The applicable text of the law to which Fontham referred is this.

> It shall be an unlawful employment practice for an employer:
> 1. To fail or refuse to hire or to discharge any individual, or otherwise to discrimi-nate against any individual with respect to his compensation, terms, conditions, or privileges of employment, because of such individual's race, color, religion, sex, or national origin;
> 2. To limit or classify his employees or applicants for employment in any way which would deprive any individual of employment opportunities or otherwise adversely affect his status as an employee, because of such individual's race, color, religion, sex, or national origin.

Section 703 (a)

It shall be an unlawful employment practice for any employer, labor organization, or joint labor-management committee controlling apprenticeship or other training or re-training, including on-the-job training programs, to discriminate against any individual because of his race, color, religion, sex, or national origin in admission to, or employ-ment in, any program established to provide apprenticeship or other training.

Section 703 (d)

Arguing against Weber's case, attorneys from Kaiser contended that in enacting Title VII Congress fully sanctioned action to remedy past exclusion of minorities (and women) from craft training programs. It was, they said, Kaiser's desire to com-ply with the spirit of the Civil Rights Act that had led to setting up the voluntary program. A lawyer for the United Steelworkers urged that the training program be upheld because Kaiser was taking affirmative action voluntarily and not acting in response to a government edict. The Kaiser plan, he said, was private and because of that it was not subject to all the constraints of government affirmative action plans where quotas might be prohibited. Deputy Solicitor General Lawrence G. Wallace represented the federal government and argued that the Kaiser program be upheld because it was a "reasonable response" to the problem of having too few blacks in the workforce.

The Supreme Court announced on June 27, 1979 in a 5–2 decision that it over-ruled the lower court and upheld the quota system for the training program. The majority decision, written by Justice William Brennan, conceded that the lower court decisions abided by the letter of the law in Title VII, but argued that they were "not within its spirit." The majority felt that, ". . . an interpretation of the sections that forbade all race-conscious affirmative action would 'bring about an end completely at variance with the purpose of the statute' and must be rejected." The majority opinion of the court read, in part, this way.

> We emphasize at the outset the narrowness of our inquiry. Since the Kaiser-USWA plan does not involve state action, this case does not present an alleged violation of the Equal Protection Clause of the Constitution. Further, since the Kaiser-USWA plan was adopted voluntarily, we are not concerned with what Title VII requires or with what a court might order to remedy a past proven violation of the Act. The only question before us is the narrow statutory issue of whether Title VII *forbids* private employers and unions from voluntarily agreeing upon bona fide affirmative action plans that accord racial preferences in the manner and for the purpose provided in the Kaiser-USWA plan . . .
>
> Respondent argues that Congress intended in Title VII to prohibit all race-conscious affirmative action plans . . . Respondent's argument is not without force. But it over-looks the significance of the fact that the Kaiser-USWA plan is an affirmative action plan voluntarily adopted by private parties to eliminate traditional patterns of racial segrega-tion . . . It is a 'familiar rule, that a thing may be within the letter of the statute and yet not within the statute, because not within its spirit, nor within the intention of its makers.' *Holy Trinity Church* v. *United States*, 143 U.S. 457, 459 (1892) . . .
>
> Congress' primary concern in enacting the prohibition against racial discrimination in Title VII of the Civil Rights Act of 1964 was with 'the plight of the Negro in our economy.'
>
> . . . it was clear to Congress that 'the crux of the problem [was] to open employ-ment opportunities for Negroes in occupations which have been traditionally closed to them,' and it was to this problem that Title VII's prohibition against racial discrimina-tion in employment was primarily addressed.
>
> It plainly appears from the House Report accompanying the Civil Rights Act that

> Congress did not intend wholly to prohibit private and voluntary affirmative action efforts as one method of solving this problem . . . Given this legislative history, we cannot agree with respondent that Congress intended to prohibit the private sector from taking effective steps to accomplish the goal that Congress designed Title VII to achieve. The very statutory words intended as a spur or catalyst to cause 'employers and unions to self-examine and to self-evaluate their employment practices and to endeavor to eliminate, so far as possible, the last vestiges of an unfortunate and ignominious page in this country's history,' *Albemarle* v. *Moody*, 422 US.S 405, 418 (1975), cannot be interpreted as an absolute prohibition against all private, voluntary, race-conscious affirmative action efforts to hasten the elimination of such vestiges. It would be ironic indeed if a law triggered by a Nation's concern over centuries of racial injustice and intended to improve the lot of those who had 'been excluded from the American dream for so long.' 110 *Cong. Rec.*, at 6552 (remarks of Sen. Humphrey), constituted the first legislative prohibition of all voluntary, private, race-conscious efforts to abolish traditional patterns of racial segregation and hierarchy.

Thus, the Court held that the challenged Kaiser-USWA affirmative action plan fell within the spirit of the law because it was designed to break down long-existing patterns of racial segregation and open employment opportunities for blacks in an occupation traditionally closed to them. In addition to these reasons, the Court majority also pointed out that:

> At the same time the plan does not unnecessarily trammel the interests of the white employees. The plan does not require the discharge of white workers and their replacement with new black hires . . . Nor does the plan create an absolute bar to the advancement of white employees; half of those trained in the program will be white. Moreover, the plan is a temporary measure; it is not intended to maintain racial balance, but simply to eliminate a manifest racial imbalance. Preferential selection of craft trainees at the Gramercy plant will end as soon as the percentage of black skilled craft workers in the Gramercy plant approximates the percentage of blacks in the local labor force.

Chief Justice Warren Burger dissented, arguing in a separately written opinion that Title VII was "a statute of extraordinary clarity. The quota embodied in the collective-bargaining agreement between Kaiser and the Steelworkers," he wrote, "unquestionably discriminates on the basis of race against individual employees seeking admission to on-the-job training programs." He further argued that:

> Often we have difficulty interpreting statutes either because of imprecise drafting or because legislative compromises have produced genuine ambiguities. But here there is no lack of clarity, no ambiguity. The quota embodied in the collective-bargaining agreement between Kaiser and the Steelworkers unquestionably discriminates on the basis of race against individual employees seeking admission to on-the-job training programs. And, under the plain language of (Section) 703 (d), that is "an *unlawful* employment practice."

A second dissent was written by Justice William Rehnquist. In 37 pages of reconstruction of the legislative history and debate of Title VII, Rehnquist quoted extensively from the floor debates in Congress to buttress his argument that the Court was making an interpretation of the law that conformed to the prejudices of the majority rather than the law's clear wording and the facts of legislative intent and Congressional debate. He concluded his strongly-worded opinion by stating that:

> With today's holding, the Court introduces into Title VII a tolerance for the very evil that the law was intended to eradicate . . . . By going not merely *beyond*, but directly *against* Title VII's language and legislative history, the Court has sown the wind. Later courts will face the impossible task of reaping the whirlwind.

Reaction to the decision against Weber was mixed. Civil rights groups cheered the decision and predicted dismissal of a rash of reverse discrimination cases by white workers currently in the courts. AFL-CIO President George Meany and other union leaders also praised the decision as a blow against racial discrimination. Kaiser was pleased that its system for selecting trainees had been sanctioned by the Court, but some business executives feared that although the decision did not require employers to set up racial quota systems there would now be pressure to do so. One board chairman of a southern company was even quoted in the national press as saying that it was not possible to produce goods and services at the lowest cost and also have affirmative action programs.

After the decision and an appearance on the "Today" show in its wake, Weber returned to work at the Gramercy plant. He was making $2,000 to $7,000 less each year than blacks and whites who had gone through the crafts training program beginning in 1974. He also had less opportunity for overtime work and, unlike skilled crafts workers, was required to take regular turns working a night shift.

CASE QUESTIONS

1. Do you agree with the majority decision of the Court? Why or why not?

2. Do you think the Kaiser-USWA plan was legal? Was it the best solution to underrepresentation of blacks in the ranks of crafts workers?

3. Do any problems or ambiguities remain in this area of law? If so, what are they and what cases may arise in the future requiring further action by the courts?

References

Read the case of *United Steelworkers of America* v. *Brian F. Weber et al.* for a more complete knowledge of the Court's arguments. Newspaper and news magazine accounts of the time provide valuable background information. Two sources of particular interest and depth are Linda Greenhouse, "The Bakke Case Moves to the Factory," *The New York Times Magazine,* February 25, 1979; and Urban C. Lehner and Carol H. Falk, "High Court Approves Affirmative Action in Hiring, Promotion," *Wall Street Journal,* June 28, 1979.

B) THE LOS ANGELES TERRACE HOTEL

It is sunrise on the West Coast. The first rays of morning light are beginning to strike the roof of the elegant Los Angeles Terrace Hotel, a 1,500-room, 61-story monolithic structure of concrete, metal, and a complex human organization. In addition to its rooms, the hotel has nine kitchens, three ballrooms, 75 meeting and conference rooms, 35 small shops and restaurants, and a tangle of pipes, pumps, compressors, electric motors, and other equipment.

The man in charge of this downtown Los Angeles landmark was Ivan Gerrold, hotel manager and vice president of Transcontinental Hotel Corp. Today, Gerrold knew, meant trouble. Yesterday he had received a call from June Friendly of the Los Angeles office of the U.S. Immigration and Naturalization Service (INS). Ms. Friendly's reason for calling was simple. She wanted Gerrold to set aside a room in which INS officials could "interview" Spanish-surnamed hotel employees to ascertain if they were legally in the United States.

Gerrold knew that there were widely publicized estimates that as many as 6 to 10 million illegal aliens had come into this country and entered the workforce, roughly three to five percent of the entire American population. They came mainly from Mexico, driven to hazardous border crossing ordeals by extremely high rates of unemployment and inflation at home. They were attracted to the United States because of the prospect of finding work, and many sent their earnings to families back in Mexico.

Most Mexican illegal aliens find jobs in Southwestern urban areas in the garment industry or in light manufacturing, such as the shoe industry in Los Angeles. They also work as domestics and fill many jobs in service industries such as the hotel industry. Gerrold was positive that he had many aliens in his employ. He had on his personnel roster well over 200 people who had Spanish surnames and many of them, he suspected, had entered the United States illegally. At hiring time the Personnel Department asked prospective employees to produce identification and work permits, but the documents were not always valid. What could he do? Besides, without the illegal aliens the hotel might as well not open for business. Most of the aliens were maids, busboys, janitors, parking lot attendants, and laborers on the maintenance crews. They were paid the lowest legal wage by the hotel, a wage that most American workers, especially those with families, would turn down. By utilizing welfare, food stamps, and family aid, American citizens could receive income within $20 a month of what the hotel paid many of its workers. Many American workers would not get out of bed in the morning for the extra few dollars. Those who did were often unreliable and unproductive.

In contrast, the "illegals" were punctual, docile, and hard-working. They had to be; if they called attention to themselves they could be deported. If they didn't do a good job they would be fired. They were an ideal source of labor for the dull and unpleasant jobs that were so vital to the operation of a major hotel like the Los Angeles Terrace.

Recently, Gerrold knew, President Carter had suggested a $1,000 civil fine be placed on employers for each illegal alien they hired who did not have a valid work permit. Gerrold thought the law would be difficult to enforce, even though it might stop some businesses from openly hiring undocumented workers. It was impossible to avoid all hiring of "illegals" short of retaining a large investigative staff to sleuth into employees' lives. Anyway, without the "illegals" the hotel and its restaurants would have to pay more to attract labor for menial jobs. Higher wages would, in turn, mean higher prices for meals, rooms, and other hotel services. The customer would pay, inflation would get worse, and the illegal aliens would probably still be around.

Gerrold doubted the AFL-CIO position that held that aliens took jobs from American workers. Americans do not want the jobs that aliens take, he believed. He repeatedly asserted that the economy needs these new immigrants.

Such general considerations did not solve his immediate problem. Should he set aside a room for the INS to use in investigating the legality of his workers? No law required that he do this. He knew he would not be popular if it became known that he had done it. However, the illegal aliens were violating the law and he could not rationalize that fact away, even if he did disagree with current statutes on immigration from Mexico. He had to make a decision.

CASE QUESTIONS

1. Should Gerrold set aside a room for the INS to use? What are the reasons for your decision?

2. Do you agree with Gerrold that illegal aliens are necessary in the American economy? Why are they an asset or liability to the economy?

3. Find out what current immigration policy toward Mexico is. What changes do you suggest in the law, if any?

DISCUSSION GUIDES ON CHAPTER CONTENT

1. Do you believe that business today has made a "commitment" to improving the position of disadvantaged minorities? Explain with specific illustrations.

2. What are equal opportunity and affirmative action? What should be the extent of corporate involvement in these programs?

3. Discuss the nature of the impact that equal opportunity and affirmative action are having on day-to-day management of business enterprises.

4. In what ways has business become involved in training and employing the disadvantaged?

5. Why do you think the proportion of minority enterprises to total business enterprises is so small? Do you approve of present private and public programs to raise this proportion? What would you recommend be done that is not being done? Defend your position.

6. There is little question that this nation has not met needs for housing for low-income groups. Why not? What should be done about it?

7. If you live in an urban area, describe ways in which business in your community is doing things to help the community resolve some of its major problems.

8. What guidelines do you suggest for a company that is interested in doing more to improve the community and help it deal with major problems?

9. Should business continue to support education? Explain.

10. What methods are currently being used by business to support education?

11. How do you define "the arts"?

12. What are the pros and cons of business support of the arts?

MIND-STRETCHING QUESTIONS

1. Identify the 10 most significant socioeconomic problems in your community.

2. You are appointed a member of the Committee of Twenty-Five. This is a group of civic-minded leaders—business, educational, religious, philanthropic, legal, and technical—in the community who have joined together to help solve its major problems. The immediate question is to establish policies and programs to deal with the major problems identified in question 1. What would you recommend?

3. Many business schools have visiting committees composed of top executives from nationally known firms. What should be the function of these committees?

4. You are asked by the chairman of the board of American Telephone and Telegraph Company to set forth basic policies for his company to use in making financial contributions to the arts. What would you suggest?

FIELD RESEARCH: COMPANY INVOLVEMENT IN COMMUNITY AFFAIRS

Arrange interviews with the top-level managers and staff of one of the larger companies in your community and prepare a report on the extent to which the company is involved in community affairs, both voluntarily and because of government regulation or union contracts. Involvement because of government regulation would include such programs as equal opportunity and pollution controls. Programs voluntarily undertaken can, of course, cover a wide range of activities. Classify those voluntary activities. Try to appraise the beneficial impact of such programs on the community. Is there a benefit to the company that appears to be greater than costs to the company? What are the primary motivations in the company leading to voluntary social programs?

19
CHANGING ATTITUDES, NEEDS, AND DEMANDS OF PEOPLE IN ORGANIZATIONS

A) THE PROMOTION OF COTTON SPRINGFIELD

Frank Converse, personnel director for the Chicago Metals Company, had a problem of sorts. A conscientious and charitable man, Converse had been one of the early advocates of minority hiring and affirmative action at Chicago Metals. He had successfully pushed to bring minorities and women into all levels of the company hierarchy, but now he was faced with an unexpected, delicate, and somewhat bizarre problem. The worst thing about the situation was that he didn't know whether any action on his part was appropriate.

The events leading up to the present difficulty were innocuous enough. Chicago Metals had a modest sized, elite corps of salesmen who traveled throughout the country demonstrating Chicago's capability to serve clients through the application of unique metals technologies. The job of the salesmen was to show a prospective client that one or more of the company's processes could fulfill a need. Each salesman, although based in Chicago, was assigned one of seven sections of the United States, which he worked with a partner. It was necessary to have the two salesmen together since the work was difficult for only one person to perform. Not uncommonly the pair would be on the road for two to three weeks at a time.

Of the 14 salesmen, not one had been a woman until Converse agreed with the decision of the Vice President of Sales, John Turner, to promote Cotton Springfield, a Vassar-educated, promising 25-year-old legal librarian within the company. Cotton was single and attractive and her buoyant personality made her a strong prospect for a successful career in sales. She was also eager for the opportunity. In an abstract sense, Converse was pleased with this decision since it not only conformed to good personnel practice but fulfilled government guidelines that specified that women and minorities should be hired in seven different job categories, including "sales." He was not, however, pleased with the flesh-and-blood consequences of the promotion of Cotton Springfield.

Turner had assigned Ms. Springfield to the only existing opening as a teammate for Anthony Gibson. Gibson was a 42-year-old veteran in the Chicago Metals sales force who worked the Southeastern sector, which included Missouri, Arkansas, Mississippi, Kentucky, Tennessee, Alabama, Georgia, and the Carolinas.

That morning Gibson had come to the personnel office to see Converse with an ardent plea for reconsideration based on his feeling that Cotton Springfield was not qualified and would cause problems. First, he had said, she had no technical background or experience in the metals business and "doesn't know carbon steel from the kitchen sink." If she didn't know the product she couldn't do the job and neither her education at an elite college nor her subsequent experience in the company law library gave her any background in metallurgy or engineering.

In addition, Gibson argued, his successful sales routine involved entertaining prospective buyers, who were all male, after business hours and the normal evening ritual included lots of off-color jokes, obscene language, and other male pastimes such as taking in a pornographic movie. Said Gibson: "How a proper and refined little filly like Cotton can handle that—I just don't know." He also pointed to a related potential difficulty. The Southeastern sector encompassed a population with conservative lifestyles and values. What would many of his customers conclude when the representative of Chicago Metals arrived with a sexy young traveling companion in tow? His and the company's image might be tarnished in the eyes of prospective customers. The inevitable kidding about their sharing a motel room might have a serious edge costly to the company. Male horseplay was okay, but to some of the "old boys" in Southern companies this might be going too far.

Gibson then became even more serious and reported an angry confrontation with his wife, who had railed bitterly against the prospect of her husband traveling across the country with a young and attractive woman for an extended period. She had threatened to leave him rather than face the ridicule of acquaintances who would assume that the two salespersons had more than aluminum in common. Gibson felt it unfair that he should be subjected to this pressure in addition to the normal pressures of a demanding occupation.

"Naturally I have nothing personal against Cotton," said Gibson as he rose to leave, "but I think you ought to reexamine your decision. She is being promoted because of her sex and not her competence and we both know it. Why don't you save me from problems with my wife and customers and save yourself and Cotton the heartache of her getting in way over her head." Although completely in earnest he dispelled the gravity of the situation by winking and adding that of course he "wouldn't mind her company on lonely nights on the road" if things couldn't be changed.

Converse sympathized with the salesman but was not sure what, if any, action he should take. Every year Chicago Metals had to fill out an EEO-1 form and, among other disclosures, Converse was required to present employment data by job category, including "sales." The *Affirmative Action and Equal Employment* guidebook on Converse's desk seemed to preclude sexual discrimination in the sales force. It stated in part that,

> For all practical purposes, almost all jobs must be open legally to men and women. The 'bona-fide occupational qualification' (BFOQ) exception of Title VII is narrowly con-

strued by EEOC and the courts. The burden of proof is on the employer to establish that the sexual characteristics of the employee are *crucial* to successful performance (such as model, actor, or actress). Only when the essence of the business enterprise would be undermined by not hiring a member of one sex exclusively is a BFOQ justified.

Converse had no doubt that women could be as effective sales representatives as men and Cotton Springfield would be given an extensive company training program to prepare her technically for the job. Furthermore, last year the company had been attacked for sexual discrimination by the National Organization of Women, which had threatened to bring suit in the courts if more women were not hired in sales and other positions. Vacancies were rare within the sales corps because of high commissions, so when a retirement left a slot open Converse had naturally looked for a woman to fill the position.

Converse knew he faced a difficult problem if he reversed his decision. Cotton Springfield might file a discrimination suit with the Equal Employment Opportunities Commission if she were removed from her new job, no matter what the reason. The Personnel Director was apprehensive. Only recently, in *U.S.* v. *Household Finance Corporation*, a company had been required to pay more than $125,000 to white-collar female employees such as Cotton Springfield, who charged that they had been denied promotion because of sex. In that case the court even decreed hiring quotas to be met until no less than 20 percent of all employees in certain job classifications were female.

Alternatively, Converse could not let Gibson or any of the other salesmen go. They were too good to be sacrificed on the altar of pressure politics. Yet he could not hire another woman sales representative to travel with Springfield. He hesitated to transfer a salesman from elsewhere into the Southeastern sector and put Gibson in another area of the country because Gibson had spent years developing and polishing contacts, as had the salesmen in other sectors. In addition, he was not sure other salesmen would be more accommodating to the idea of working with a young woman.

CASE QUESTIONS

1. Should Converse act to reverse his decision about putting Cotton Springfield in the sales force with Gibson? What mistakes has he made, if any, and how could they have been avoided?

2. If Springfield remains in the sales position what problems is she likely to face in the future and what can Converse or the company do to support her?

3. Does this case illustrate any special problems that women face in moving into traditionally male-dominated business positions? If so, what are they? See Rosabeth Moss Kanter and Barry A. Stein, "The Gender Pioneers: Women in an Industrial Sales Force," in Kanter and Stein, eds., *Life in Organizations* (New York: Basic Books, 1979), pp. 134–160; and Mary P. Rowe, "Case of the Valuable Vendors," *Harvard Business Review* (September-October 1978), pp. 40–63.

B) BRENNAN'S BIBULOUS BREAKDOWN

In 1943 an unskilled laborer named John Brennan joined the Ford Motor Company. For the next 31 years Brennan's career appeared to be an enviable success story. He rose from his first unskilled position through a series of jobs in sales and administration until he became chairman of Ford of Switzerland.

Unfortunately for Brennan, however, the jobs that he held in later years at Ford placed him in an environment where alcohol was an integral part of the daily routine. He began drinking "seriously" in 1950 when he represented Ford in Washington, D.C., making the rounds of Washington cocktail parties and bars. Later Brennan served as the company's liaison at the United Nations in New York where he conducted business at the delegates' bar and during long martini lunches. Brennan was subsequently promoted to higher posts in The Netherlands and Austria which confronted him with further social drinking in the course of his duties. By the time he had assumed his position as chairman in Switzerland he had begun drinking alone and realized he had a serious problem.

Brennan sought help from the company. When his problem became known he was met in a Zurich hotel room by high Ford officials and, over a bottle of Johnnie Walker Black Label, persuaded to take early retirement.

In 1975 Brennan sued the Ford Motor Company for $1.3 million. His contention was that his work environment was responsible for starting him down the path to alcoholism and that when he sought help from company officials he was persuaded to take early retirement rather than to seek rehabilitation.

CASE QUESTIONS

1. Does Brennan have a legitimate grievance?
2. If you were a lawyer for Ford Motor Company what arguments could you make to absolve the company of liability?
3. Explore the attitudes of American business toward the alcoholic employee. Generally, are such employees treated in an "enlightened" way?

Reference

There are numerous articles in business-oriented magazines and journals about alcoholism. See, as one example, Marion Sadler and James F. Horst, "Company/Union Programs for Alcoholics," *Harvard Business Review,* Vol. 50, No. 5 (September-October 1972), pp. 22–34, 152–56; and Joseph F. Follmann, Jr., *Alcoholics and Business: Problems, Costs, Solutions* (New York: AMACOM, 1976).

C) BIG COMPANIES: OPPRESSORS OF INDIVIDUAL EXPRESSION OR SOURCES OF SELF-SATISFACTION?

A Case for Role Playing

Businesses in general, but large companies in particular, have for a number of years been strongly attacked for forcing conformity, stifling self-expression, thwarting creativity, repressing natural drives, and in numerous other ways oppressing the individuals whom they employ. Businesspeople themselves, however, do not accept this picture. They say that an individual can lead a very satisfying life in a large company. They say there are many institutional arrangements present in large companies that not only permit but stimulate individual creativity, innovation, and participation.

Role 1. You are on the side of the critics of business: You accept the basic thesis in the first part of the introductory paragraph. Your assignment is to talk with your friends and read to build up a concrete list of ways in which large companies do, in fact, repress the individuals who work in them.

Role 2. You take the position that "life can be beautiful in a large company." Your task is to explain exactly how large companies today do help individuals to lead more satisfying lives.

Role 3. You take the position that there is truth in both statements. Your assignment is to think ahead and explain what a big company can do, aside from what it is now doing, to improve the personal self-satisfactions of individuals who work there and also advance the welfare of the company. *Note:* In the development of these three positions, it may be useful to classify people in groups, such as blue-collar workers, white-collar workers, lower-level managers, middle-level managers, and top managers.

References

Melvin L. Kohn, "The Benefits of Bureaucracy," *Human Nature,* August 1978.

George Strauss, "Organization Man—Prospect for the Future," *California Management Review,* Spring 1964.

Leonard R. Sayles, *Leadership: What Effective Managers Really Do . . . and How They Do It.* (New York: McGraw-Hill Book Company, 1979).

Samuel A. Culbert, *The Organization Trap.* (New York: Basic Books, Inc., 1974).

DISCUSSION GUIDES ON CHAPTER CONTENT

1. What is work? How have definitions of work changed over time?

2. Explain Maslow's hierarchy of needs classification. What importance do you attach to this classification?

3. Herzberg says that job dissatisfaction is not the opposite of job satisfaction. What does he mean? Of what significance is this observation?

4. Explain why there is dissatisfaction among blue-collar and white-collar workers, managers at different levels, new MBAs, young workers, women, and minority workers.

5. According to Eli Ginsberg, chairman of the National Commission for Manpower Policy, "the single most outstanding phenomenon of our century is the flood of women into jobs." Do you agree? Explain.

6. What are some methods that large organizations employ to stimulate individual creativity, innovation, and imagination?

7. What is meant by quality of working life?

8. What do you think can and should be done by business to improve QOWL? Explain.

9. What is the concept of job enrichment? What promise does it hold for improving QOWL in business organizations?

10. It has been contended by many authors that future organizations will be more democratic and participative. Do you agree?

MIND-STRETCHING QUESTIONS —————————————————

1. Many organizations are currently considering adoption of the four-day work week. What implications does this have for business and for society?

2. It has been stated that today's youth emerging from college and entering business will have a profound effect on organizational structure and goals. How will this come about? How would you, fresh from school and entering a company at or near the bottom of the ladder, go about introducing the concepts you have learned and the values that you hold?

3. Do you think that there are certain "proper" attitudes that tend to help a person in the business world? Is it permissible for organizations to expect employees to cultivate these attitudes? How far do you think this expectation should go? Defend your position.

20
LABOR UNIONS AND MANAGERIAL AUTHORITY

DISCUSSION GUIDES ON CHAPTER CONTENT

1. What is the difference between collective bargaining and arbitration? What are their relative merits?

2. Many managers express concern about the power of unions over their "managerial prerogatives." How has union power restricted managerial authority?

3. On the other hand, there are limitations on the exercise of power by unions. Describe some of the more important limitations.

4. Despite the antipathy that often exists between managers and unions, there is an acceptance of unions on the part of managers, and unions are much less militant and more amenable to peaceful negotiations today than ever before. Why?

5. Explain the nature and potential significance of the agreement the United Steelworkers of America made with management not to strike and to submit disagreements to arbitration.

6. What are the pros and cons of union representation on corporate boards of directors? How likely is it that this system will be adopted in the United States?

7. What might be some of the more significant future demands of labor unions in the United States?

MIND-STRETCHING QUESTION

1. While labor unions have been growing over the years, and managers have been accepting them more easily than in the past, would you say that it would be better for industry in this country if labor unions were more widespread? Or would you contend otherwise?

21
ETHICS IN THE BUSINESS SYSTEM

A) MARTIN'S CAMPAIGN CONTRIBUTION

Jack Martin is speaking to his wife Mary. "Yesterday I had lunch with Ed Wilson. You remember him. You saw him at the country club party last year."

Mary: "Yes, but very vaguely. What did you talk about?"

Jack: "Oh, mostly business. But did you know he is backing Bill Smith for mayor?"

Mary: "Bill Smith! How could he? Smith is a crook, and you know it."

Jack: "Yes, I know it. That's why I am backing Joe Donaldson."

Mary: "Our League of Women's Voters' Committee on Candidates is backing Donaldson, and I'm going to campaign actively for him."

Jack: "That's good. But try to maintain a low profile, would you?"

Mary: "Why?"

Jack: "Well, Ed Wilson feels pretty strongly about Bill Smith. I don't want to offend him because he's my biggest customer. He just gave me another $100,000 contract. As a matter of fact, he asked me for a contribution to Smith's campaign, since he is treasurer of the businessman's committee for Smith."

Mary: "Jack, how could you? You don't want Smith for mayor, so why help with a campaign contribution?"

Jack: "Mary, you don't understand. We talked about the new order before talking about Smith. Ed was all set to sign the contract when he raised the question about a $100 contribution for Smith's campaign. I gave him a check right there and then. Having him agree on the contract after that was as easy as silk. This means a great deal to the company and to us. I don't see how we could break even during the next six months without this contract."

Mary: "If you had been honest with Ed Wilson, I am sure he would have accepted the fact that you don't want Smith and don't want to help him campaign. This is a democracy. Why should Ed Wilson resent your views? Why should he hold it against you if you don't contribute to Smith's campaign?"

Jack: "Mary, I'm sorry I mentioned the matter. You don't understand. If I had refused to contribute, Ed would have smiled and said, 'Jack, I fully understand and respect your views.' But, he would as likely as not have also said he wasn't quite ready to sign the contract, that he had a few details to check out before making the commitment. There are others in this business who can fill his order as cheaply as our company can. We would have parted with a friendly handshake, and Ed would have said to call him in a few days. I would call, and Ed would say that he wasn't really ready yet. A few weeks later, I would call again but be unable to reach him. Then I would learn through the grapevine that he had given the contract to my competitor. Mary, this is a dog-eat-dog business. It was a 'come-across-or-lose-my-contract' situation. I could tell by Ed Wilson's way of speaking. We simply could not risk losing his business. I would have given him $500 had he asked me."

Mary: "You should have stood up to him. What kind of a man is Ed Wilson? I wouldn't do business with him. If he is that stubborn and indifferent to the rights of others, let him take his business elsewhere. Jack, you are not the man I thought you were. Where is your moral backbone?"

Jack: "Oh boy! Why did I ever mention it?"

Mary: "Something is very wrong with business when you have to submerge your real convictions to get a contract. Something is wrong with business, when you are forced to choose between your family's well-being and your moral convictions! If this is possible then business is immoral."

CASE QUESTIONS

1. Compare Mary's viewpoint to Jack's. Is there a difference between business ethics and ethics in other walks of life?
2. Can you support Jack's action?
3. It has been argued that doing business is often like playing poker. Do you agree? See Albert Z. Carr, "Is Business Bluffing Ethical?" *Harvard Business Review,* January-February 1968, pp. 143–153. (This case was drafted from the article. See also Timothy B. Blodgett, "Showdown on 'Business Bluffing,'" *Harvard Business Review,* May-June 1968, pp. 162–170.)

B) BEHAVIOR MODIFICATION COMES OF AGE*

Out of the psychologist's laboratory and into factories and offices has come "positive reinforcement" or PR. Like a fecund plant it has spread from a single seed to take root in businesses across the country. The business value of the concept of PR is undeniable and one consulting firm even gives a written guarantee to save companies at least $30,000 in the first year of a PR program. However, the social and moral consequences of the technique cast a shadow on its gleaming successes.

The Origin of Positive Reinforcement

The concept of positive reinforcement is associated with the work of psychologist B. F. Skinner, a prolific author and experimenter on human behavior. Skinner's belief, briefly stated, is that the behavior of animals and people can be altered through what he calls "operant conditioning," or the immediate reinforcement of

*Prepared by John F. Steiner

desired behavior with rewards. Operant conditioning (or positive reinforcement) is more effective, argues Skinner, than "aversive conditioning," or the attempt to shape behavior through punishment.

In one of his early works Skinner describes how this technique works with pigeons.

> I watch a hungry pigeon carefully. When he makes a slight clockwise turn, he's instantly rewarded for it. After he eats, he immediately tries it again. Then I wait for more of a turn and reinforce again. Within two or three minutes, I can get any pigeon to make a full circle. Next I reinforce only when he moves in the other direction. Then I wait until he does both, and reinforce him again and again until it becomes a kind of drill. Within ten to fifteen minutes, the pigeon will be doing a perfect figure eight.[1]

Skinner became so enamored with the potential application of this concept to shaping human behavior that he wrote a controversial novel, *Walden Two*, portraying a utopian society where positive reinforcement is used to control behavior toward socially desirable ends.[2] The book attracted a host of critics who argued that the behavioral reinforcers running the Walden Two community were manipulators with no special knowledge of what socially desirable goals were.[3]

Business Discovers Positive Reinforcement

In the late 1960s, Edward J. Feeney, then with Emery Air Freight Corp., pioneered the systematic use of positive reinforcement to cut costs and raise worker productivity. His methods were based on Skinner's theory. Here is how he did it.

Emery flies many small shipments to the same destinations and these cost less when placed in large containers than when shipped separately. A performance audit showed that only 45 percent of shipments were containerized, but Feeney set a goal of 95 percent utilization. This would save freight costs.

Feeney developed a program to motivate workers through PR techniques. Managers received elaborate books of instruction about how to give recognition and rewards to employees. The workbooks listed 150 types of reward from a simple smile or nod of the head to buying the employee a cup of coffee to detailed and specific praise. Supervisors were told how to use sentences like, "Joe, I liked the ingenuity you showed just now getting those crates into that container. You're running pretty consistently at 98 percent of standard. And after watching you, I can understand why."[4]

Desired behavior was to be reinforced as soon as possible and, in the beginning, with high frequency. Specifically, Feeney urged supervisors to give praise to employees twice a week during the early weeks of the program. Workers with below-standard performance were not censured or punished. Subpar behavior was not commented upon and supervisors were instructed to look for and reward any positive actions, even the smallest.

Later in the program supervisors were told that they could reinforce less frequently and at random intervals. This was judged to be just as effective after the early groundwork had been laid.

The results were dramatic. Container utilization jumped to over 90 percent and stayed there. Emery saved over $650,000 a year in shipping costs. Employee morale rose and poor performers became a rarity. The behavior-shaping techniques were expanded to other departments and operations.[5]

Since the initial application of PR at Emery, Feeney and others have set up consulting operations to proselytize the new management religion. In the early 1980s, PR has started to catch on with dozens of companies. It is used by such familiar corporate names as AT&T, B.F. Goodrich, Ford, Frito-Lay, General Electric, Western Air Lines, and Weyerhaeuser. Minnesota's 3M claims annual cost savings running into the millions. Even small businesses are getting into the act.

The behavioral-shaping potential of certain types of reinforcement is extremely powerful. Gambling devices, which operate on random reinforcement schedules, are particularly addicting, as ranks of hooked gamblers will attest. Some PR programs take advantage of this irresistible appeal.

One such project, designed to reduce absenteeism, offered a lottery to 215 hourly employees in a manufacturing plant. Every day those employees who came on time were able to select a playing card from a deck. At the end of each week a punctual employee would have accumulated a poker hand of five cards and the highest eight hands won $20 each. Absenteeism dropped 18 percent.[6]

The Critics of Behavior Modification

Positive reinforcement and other behavior modification techniques in business, despite proven financial advantages, are not without their critics. The critics make four basic points.

First, they argue that with PR, people are being manipulated to achieve the goals of others. They are deprived of their full freedom and treated like automatons with no purposeful will of their own. Behavior modification techniques demonstrate little concern for the integrity of individuals or respect for their free will. Furthermore, they insult the intelligence of all those beyond the most incapacious and behaviorally impaired. Normal people should not be treated like Skinner's mice and pigeons.[7]

Second, while a few isolated programs of behavior modification in industry may be largely unobjectionable, the use of PR may spread and threaten the freedom of large numbers of workers. Widespread use of PR in business might pave the way for application of new behavioral modification techniques by government and lead to mass control of populations. Could Americans save more energy, for example, if behavior modification techniques were developed for use by government bureaucrats? Such a "benevolent" application of PR might be tempting to legislators, especially if it had become widely accepted in business.

Third, some critics argue that behavior modification techniques utilizing random reinforcement, like the aforementioned project that used the deck of cards, may addict susceptible persons to gambling. Employers, say these critics, wouldn't give a person a drink for doing a good job. If they did, they soon would have a number of alcoholic employees. Likewise, why turn workers into gamblers by tempting them in the process of increasing productivity?

Fourth, some management theorists say that PR techniques are overrated and faddish. They argue that PR will not even work in many situations, a reference to the difficulty of applying it where performance cannot be precisely measured. Western Air Lines, for example, has had difficulty applying PR to flight attendants because a quantitative measure of performance is elusive.

Advocates of PR respond that behavior modification is a new and valuable management tool that can increase productivity, reduce absenteeism and turnover, and even provide greater job satisfaction among employees in most cases. Because of the praise they receive, workers have reported feeling better about their jobs and morale often rises where PR is applied. The central theme of PR advocates is that it pays off. Says Feeney:

> With savings this large we can't afford to worry about charges that we're manipulating our employees . . . . People in business manipulate their employees all the time—otherwise they would go bankrupt. The only questions are, how effective are you as a manipulator and what ends do you further with your manipulation? Our end is improved performance, and we've deen damned effective in getting it.[8]

With more and more PR programs being adopted in industry this debate is likely to become hotter. Is PR a genie in a bottle or a hidden army inside a wooden horse of management rhetoric?

CASE QUESTIONS

1. Is behavior modification a desirable management tool? Why or why not?
2. Is there a real threat to individual liberty from the adoption of behavior modification techniques by business?
3. Since our nation (and others) is currently in a productivity slump is it desirable to make a trade-off between increased worker productivity and individual freedom?

Notes

1. Quoted in Kenneth Lamott, "On Controlling Human Behavior," *Horizon,* Vol. XVIII, No. 1 (Winter 1976), p. 7. For more information on Skinner see Richard I. Evans, *B. F. Skinner: The Man and His Ideas* (New York: E.P. Dutton & Co., 1968).
2. B. F. Skinner, *Walden Two* (New York: Macmillan, 1948).
3. See, for example, Joseph Wood Krutch, *The Measure of Man* (New York: Grosset and Dunlap, 1953).
4. Edward J. Feeney, "At Emery Air Freight: Positive Reinforcement Boosts Performance," *Organizational Dynamics,* Winter 1973, pp. 41–50.
5. *Ibid.,* p. 43.
6. Ed Pedalino and Victor U. Gamboa, "Behavior Modification and Absenteeism: Intervention in One Industrial Setting," *Journal of Applied Psychology,* December 1974, pp. 694–698.

7. Fred L. Fry, "Operant Conditioning in Organizational Settings: Of Mice or Men?" *Personnel,* Vol. 51, No. 4 (July-August 1974), pp. 17–24.
8. Feeney, p. 45.

C) AERIAL ESPIONAGE OR AMERICAN ENTREPRENEURSHIP

One sunny day in 1969, in Beaumont, Texas, a small airplane was seen circling over a plant being constructed by E. I. DuPont de Nemours and Company. Once finished, this plant would produce methanol, a chemical used in making antifreeze by a secret and unpatented process. There was a photographer in the airplane who freely admitted taking pictures of the plant and delivering them to a third party.

DuPont sued the photographer and others, alleging that trade secrets had been obtained wrongfully, and asked for damages and an injunction from the use of the photographs. DuPont said that since the plant was under construction, a skilled person could tell from the photographs the secret process that would be used in making methanol. It claimed the process had been developed at great expense in time and money and gave DuPont a competitive advantage over other producers.

The defendants claimed there was no wrongdoing. They said the photographs were all taken in airspace in the public domain. No government aviation laws or standards were violated, and there was no trespass or breach of confidential relationships. Indeed, they asserted, there was nothing more involved than good old American entrepreneurship.

The court agreed with DuPont, and observed:

> Our devotion to freewheeling industrial competition must not force us into accepting the law of the jungle as the standard of morality expected in our commercial relations. . . . One may use a competitor's process if he discovers it by his own independent research; but one may not avoid these labors by taking the process from the discoverer without his permission at a time when he is taking reasonable precautions to maintain its secrecy. To obtain knowledge of a process without spending the time and money to discover it independently is *improper* unless the holder voluntarily discloses it or fails to take reasonable precautions to ensure its secrecy.[1]

CASE QUESTIONS

1. In your view, was the photographer acting unethically?

2. In the case, the judge said: "'Improper' will always be a word of many nuances, determined by time, place, and circumstances. We therefore need not proclaim a catalogue on commercial improprieties. Clearly, however, one of its commandments does say 'thou shall not appropriate a trade secret through deviousness under circumstances in which countervailing defenses are not reasonably available.'" Name some practices that you think are improper ways to obtain trade secrets. Name some that go on in industry that you think may be proper. (See, Michael S. Baram, "Trade Secrets: What Price Loyalty?" *Harvard Business Review,* November-December 1968, pp. 66–74.)

3. How much espionage is going on in industry and what do executives think about it? (See Jerry L. Wall, "A Survey of Executives' attitudes, practices, and ethics vis-a-vis espionage and other forms of competitive information gathering," *Harvard Business Review,* November-December 1974.)

4. What can an employer do to protect the firm from espionage? (See Roger M. Milgrim, "Get the Most out of Your Trade Secrets," *Harvard Business Review,* November-December 1974; William F. Glueck and Robert A. Mittelstaedt, "Protecting Trade Secrets in the Seventies," *California Management Review,* Fall 1973; and J. Roger O'Meara, *How Smaller Companies Protect Their Trade Secrets,* New York: The Conference Board, Inc., 1971.

Note

1. E. I. DuPont de Nemours vs. Christopher (431 F. 2d 1012, 1972).

D) CRISIS AT XYZ

National Electronics Company, the parent of many subsidiaries, was embarrassed by having to report substantially lower earnings than had been previously forecast to the public. Shortly after the report, XYZ Company, one of National's subsidiaries, announced the selection of a new president and a new vice-president of finance (replacing the controller). John Smith, former president of XYZ, and George Logan, former controller, had been withholding information from the parent company about the poor financial condition of XYZ.

Smith had made a decision to go after two large contracts. Smith's managers disagreed on his optimistic estimate of the probabilities of getting them, but he persisted and became more and more committed financially. Finally, XYZ failed to get the contracts, and the poor financial position of the company had to be made known to headquarters. Had XYZ won the contracts, Smith would have been a hero. As it turned out, he resigned under pressure and his resignation was accepted.

One director of National said that out-and-out fraud was involved, while another thought this was a situation directly attributable to the pressures on people like Smith to make profits. In such instances, this director felt, they tended to take the optimistic view.

A major question that arose was why a number of top managers at XYZ, who had close affiliations with men at National, did not go above Smith and make the situation known. Investigation showed that loyalty to Smith was high, and, as a result, his staff accepted his position.

CASE QUESTIONS

1. Was there a violation of common standards of ethics in this situation?

2. Who was to blame for the fiasco?

3. What would you have done had you been the controller?

References

For detailed discussion of this subject see John J. Fendrock, "Crisis in Conscience at Quasar," *Harvard Business Review,* March-April 1968; and John J. Fendrock, "Sequel to Quasar Stellar," *Harvard Business Review,* September-October 1968.

E) WILLARD ATKINSON

Willard Atkinson has been with the Tiller Container Corporation for forty years and is now in charge of production for a very large division. When Atkinson first worked for the company he was quite capable of dealing with the problems of production that he encountered, but he has not bothered to keep abreast of new production techniques. However, he was successful in hiring two bright young MBAs who are highly competent in production techniques and excellent general managers as well, and he has tended to delegate more and more of his responsibilities to these men. There is little if any doubt that he could not manage the affairs of his department without the talents of these young men. Unfortunately, they have made it known that they may leave unless brighter opportunities are opened for them, and the management knows they would be extremely difficult to replace. About the only place they would fit in the company would be in Atkinson's job.

Atkinson is now sixty years of age. The voluntary retirement age at the company is sixty-five. Atkinson has made it known that since he is in good health he intends to stay. The president is thinking seriously of asking him to take early retirement in order to save one of the two young men on his staff whose talents are sorely needed in the company. Early retirement will give Atkinson 40 percent of his salary, whereas voluntary retirement at sixty-five would give him 50 percent.[1]

CASE QUESTIONS ─────────────────────────────

1. Do you think Atkinson is behaving ethically?
2. If the president of the Tiller Container Corporation forces Atkinson to take early retirement, do you think he is acting ethically?
3. If you were one of the younger men, what would you do?
4. In your opinion what impact will the elimination of the mandatory retirement age have on the managerial evaluation and promotion processes in companies?

Note

1. For a detailed discussion, see John J. Fendrock, "Crisis in Conscience at Quasar," *Harvard Business Review,* March-April 1968, pp. 112–120. John J. Fendrock, "Sequel to Quasar Stellar," *Harvard Business Review,* September-October 1968, pp. 14ff.

DISCUSSION GUIDES ON CHAPTER CONTENT ————————

1. What is business ethics? What are some of the major reasons ethical problems arise in business?

2. Surveys have more or less consistently shown that managers say pressure from superiors to achieve higher results is one of the main causes for resorting to unethical behavior. Would you agree with this finding?

3. According to one observer, "business behavior is more ethical than it was 15 years ago." Assess this statement.

4. What are the principal sources of values that constitute the business ethos? Which is most influential today?

5. The possibility of business becoming more ethical is bound up with the possibility of its professionalization. Comment.

6. What can and should a company do to improve the ethical and moral conduct of people working for it?

MIND-STRETCHING QUESTIONS ————————————

1. Critics often say that the managers of a business, unlike members of other professions, primarily seek cash and emphasize materialistic values. Other professions, on the other hand, seem to have lofty primary purposes and high ideals of public service from which, as a side-line, money flows. Comment.

2. The president of a local construction company asks your advice in developing a code of ethics that may be used to guide the actions of all employees in his company. What would you suggest?

22
MAKING ETHICAL
DECISIONS IN BUSINESS

A)   WHISTLE BLOWING AT HI-QUALITY AIRCRAFT*

James Sinclair, president of Hi-Quality Aircraft, was pacing in his office, deep in thought and obviously concerned. He was pondering what to do to stop the controversy raging in the press about the safety of his new Exec-Six airplane. Somehow he did not seem able to stop this controversy, and if it did not stop, sales were not likely to reach the breakeven point, with a resulting substantial loss to the company. What could he do? What should he do?

He had somehow lost control of the situation. He still couldn't believe it had happened. Maybe if he tried to review this terrible fiasco again it would help. Yet after reviewing the problem so many times before, this seemed like an exercise in futility.

The newspapers had called Phillip Evans a "whistle blower." Sinclair had never liked that term and, in most cases, the people associated with it. Evans was becoming a hero around the country, with Hi-Quality Aircraft playing the role of corporate villain. Before this incident was closed, many people would be hurt.

Success Story

James Sinclair had assumed the presidency of Hi-Quality late in 1969. Jim had an engineering background, but his impressive credentials in corporate finance assured his appointment. He had established a reputation with two other aviation firms as a hard-driving, competent manager.

During the last 10 years, Hi-Quality had grown from obscurity to become the major producer of executive aircraft. Superior engineering, coupled with attractive pricing, enabled the firm to record constantly rising sales and profits. The firm had always followed a policy of generously supporting its research and development programs. It took pride in its engineering and design excellence.

Project HQE-6

Early in 1970 Hi-Quality embarked on Project HQE-6—the design and manufacture of the Exec-Six aircraft. This airplane would be the most advanced and fastest

*Prepared by George A. Steiner

155

six-passenger executive aircraft yet conceived. It would also be priced at least 10 percent lower than its closest competitor. As always, design and engineering would be the best Hi-Quality could offer. Profit margins would be the lowest in 10 years, however, because of the low price tag, and competitive pressures would exert much more influence on cost-benefit analysis of engineering design requirements than ever before.

This new project necessitated a 20 percent increase in personnel in the engineering section. Phillip Evans was hired as a project engineer in March 1970. Evans was 28 years old and had already established himself as a real "comer" in aircraft fuselage and airfoil design. His previous experience had been with a large military contractor in the aerospace industry. Some of his designs were largely responsible for the speed and superiority of American fighter-bombers.

Cost versus Design Considerations

The HQE-6 prototype was completed in late 1971. Preliminary testing indicated that it was indeed a superior aircraft. Bernard Collins, the veteran senior project engineer, was very pleased with the work his engineering section had done. He was especially happy with Phillip Evans, whose wing design enabled the aircraft to take off and land in 25 percent less distance than conventional aircraft. Also, the cruising speed of 625 miles per hour was well above design requirements and the competition.

Keith Mitchell, general production manager, was not quite as enthusiastic as Collins. The accounting department had just completed costing the HQE-6 and found that its construction costs were 15 percent higher than the targeted price. While costs exceeded projections on several features of the aircraft, the wing design was estimated to be 60 percent over budget. In addition, manufacturing lead time on the wing construction was estimated to be three times original projections.

Mitchell and Collins had always been able to work out such problems in the past, and it looked as if it would be possible to bring costs into line on most of the sections of the aircraft except the wing section. Collins agreed that substantial redesign was in order for the wing section.

Quality Level Becomes Critical

Evans seemed to accept the situation that Bernard Collins presented to him. He began redesign work immediately, but did seem somewhat puzzled as to why the original design was unacceptable.

After two weeks of long work days, the engineering section presented two proposals for redesign. The first design, worked out almost entirely by Evans, was a substantial departure from the prototype design. It was potentially a dramatic breakthrough in design characteristics, but once again costing estimates indicated that it would be around 30 percent over budget.

The second proposal was a joint effort of three engineers in the section, working closely with senior project engineer Bernard Collins. This proposal involved using the original design with modifications. These modifications involved: (a) reducing the number of reinforcing stringers between the inner and outer skins of the wing assembly; (b) changing the material specifications from steel and inconel to titanium-steel construction; and (c) increasing the angle of jet flap on the trailing edge of the wings.

Preliminary wind-tunnel experiments indicated that the second proposal would meet accepted safety factor limits of five to one at cruising speed and three to one at take-off and landing.

Proposal 2 was given the go-ahead for final testing and manufacture, since the modifications brought the construction costs within budget limits.

Confrontation

Mr. Sinclair recalled the conversation that Bernard Collins said he had had with Phillip Evans the following week. Collins was in his office going over test results of the revised design, when Evans abruptly charged in.

"Mr. Collins, I've got to talk to you about this new design," said Evans.

Collins: "Sure thing, Phil, what's on your mind?"

Evans: "Well, to put it simply, that wing design won't do the job. As a matter of fact it's so bad it's not safe."

Collins: "I don't understand, Phil. All test results show that it meets safety requirements, and after all, it's only a modification of your own design, which we know was far superior to anything in the industry."

Phil: "Mr. Collins, that's just the problem, it's not the same design. Those modifications virtually destroy the design of the prototype. I've made some trial experiments with models of the proposal, and my suspicions are confirmed. Its wings exhibit slight vibration characteristics on steep ascents and descents and during prolonged flight at low altitude. Likewise, temperature rise approaches the danger level on the leading edge of the wing, which could cause skin separation. Most importantly, the friction drag coefficient transfers from the laminar flow curve to the turbulent flow curve because of the change in material specifications and trailing edge design."

Collins: "Wait a minute, Phil, we've had several engineers running tests on the model, too, and they have all been favorable. From what you've told me, it seems that you don't really understand how this plane will be used in actual service. It doesn't have to be capable of operating like a navy fighter-bomber."

Evans: "But Mr. Collins, what about emergency situations? Operating characteristics must be considered there also."

Collins: "They are. That's why we calculate in a safety factor. Look, Phil, we've been in business quite a while now, and we take it seriously. We stand by our planes, our record speaks for itself!"

Evans: "Maybe so, but I know about wing design, and I say that in certain situations, conditions may exist to cause the wing sections to separate from the fuselage. And if that happens, someone is going to die, and it will be too late. I don't want any part of it."

Evans immediately left Collins's office without giving him a chance to answer. Evans resigned that afternoon.

The Engineer Takes Other Action

The first flight of the airplane was made in early 1972, and by the fall of 1972 the airplane had recorded 750 hours of flight time. In October 1972 all tests had been made, and final certification by the Federal Aviation Agency was given. This meant that the airplane had passed all federal air regulations and requirements.

At the time of FAA certification, the company had received orders or options for 50 airplanes. This was enough to convince the company it should proceed. The breakeven point was calculated to be 150 aircraft, and it was hoped that this number of aircraft would be sold by the end of 1973. The total sales of the airplane were conservatively estimated to be 410 over a five-year period.

Manufacture of the Exec-Six began in November 1972, with the first deliveries to be made in early 1973. A few days after production began, Sinclair received a registered letter from Phillip Evans that outlined his objections to the project and demanded that production be stopped. Sinclair again reviewed the situation with his top management and the engineering department, and a decision was made to continue production. In his letter Evans stated that if production was not halted, he would present his case at the annual stockholders meeting to be held in three weeks.

Sinclair could hardly forget what happened at the annual meeting. Evans, a stockholder, demanded to be heard. Sinclair had been prepared for the confrontation and was convinced he could handle it effectively.

Evans began: "Mr. Sinclair, as president of Hi-Quality Aircraft, isn't it true that you have been aware for some time of the potentially dangerous design specifications of this new aircraft?"

Sinclair: "I am thoroughly familiar with the design specifications of the Exec-Six, and I am convinced that the aircraft meets all existing safety standards. It indeed is a superior aircraft."

Evans: "Mr. Sinclair, I worked on the design of that aircraft and I know of several weaknesses that can cause structural damage under certain conditions."

Sinclair: "Ladies and gentlemen, I must emphasize that these allegations are unfounded. The aircraft has successfully passed all model testing and prototype experiments by us and the government and clearly meets or exceeds standards for design performance. We all know that under severe testing it is possible to fail any design if the conditions become too extreme. This aircraft is built for specific civilian functions, and it is inappropriate to evaluate its performance in extreme experiments meant for military aircraft, which is what Mr. Evans has done."

Evans: "Then you admit the plane did fail design tests."

Sinclair: "No, I don't."

Evans: "Do you admit that under certain conditions, even though abnormal, the design could fail?"

Sinclair: "I can simply restate that no aircraft can perform perfectly under *all* conditions. The cost to build such an aircraft would be so high that no one could afford to build it or buy it."

Evans: "Then you're saying you can't build a safe plane because it costs too much."

Sinclair was able to bring the argument to an end, but the damage had been done. He hoped that his persistent, rational arguments had prevailed. After watching the local TV newscasts of the proceedings, however, he wasn't so sure. The newscasts, while accurate, seemed to raise doubts in the viewer's mind about the safety of the airplane. The story was picked up by national news media and was continuously in the news as a result of what amounted to a crusade by Evans to stop production of the airplane. Evans kept writing letters to Hi-Quality management, its board of directors, newspapers, and the FAA.

The Crisis

In June 1973 a recently delivered Exec-Six crashed on landing. In the airplane were three engineers employed by the company owning the plane. Neither they nor the pilot were injured, but the airplane was seriously damaged. The official determination of what caused the accident would not be known until the National Transportation Safety Board made its report some months hence. The engineers in the airplane, however, all agreed that pilot error in slowing down the airplane too much had caused an engine stall.

The crash gave impetus, however, to Evans's public outcry against the airplane. A national consumer activist group joined Evans, and once again the story of Exec-Six was featured in the headlines.

Sinclair was still absolutely sure of the reliability of the aircraft and sought in every way possible to counter assertions by Evans and all others now involved in the debate. Sinclair obviously was not completely successful. While the Exec-Six was still being sold, the orders were far below the projections. Some of the original options were not picked up, and new orders were slow. Indeed, by the fall of 1973, only 75 firm orders had been received, one half of what was anticipated. There was no doubt in Sinclair's mind that poor sales were directly attributable to Evans's campaign.

CASE QUESTIONS

1. Did Phillip Evans handle his grievance appropriately?
2. What should be management's strategy in handling such incidents?
3. What would be the effect on business enterprises if this type of whistle blowing became recognized as appropriate employee behavior?
4. Analyze in general terms the cost-benefit trade-offs generated in this case. Who comes out ahead? Who loses?

References

Tony McAdams, "Speaking Out in the Corporate Community," *Academy of Management Review,* April 1977.

David Ewing, "Who Wants Corporate Democracy?" *Harvard Business Review,* September-October 1971.

David Ewing, *Freedom Inside the Organization* (New York: E. P. Dutton, 1977). For a critique of this book see Max Ways, *Fortune,* October 1977.

Ralph Nader, Peter Petkas, and Kate Blackwell, *Whistle Blowing* (New York: Bantam Books, 1972).

Charles Peters and Taylor Branch, *Blowing the Whistle: Dissent in the Public Interest* (New York: Praeger, 1972).

B) SELLING ETHICS AT CONTINENTAL CHEMICAL*

Continental Chemical Company is a multinational refiner and distributor of chemical supplies for industry. The company, which had revenues of $5 billion in 1980, produces and delivers supplies of sulfur, sulfuric acid, phosphate, magnesium, chlorine, and other products to factories around the world which use them in various industrial processes.

The headquarters of Continental are in New York, but it also has 25,000 employees in six major factory and office complexes in the United States and another 6,000 personnel overseas.

Continental always has had a highly regarded training and development program for management personnel. It offers company training programs to managers in traditionally popular areas such as management theory and practice, marketing concepts and techniques, and financial and accounting methods. Ambitious managers at Continental find it both useful and politic to avail themselves of training opportunities.

Early in 1980, Robert Collins, director of Continental's training and development staff, received a memo from Thomas Johnson, president of the company. The memo directed Collins to submit a proposal for a management training program focusing on business ethics and social responsibilities. The essence of Johnson's memo is in the following excerpted paragraphs.

> Changes in public attitudes and expectations, the broad social impact of Continental Chemical Corporation, and the growing complexity of ethical programs have all created a need for managers trained to cope with the turbulent and sensitive social environment. At all levels, Company managers are faced with situations and problem areas where it is difficult to write stringent policy guidelines due to the value-laden nature of the issues that arise.
>
> Specifically, I refer to compliance with environmental regulations, compliance with worker health and safety regulations, the puzzle of foreign political payments, questions of organizational loyalty, the challenge of female and minority hiring practices and affirmative action programs, the development of voluntary social programs exceeding responsibilities under the law, the difficult decisions posed by human factors in cost-benefit studies, and the general determination of corporate social responsibility. In

*The authors are joined by Herbert Schick.

addition to these areas, there are perennial problem areas with ethics involving such things as employee privacy, conflicts between organizational loyalty and family life, and conflicts between the values of co-workers within the firm.

I believe we can, through training, better equip our managers to confront the growing ethical challenge in business. Please develop a proposal for a training program that will give managers the mental tool kits needed to cope with ethical problems. I believe this area of training is no less important than such traditional areas as worker motivation, supervisory leadership, time management, and sales techniques.

Submit to me, in two months, an outline of an ethics training program along with a preliminary budget.

Collins enthusiastically outlined a training program on ethics and social responsibility for middle- and top-level managers. Over a five-year period Continental's domestic managers would, on a rotating basis, attend an intensive two-day seminar at the company's training and development institute on the Hudson River in New York. Within three years of attending the first two-day seminar, each manager would also be rotated into two additional one-day seminars on special topics in ethics and corporate social responsibility at training sites dispersed throughout the country. Thus, each Continental manager would receive four days' training and, in theory, all managers would have completed the program within three to eight years.

The cost of the program, which some members of Collins's staff jokingly referred to as a "product recall campaign," was steep. Travel to the two-day seminars was a major expense, but most Continental managers visited New York headquarters at frequent intervals. The on-going salary paid each manager for the four days in training, or the opportunity cost of the program, was also steep. However, most Continental managers took training programs at regular intervals and would simply be taking ethics training in lieu of something else. Some would, of course, take ethics training on top of other offerings.

In addition to the normal costs of running the seminars and programs, such as coffee, meals, pencils and paper, speakers' fees and film rentals, Collins needed to hire two new training staff members and a secretary to handle the increased load. In sum, Collins estimated the cost of the program to be $70,000 a year for the first five years and $40,000 a year for the next three years. Over an eight-year period, then, the total estimated cost of the program was $470,000, not including the opportunity costs of the attending managers' time. Collins estimated that not more than 10 percent of this cost would be offset by lowered attendance at more traditional programs.

Two months after submitting his proposal, Collins received a memo from Johnson that posed an unexpected obstacle to the start-up of the program. Here is the pertinent text.

I brought your recommendations and budget for the training before the Board of Directors at the last monthly meeting. The Board has postponed action on the proposal until its next meeting. In the meantime, I request that you submit to me written answers to the following questions that were raised by Board members about the proposal.

1. What effect would the training have on the productivity and profitability of the Company? Would productivity and profitability be enhanced?

2. Why is there a more compelling need to address ethical problems today than in the past? If Continental managers have ethical difficulties why should we not tighten up hiring practices in personnel and write stiffer policy guidelines for employees? Would an ethics training program work if these things were *not* done?
3. How do you propose to measure the results of your program? What indicators exist to reflect results in such a training program? Can you suggest an evaluation measure?

Please submit your answers prior to the next Board meeting, on July 1.

As Collins examined the questions he could sense between the lines underlying hostility to the training program. From what he knew of the board's members, they were an elderly, cost-conscious, and conservative lot. He guessed they were giving Johnson a hard time and he knew his answers would have to be convincing if President Johnson were to sell the program.

CASE QUESTIONS

1. Do you think the program developed by Collins is a good response to the problems pointed out by Johnson in the first memo?
2. How would you answer the questions posed in Johnson's second memo?
3. What suggestions do you have for the specific content of the four days of training?
4. What alternatives to an ethics training program exist for elevating ethics at Continental?

DISCUSSION GUIDES ON CHAPTER CONTENT

1. Discuss Chester Barnard's views on business moralities, with particular reference to the fact that there are usually different types of business moralities in a company.
2. Considering the apparent fact that the ethical content of business decisions is increasing and, at the same time, the consensus of ethical standards is being eroded, what do you think ought to be done to reconcile the two trends to achieve a more practical framework for guiding managers?
3. Identify the guides for ethical business conduct presented in the textbook and comment on the strengths and weaknesses of each.
4. Compare and contrast Purcell's three-stage model for making ethical decisions with the balance-sheet approach of Janis and Mann.

MIND-STRETCHING QUESTIONS

1. Draw up a personal code of ethics that you would like to follow when you enter the business world. Do you think you will be able to follow it? Explain.
2. What connection do you see between technical morality and consumer complaints over product quality?

23
TECHNOLOGY

DISCUSSION GUIDES ON CHAPTER CONTENT ─────────

1. What is meant by "technology"?

2. There is a strong feeling among many people in society that technology is and will continue to be the savior of humanity. A growing groundswell of voices, however, is claiming that technology is destroying society. What are the bases for these conflicting views? Where do you stand?

3. What is "technology assessment"? To what degree should a company be responsible for detecting and preventing primary impacts when it introduces new technology? To what extent should it be responsible for detecting and avoiding secondary impacts? ("Primary" may be defined as impacts on things such as landscape, on interrelationships between people, on the way business is done, on ideas and values of people, and so on. "Secondary" refers to subsequent impacts.)

4. Since the United States has prided itself on having a private free enterprise system, what justification is there for government-sponsored and financed research and development in business?

5. Is technological unemployment to be feared?

6. How has technology affected the structure of and managerial processes in business?

MIND-STRETCHING QUESTIONS ─────────────

1. In the short run, technological unemployment is a real threat to some workers. To what degree should companies that are introducing labor-saving improvements be responsible for the retraining of displaced workers and for placing them in jobs suitable to their new talents?

2. Should the federal government have policies to finance research and development in the private sector so as to assure sufficient progress in such areas as defense? electronics? automobiles? energy? Would such policies undermine or encourage the initiative of private business organizations? Would such policies weaken or strengthen the free enterprise system? Explain.

V

SELECTED POLICY AREAS IN THE DIRECT BUSINESS-GOVERNMENT INTERFACE

24

FAILURES OF GOVERNMENT REGULATION AND PROPOSALS FOR REFORM

A) AMERICA'S ENERGY FUTURE*

Introduction

The following is an edited transcript of a conference held at your state university on September 7, 1979. It was called by the school of business to discuss major issues in America's energy future. Attending the conference were the following people, in alphabetical order.

Dr. John Engineer, Professor of Engineering

Ms. Mary Govern, United States Department of Energy

Dr. James Margin, Professor of Economics

Ms. Jane Newham, Congresswoman from New Hampshire

Dr. Harry Oiler, Representative from a major oil company

Mr. George Plummer, Representative from a local labor union

Dr. William Porter, Chairperson from state university

Ms. Alice Sierra, Representative of the Sierra Club

Dr. Porter: Our school brought this group together to discuss the many issues relating to energy in the United States. From any angle energy is a major concern today and will be for many years to come. Unfortunately, there is no consensus about what the problem is; whether or not there really is a problem; what impact

*Prepared by George A. Steiner

166

energy will have on our economy, life styles, and other areas of our society; and what public policy ought to be.

The basic purpose of this conference is not necessarily to resolve these questions. It is rather to provide a forum for airing different points of view about major issues in America's energy future.

May I begin this conference with a few personal observations about our energy situation? No one should approach the energy situation, in my opinion, without some recognition that it is an enormously complex subject. It covers a very wide range of subject matter, far more than we can cover at this conference. For most of the major issues there is controversy not only about the nature of the issue but what public policy should be with respect to it. There is a distressing lack of consensus about the nature of the energy problem and what should be done about it. We lack much information that is needed to come to objective evaluations. For example, there are many different models of our energy situation—current and future. We must be wary of them for each has a different set of premises and it is very important to know what they are and whether or not they are credible.[1] Also, equally skilled experts can take the same set of data and come to radically different conclusions.

As a reference point for our discussion I present a few statistics about which there can be no controversy. Exhibit 1 presents a distribution of energy consumption in the United States in 1977 and the quantity in units commonly used for each source. Exhibit 1 makes it quite clear that one half of our energy consumption is derived from oil, with natural gas and coal making up the bulk of the remainder.

EXHIBIT 1

U.S. ENERGY CONSUMPTION, 1977

Sources	Millions of Barrels per Day of Oil Equivalent	Percentage of Total	Quantity in Units Commonly Used for Each Source
Petroleum	18.4[a]	50	18.4 million barrels per day
Natural Gas	9.2[b]	25	19.2 trillion cubic feet per year
Coal	6.7[c]	18	625 million tons per year
Nuclear	1.3	4	251 billion kilowatt hours per year
Hydro	1.1	3	230 billion kilowatt hours per year
Total	36.7	100	

[a]Includes imports of 8.7 million barrels per day (mbd), or 47 percent of total oil consumption; excludes 0.2 mbd of exports.
[b]Includes imports of 0.5 mbd oil equivalent, or 5 percent of total natural gas.
[c]Excludes exports of 0.6 mbd oil equivalent.

Source: Department of Energy, Energy Information Administration, *Annual Report to Congress, Volume III, 1977* (Washington, D.C.: Government Printing Office, 1978), pp. 5, 23, 51, 145.

In this light it is informative to note how other than oil energy sources convert to one million barrels of oil daily. Conversion factors are: natural gas: 2.08 trillion cubic feet (TCF) per year; coal: 94 million tons per year; nuclear: 199 billion kilowatt hours (kwh) per year; and hydro: 203 billion kilowatt hours (kwh) per year.[2]

The average annual rate of growth of energy usage in the United States from 1950 to 1970 was 3.4 percent. At this rate energy consumption would almost double between 1970 and 1985 and come close to doubling again by the year 2000. To increase energy output to meet such a demand would raise great questions of supply.[3]

To conclude, look at recent trends in imports of oil. In 1957 the United States was a net exporter of fuels and lubricants. Since then imports progressively have exceeded exports until today we depend upon foreign countries for about 47 percent of our oil. At the same time the price has escalated significantly. In 1979 our average daily consumption of oil will be about 19 million barrels. Of that amount we will produce ourselves about 10 million barrels, leaving 9 million to be imported. Our largest supplier is Saudi Arabia, supplying some 18 percent. Next is Nigeria, supplying 13 percent. Then in successively smaller quantities are Libya, Algeria, Canada, the Virgin Islands, Mexico, Indonesia, and the United Arab Emirates.[4]

In 1973 Saudi Arabian light crude oil, a benchmark oil for pricing, was $2.41 per barrel. In 1974 it jumped to $10.95 and in a series of increases moved to $18.00 to $23.50 per barrel on July 1, 1979. The spread is due to the fact that the Organization of Petroleum Exporting Countries (OPEC), whose cartel now controls world prices, set the base price at $18.00 with permission to members to add surcharges to a maximum of $23.50. These are contract prices. Spot prices, or those charged for a current one-time sale of a particular oil, have been considerably higher.

Is There An Energy Crisis?

Now, I would like to raise the question: Is there an energy crisis?

Mr. Plummer: Well, I for one think there is. When I have to stand in line for a few hours to get a tank of gas I say there is a crisis.

Ms. Sierrra: That's temporary. When the price goes up enough the oil companies will see to it that there is enough gasoline so that their profits will increase. Remember that in May/June 1979 gasoline sold for around 70 cents a gallon. Now in September it is over $1 and there are no gas lines.

Mr. Oiler: I can't agree with that. What really happened in the spring of 1979 was that the world lost three million barrels of oil a day when the Shah of Iran was overthrown and that country was in the throes of revolution. To make matters worse our government asked the oil companies to increase reserves of heating oil to make sure there would be no shortage next winter. That cut gasoline output from the refineries. Furthermore, government allocations of gasoline around the country were based on 1978 data and a few erroneous assumptions. A few other technical factors also reduced output, such as the fact that you get fewer gallons of gasoline out of a barrel of oil if you make unleaded instead of leaded. We all know the demand for unleaded is rising.

Mr. Plummer: Granting all that, how do you explain the fact that I don't have to wait in line for gasoline today? Also, is that not due to the fact that higher prices have lifted oil company profits so they now produce more gasoline?

Mr. Oiler: Your cause and effect is way off. Price has gone up because OPEC said it was up. The benchmark oil price for Saudi Arabian light crude on June 30, 1979, was $14.54 plus surcharges, ranging from $1.20 to $7.00 per barrel. Then, suddenly, July 1, 1979, the price was raised 65 percent or more, as I noted before. That's why gasoline prices are up.

At the same time Saudi Arabia agreed to increase its exports by one million barrels per day over the OPEC limits that were set at that time. That relieved enormously the world demand/supply balance. At the same time there was some modest increase in Iranian output. Let me point out also that gasoline consumption in 1979 has dropped from 1978 levels. Oil companies are delivering about 10 percent less gasoline to the pumps today than last year, yet the demand/supply balance is roughly all right. Why? People are using less gasoline.

Now, let me say something about profits. Profits is a dirty word in many areas. However, profits in the oil industry are not wild, as some people think.

Mr. Plummer: You can juggle the figures all you want but I still say that if prices go up and profits go up you will get more gas.

Mr. Porter: I would like to have us move away from the current situation and look ahead. Do we have an energy crisis in the future?

Is There An Energy Crisis In Our Future?

Ms. Govern: I would like to comment on that question. We do indeed have a serious energy crisis ahead. To begin with the mere fact that we depend upon foreign countries for close to half our oil, a trend that is rising, is very serious. It means that the United States is no longer in control of its destiny. It is quite possible that we shall be the subject of oil blackmail. By that I mean the Arab nations can threaten to shut off oil production if we do not knuckle under to their political demands. Anyway, most of the world's imported oil, including ours, comes from countries with unstable or potentially unstable governments. Look what happened to what we thought was a stable Iran. A further danger is that sabotage of tankers in the Strait of Hormuz could cripple our economy. Why? Because two thirds of the world's oil passes through that narrow water passage by tanker, and a sinking of a tanker there could delay shipments for days, if not weeks.

Aside from the political threats to our high oil imports, look at the costs. The dollar value of revenues to OPEC countries for their oil production was $28 billion in 1973. Today the estimate for 1979 is $185 billion. We are witnessing a massive shift of wealth to these nations at the expense of other nations, especially the lesser developed countries. United States costs for imported oil were $8.3 billion in 1973 and are expected to be $56 billion in 1979. These transfers have upset our balance of payments, have significantly added to our inflation problem, have lowered substantially the value of the dollar in relation to foreign currencies, and have led to massive Arab investments in the United States.

If that is not enough to convince anyone that we have a crisis, look at the scenario of demand and supply. Now, I agree with our chairman about the limits of models but the highest probabilities attach to a rather bleak outlook. Let me explain.

Neither the United States nor the world will suddenly run out of oil. We do not now nor are we likely to have in the 1980s or the 1990s an absolute physical shortage of oil. Rather, what we face is a world demand for petroleum that exceeds the supply of oil that producers can or will be willing to produce.[5]

Since OPEC accounts for about 90 percent of the world's exports of oil today and will most likely for some time ahead, we may start there. At slightly higher prices a current reasonable estimate of demand for OPEC oil in the 1980s will run from 34 to 44 million barrels per day (MBPD). At the end of the 1980s capacity is not likely to exceed 44 MBPD. Saudi Arabia's capacity at that time is assumed to be 19 MBPD. In 1979 Saudi Arabia produced about 11 MBPD. A very large question is whether OPEC nations, especially Saudi Arabia, wish to increase their production to these levels. There is much discussion, especially among the younger members of the Saudi Arabian ruling family, about the need to restrict oil output in order to preserve that national asset. Even assuming that there will be no arbitrary reduction of OPEC output the price is likely to be increased anywhere from 50 to 75 percent over today's prices.

The problem is not one of reserves, since Saudi Arabia alone has an estimated 166 billion barrels of reserve. It is a matter of capacity and willingness to produce.

Prospects for increased output of oil in the United States are not bright. More drilling took place in the United States in 1978 than in any other year in the past two decades, yet our estimated reserves continue to decline. They have been declining since 1969.

There are some optimists, in and out of the oil industry, who believe that new major strikes either in the United States or in non-OPEC countries may well resolve our need for oil for a long time to come.[6] On the basis of past experience, however, a national policy based on such projections could be disastrous.

I won't get into the possibilities of substitutes that might reduce our demands for oil. We may get to that later. Altogether the prevailing wisdom today is that we face an energy crisis in the sense that we depend too heavily on oil from foreign sources, and the possibilities of correcting that condition are not within easy grasp or a reasonable period of time. There is no quick-fix solution.

Mr. Plummer: I disagree with your last sentence. The solution is to take over the oil companies.

Who Is To Blame for The Crisis?

Mr. Porter: That, Mr. Plummer, is of course one solution. Are you blaming the oil companies for our troubles?

Mr. Plummer: I certainly am. The oil companies have been in the driver's seat. They are a monopoly and they have used that power to increase prices and profits at the expense of the public. They could have averted the crisis.

Dr. Margin: A very good case can be made that the major blame for our current and projected crisis rests with the federal government. As Walter Mead has so clearly pointed out the federal government over a 50-year period of time has developed one policy after another that inevitably has led to the present situation. Fundamentally, the federal government for years favored oil producers (through depletion allowances, for example) and diverted investment into oil rather than competing energy sources. Also, the federal government has followed deliberately a low-price energy policy which has inhibited the development of competing energy supplies. As a matter of policy we have shielded the economy from the real costs of energy.[7] For example, from 1950 to 1973 the real price of energy in this country, adjusted for inflation, dropped 1.8 percent a year. The price of gasoline in 1978 in the United States was no higher in real terms than in 1967. In 1967 the price of gasoline in the United States was the lowest in the world. If the oil companies had a monopoly they did not know how to use it for their own selfish interests. More recently, look at the mess the federal government is now in trying to forge an energy policy. No, I believe that the basic blame for our problems rests with the federal government.

lieve that the basic blame for our problems rests with the federal government.

Dr. Oiler: Thanks. I agree fully with you. I would like to add to your comments that government price controls on oil and gas during recent years clearly have inhibited production of old oil and drilling for new oil and gas. Since 1975 the index price of oil at the wellhead has been progressively below the index of drilling and production costs.[8]

Ms. Sierra: I would like to suggest that the typical American consumer must share much of the blame. We have been a profligate people, unconcerned about the world's scarce resources.

Dr. Margin: Let's not forget the OPEC cartel. We would have no current problems if they produced what they are able to produce. Furthermore, their production costs are in the range of 25 cents a barrel yet they sell the stuff to us for $25 a barrel. Talk about your monopolists!

Dr. Porter: It seems to me that the core of what has been said here so far is that we do have an energy crisis. However, that does not adequately describe our future. Even though we and the remainder of the world may not find new major sources of oil, we in the United States particularly are blessed with other energy sources. Our problem, of course, is to make a transition from current reliance on oil to these other energy sources. If this is done well, we may have problems with respect to oil during the next decade or so but after that our technology should provide us with sufficient energy supplies to meet our needs at reasonable costs.

If we can agree on that point, at least for the sake of continuing our dialogue, let's focus now on the President's energy policy.

President Carter's Energy Policy

Dr. Porter: Jim Margin, would you outline that policy for us?

Dr. Margin: Briefly, President Carter announced an energy policy when he first came to office. It had some good things in it and some that were completely impossible politically. Fundamentally, he leaned too little on stimulating production and too much on conservation. In May-June 1979 when gasoline became so short at the pumps that, first in California and then in eastern states, motorists formed long lines to get gasoline and some were denied gasoline, the President spent several days at Camp David talking to scores of people from different walks of life about what he should do. He returned from Camp David with a program. The main points of his program, announced on July 15 and 16, are as follows:

1. Place a flat ceiling of 8.2 MBPD on oil imports and keep it at that level indefinitely.

2. Establish a government-chartered energy-security corporation to develop a synthetic fuel industry. The goal by 1990 is production of at least 2.5 MBPD of oil substitutes from shale, coal and other sources. The corporation would be allocated $88 billion for this task.

3. Set up a new cabinet-level energy mobilization board with power to insure that environmental, procedural, and other federal and state regulations do not delay the development of plants, ports, pipelines, or other energy facilities.

4. Prepare a standby gasoline rationing program to be ready when needed.

5. Give each state a target for reducing the use of gasoline and other fuels within its borders. If any state fails to develop a plan to meet the targets the federal government will prepare a plan for the state.

6. Provide interest subsidies of $2 billion to induce owners of homes and commercial buildings to insulate and convert from oil heating to natural gas.

7. Establish a goal for utilities to cut their use of oil by 50 percent over the next 10 years. Conversion to coal, nuclear power, or other energy sources will be financed partly through grants and loan guarantees.

8. The 94 nuclear power plants now being built or planned will be completed. Any commitment beyond this will be delayed until there is a full report of the Three Mile Island nuclear accident.

9. Set aside $10 billion to improve bus and rail networks.

10. Set aside $6.5 billion to upgrade the gasoline efficiency of automobiles.

11. Provide $2.4 billion dollars each year to low-income people to help them cope with higher energy prices.

12. Set up a government "solar bank" to subsidize loans for installation of solar-energy systems in both homes and businesses. Also provide tax credits.

13. Total costs amount to about $142 billion which will come from an energy-security trust fund financed by a tax of 50 percent or more on the windfall profits earned by United States oil companies as price controls are phased out. In addition, the government will sell up to $5 billion in energy-security bonds to the public for use by the energy-security corporation.

Dr. Porter: Well, there you have the proposed policy to solve our energy crisis. Will it fly?

Ms. Sierra: I think it stinks. It says nothing about preserving the environment while we dig up more coal, build nuclear power plants all over the place, and pollute the air with more coal-burning electric power plants. Not only that, but he wants to set up a super-bureaucracy to violate the environmental protective laws that we now have. That's terrible.

Dr. Margin: Well, Alice, I guess we have to face up to some tough trade-offs. Do we want a cleaner environment and an energy crisis? Or, will we accept a little less clean environment and have no energy crisis? We must make a choice. There is no question about the fact that our environmental protection laws have impeded the development of new energy sources. Furthermore, as you know, intransigent environmentalists have stopped some new power plants for presumably trivial reasons.

Dr. Engineer: One thing that disturbs me about the new plan is that it is very short on some critical things the government itself might do. For example, if California accepted the lower emission standards that now apply to the remainder of the country we could save the equivalent of hundreds of thousands of gallons of gasoline a day. Also, the federal regulations are filled with impediments to reduced gasoline consumption. Most are not major but when combined add up to enormous savings if they are corrected.

Dr. Porter: Return to my original question. Will it fly? Congresswoman Newham, how will the Congress look at this plan?

Ms. Newham: Well, one never knows for sure what the Congress will do but we all know that President Carter's past energy policies have had tough going in the Congress. One of the major reasons is that there is no consensus about what an energy plan should contain. There is no consensus in the country generally, there is no consensus in business and there is no consensus in the Congress. I doubt that there is a consensus in the Administration itself.

I would expect that my fellow members of the Congress will be wary of creating new powerful peacetime boards that would operate independently of the Congress. In today's charged battle for power between the Congress and the Executive Branch, Congress might see this as a diminution of its power, and object.

Objection in the Congress to an energy-mobilization red-tape-cutting board will be reinforced by environmental groups. Indeed, a coalition of about a dozen environmental groups was formed very soon after the President's speech to reject or seriously limit the authority of this board. These groups fear that the board will scuttle current environmental safeguards.

The Congress today is very sympathetic to the development of synthetic fuels. Actually, on June 26, 1979, the House approved a $3 billion program for synthetic fuels, and at this moment an omnibus energy bill is pending in the Senate. So, that part of the President's program may be accepted. However, the Congress will look warily at a new government-chartered corporation designed to create a new industry. Conservative members of the Congress may view this development as a violation of our free enterprise philosophy.

As you know, the Congress has little difficulty, generally, in subsidizing individuals and groups especially if the largesse can be spread nationally. So there are parts of the program that will receive little objection.

Dr. Margin: I'd like to comment on the import quota. If the limit is maintained it surely will lead eventually to much higher prices for gasoline and may, if we do not do something to match energy demand and supply, create serious demand-supply imbalances. At the moment we are importing less than 8.2 MBPD, but soon we shall want more. Let me hypothesize a bit.

We are now in the process of deregulating oil, a process that will be completed after 1981. Now suppose that our import limit in 1982 will be 1 MBPD less than we need. Are we likely to meet that deficiency by increased American output? I doubt it. The result will be, if that is the case, a rise in domestic oil prices. Will this, in turn, trigger a rise in OPEC prices?

Why impose a quota instead of a tariff? One answer is that politicians choose quotas over tariffs because, while each raises domestic prices, tariffs as cause of price increases can be directly attributable to politicians, whereas the linkage of quotas with a price rise is not clear to the ordinary person.

Dr. Porter: We have not discussed a key feature of this plan, namely a windfall profits tax which will provide the basic financing for the plan. How may the Congress view this tax?

Ms. Newham: Much may depend on the mood of the country and events. I have some reservations about whether or not the Congress will pass a windfall profits tax that will yield the revenue needed for this plan. There already is some talk in the Congress about exempting independent producers from such a tax if it is imposed. That could reduce the revenue at least $20 billion. Also, there is some disposition to exempt newly discovered oil. That might exempt an additional $40 billion. The Congressional Budget Office, in a careful study of windfall profits, has concluded that if the President's proposal to apply a 50 percent tax rate to additional producer revenues is approved, the revenues would not be as large as in his plan. Between now and 1985 this Office calculates that windfall revenues would be about $69 billion. Of this amount only about $30 billion would be taxed away as windfall profits under the President's play.[9]

On the other hand there is a recognition in the Congress that with rises in OPEC prices there has been an automatic increase in the value of United States-owned oil and gas reserves. The increase of the two could amount to $800 billion or about $10,000 per family.[10] These are big numbers. The question of how much of the gains, if taxed, should be distributed will raise strong controversy in the Congress. For example, there are those who favor giving most of the windfall to consumers by keeping prices low. On the other hand are those who want the producers to keep the windfall on the grounds that it will induce them to further exploration. There are, of course, many other positions.

Are Oil Company Profits Excessive?

Dr. Porter: This brings us back to the question of current profits. Have oil company profits been excessive, as alleged?

Dr. Oiler: It should be said at the outset that earnings in the second quarter of 1979 for the 23 largest United States oil companies were $5.47 billion, up 66 percent over the same period last year. Texaco's earnings leaped 132 percent during the same period. However, it should be pointed out that earnings in the second half of 1978 were soft because of the then temporary oil glut. However, there is no doubt that the companies have profited from the rise in OPEC prices.

Over a longer period of time, however, the figures are not that great. For example, from 1958 to 1973 the rate of return on equity of all petroleum companies was 10.0 percent while that of all manufacturing companies was 9.3 percent. From the first half of 1975 to the first half of 1978 the combined profits of the five major United States oil companies fell, after adjustment for inflation. A significant question is, of course, which trend will take place in the future; that of the longer-range past or that of the very recent past?

I should like to add a point here that I think is important in the debate about profits. The President has stridently called for a windfall profits tax yet has said that he does not object to company profits if they are reinvested in exploration for oil and gas in the United States. Rather, he has accused oil companies of taking oil profits and not putting them back in the ground to develop more energy. The chairman and chief executive officer of Conoco responded in an open letter dated August 1, 1979, to these considerations. He said that "Conoco's outlays to increase energy supplies and expand its operations have exceeded net income by more than a two-to-one margin over the past ten years . . . . Furthermore, Conoco's policy will be to plow back into domestic energy development all income derived from oil price decontrol."[11] This is a position that I believe other oil companies have taken.

The Outlook for Oil Supplies

Dr. Porter: From what has been said it looks like tough sledding for President Carter's energy program in the Congress. Perhaps it would be fruitful at this point to examine prospects for some of our major energy sources over the next 10 to 20 years. Mary, how do you and your associates view the outlook for oil and gas in the future?

Ms. Govern: We anticipate that with oil price decontrol, enhanced recovery methods from old fields, and new drilling, at the turn of the next decade we shall be producing approximately 10 MBPD, which is our current rate of production. Obviously this is based on the premise that we shall make no new large discoveries in the United States. Such discoveries are possible, of course, but highly improbable.

Why this gloomy projection? To begin with it takes something like four billion barrels annually of new discovery to maintain current production, but there has been only one year in the last 30 in which more than three billion barrels of reserves have been found.[12] Also, as we noted earlier, higher drilling in the past few years has not resulted in stopping the decline in our oil reserves. As some of you know, much oil—in many instances as much as half—is left in the ground following conventional recovery methods. New methods of recovery can recoup some of the vast stores now below ground, but probabilities are that little more than 1 MBPD from such recovery will be available in the late 1980s.[13]

Our great reserves of oil in shale rock have been thought of as our ace in the hole. It has been estimated that we have something in the neighborhood of 400 billion to 700 billion barrels of exploitable oil locked in shale. This may be true but the price of getting it remains elusively high. It seems, literally, that each time costs are calculated they are from $5 to $15 per barrel higher than the world oil price, whatever it is at the moment. Costs of production are high. With present technology it is calculated that to produce 100,000 barrels of shale oil a day, which would be one half of one percent of our oil consumption, an investment of $1 billion and a decade for development would be required.[14] Environmentalists are strongly opposed to mining our shale rock, as are agriculturalists, because of the vast quantities of water required to produce it. Here is a major barrier.

We also have reserves of perhaps 10 billion barrels in heavy oil. Canada is calculated to possess the equivalent of two trillion barrels of heavy oil in tar sands, but again the problem is to get it out at a cost that is acceptable. No oil company is going to invest the huge sums required to get large quantities of this oil with the eventual cost and price so uncertain.

So I see no way for us to overcome the gap of 9 MBPD that exists today nor any increment of a widening gap in the years ahead. There is no doubt that demand for oil will grow in the years ahead, given current policies, and since production is not likely to rise, the gap of domestic imported oil will widen.

Dr. Porter: Mary, you mentioned decontrol. Our conference participants should be reminded, if they do not already know, that early this year the President did decontrol oil prices, a policy that will be implemented gradually up to 1981, after which there will be no government controls. In mid-1979 the President also decontrolled the price of heavy oil. Decontrol will increase production, but not enough to lessen our dependence on foreign countries.

Ms. Newham: It should be pointed out that if this projection is correct, and it seems to enjoy a high probability at the moment, we will have a serious energy crisis. It means higher oil prices, perhaps slower economic growth, tensions with other nations over supply, and the possibility of a serious disruption of the flow of oil which would cause a disastrous shock to our socioeconomic system.

Dr. Engineer: One thing we can do to lessen the latter risk is to stockpile oil. That is our national policy today but we have stockpiled very little. We should have at least a six-month supply. It would be very expensive to do this, of course, but the insurance it would give is worth the price.

Dr. Porter: Before yielding to despair about oil let's take a look at other energy possibilities to give us relief. How about natural gas, the so-called prince of hydrocarbons. Here is a fuel free of many of the disadvantages of oil, coal, and nuclear power.

Dr. Oiler: Before getting into the gas picture I want to take issue with these oil supply projections. There is much optimism in the petroleum industry about potential new discoveries and increased production from old wells if government lands are opened for exploration and prices are decontrolled. Not only are there vast lands in the United States that are government owned (and have not been explored) but there are vast areas throughout the world that are unexplored. No one knows, of course, how much oil exists in unexplored areas, but it is difficult to believe that there will not be large new pools of oil discovered in the future. Furthermore, there are some 30 billion barrels of oil in existing fields in the United States. It is now uneconomic to produce them because of cost. Given higher prices and new recovery techniques a good bit of this oil will be available for use. So I can't go along with Ms. Govern's low potential oil supply.

Let's turn to shale oil for a moment. I admit that getting firm cost estimates for shale oil is elusive, but there are many experts who believe that the price ultimately may be as low as $15 per barrel but no higher than $30 per barrel. Furthermore, whatever the price, it is likely that the cost will be anywhere from $10 to $15 per barrel under synthetic fuel made from coal. Dr. Armand Hammer, chief executive officer of Occidental Petroleum, a pioneer in shale oil technology, believes that technology now is so well developed that two million barrels a day of oil from shale is quite possible by 1990.[15] If we can tap our shale reserves we can resolve the energy problem.

Ms. Govern: I agree with your last statement, but we certainly cannot in the next few years; there are grave problems in rapidly increasing shale oil production aside from uncertainties about price. A million barrels of oil from shale would require processing about two million tons of rock per day. Aside from the physical problem of moving the rock we would raise plenty of dust in the atmosphere. Furthermore, a 100,000-barrel-a-day plant would require 29,000 acre-feet per year of water. In the western states, where recoverable shale oil is bountiful, water is scarce and water rights already have been allocated. Changing them would be extremely difficult. So, because of such problems I still stick to my forecast.

Ms. Sierra: I am glad you raised the issue of environmental quality. This is a serious problem with shale oil production.

Ms. Newham: One problem oil companies have in investing in shale oil is that whatever price is finally decided upon it will be higher than the OPEC price. To help resolve this problem several proposals have been put before the Congress. One is to guarantee to the oil companies a minimum price. Another is to give the oil companies a credit for tax purposes of, say, $3 per barrel. That would be equivalent to $5.15 before taxes. With that the president of Union Oil Company's mining division says his proposed 9,000-barrel-a-day facility would yield 15 percent return on investment.[16] Should the government guarantee prices and/or give tax credit support for shale oil production? Should the government team up with private industry to expand shale oil production? Remember that President Carter in his Camp David energy plan calls for 2.5 million barrels of oil a day from synthetics, such as oil from shale and coal. He also is asking the Congress to appropriate to an Energy Security Corp. $88 billion to achieve this end. If Congress approves this plan there will be much money available to expand oil supplies from shale rock and coal. A tough question arises as to whether a good part of this $88 billion would be better spent on other energy-producing or energy-saving programs.

The Outlook for Natural Gas Supplies

Dr. Porter: Let's get back to natural gas.

Ms. Govern: We consume about 20 trillion cubic feet (tcf) of natural gas a year, of which we import only five percent. Unfortunately, our reserves of natural gas have been declining. Reserves peaked in 1967 and by 1978 they fell some 25 percent to a level equal to only 10 years' consumption at current rates. This decline in reserves, fortunately, does not mean we are running out of gas. There is general agreement that we have rather large reserves, at least a 25-year supply, at current rates of production. To get these new reserves will, however, require higher prices.

Gas price has been controlled in the United States for many years, but the Natural Gas Policy Act of 1978 created a framework for gradual decontrol. The act is complicated but in general it results in higher prices for consumers but provides benefits to producers and distributors. The latter, for example, will be able to charge a higher price for interstate gas than was legal before. Heretofore we had a two-tier pricing system. Intrastate gas that was not controlled was higher-priced than intrastate gas that was under government control.

No one knows today how much gas will be decontrolled and what impact this will have on gas supplies. There are strong pressures for continued controls both by consumers who want low prices and who believe there is no gas shortage and by the government, which believes limited supplies require price control. It is my guess that new annual discoveries will be in the range of 10 tcf to 25 tcf per year with the figure closer to the lower number. If so, and if there are no other sources of gas, we shall be faced with reduced industrial use of gas for boiler fuel and more conversion to coal. If discovery is in the higher range our gas-consuming patterns will be comparable in the future to those of today.[17]

We can and are likely to import more gas to supplement domestic reserves. Mexican supplies are an obvious potential. In 1977 Energy Secretary Schlesinger rejected a contract price of $2.60 per 1,000 cubic feet for Mexican gas. Now the United States is talking about a price of around $3.60; the Mexicans go much higher, no less than $4.00, they say. There is gas for sale there as well as in Canada, for a price.

Another possible source is synthetic gas (SNG). Processes for producing gas from coal have existed for a long time. However, the cost is considerably above world prices for gas and oil equivalents. Furthermore, the federal government has hindered development of such fuels by refusing to allow what investors consider to be an adequate price. SNG in any large quantities is only likely in the more distant future.

Another possibility is liquefied natural gas (LNG). At the present time we are importing LNG but the total contribution to our gas supplies is less than one half of one percent. Early this year, however, the Department of Energy denied applications by Tenneco and El Paso Natural Gas for permission to construct two large LNG import projects. There are three significant problems with imported LNG. One is safety. Accidents to LNG tankers, storage facilities, or transport vehicles could be very serious. Equally reputable scientists come to different conclusions about risk. Some think risks are under control but others think the hazard is great.

Cost is also an obstacle. Today it would cost $2 billion to build facilities for a typical LNG import project that would include a liquefaction plant and special ships. It is estimated that the full cost of LNG delivered in the United States would be from $5 to $7 per thousand cubic feet.[18] A third shortcoming is that if we imported much LNG we would be moving into the same position with gas that we are in with oil in terms of foreign dependence.

Dr. Porter: That scenario is not as optimistic as I thought it might be. How about coal? Here is a potential that many people believe is our salvation. John, what is your projection here?

Dr. Oiler: Before moving on I want to take issue with that forecast. We have plenty of gas downstairs, as Ms. Govern observes. The problem is price decontrol. Decontrol prices and we shall have gas.

Ms. Govern: There is certainly a possibility that decontrolled prices will generate more gas supply, but there is little current basis for optimism. As a result we should not base public policy on such soft projections.

Ms. Sierra: I see a major problem for environmentalism if Ms. Govern's projections are accepted. Just last week (September 7) the Environmental Protection Agency allowed refiners to reduce the amount of lead in gasoline in order to increase available gasoline. (Relaxed standards for lead will increase available supplies by 340,000 barrels of gasoline per day.) I hope that pessimistic estimates for oil and gas supply do not lead to environmental degradation as a matter of public policy. There must be protection of the environment.

Ms. Newham: We should not underestimate the pricing problem of natural gas. There is strong pressure in government and with the general public not to decontrol gas prices. The extremely complicated ceiling pricing mechanisms in the Natural Gas Policy Act of 1978 are in themselves inhibiting to production. My question is, given the politics of the situation: will we ever get to a free-market pricing system for natural gas in 1985?[19]

The Outlook for Coal Production

Dr. Porter: Let's proceed now with our coal situation.

Dr. Engineer: In the spring of 1977 President Carter announced his first National Energy Plan. Among other things it called for a doubling of United States coal production (to 1.2 billion tons per year) by 1985. How strange it was, in this light, to learn in early 1979 that the coal industry was in a slump. At the same time Secretary Schlesinger was urging industry to use natural gas instead of coal in order to reduce reliance on oil.[20]

The United States is blessed with an abundance of coal. We have approximately one third of the total world coal reserves, or a range from 150 to 450 billion tons. Unfortunately for us, however, coal carries with it an abundance of problems that will serve to limit its full potential to solve our energy problems. A few major ones follow.

To meet the President's goal would require a doubling of the mining force which recently numbered about 1,500 mining engineers and 160,000 miners. We would have to open up from 200 to 400 new mines and find capital investment of about $25 billion. For comparison, the outlay of capital from 1965 to 1974 in the industry was $6.5 billion.[21]

There are well-known environmental problems, especially with the western strip mines. Another problem stems from the potential "greenhouse" effect of dumping carbon dioxide into the atmosphere. Build-up of carbon dioxide lets radiation from the sun pass through to the earth but blocks radiation from the earth with a resulting build up in earth temperatures. This, of course, is serious.

There are other problems. The railroad system is not built to carry the needed quantities of western coal to eastern users. If they did try to meet the need they would face serious community problems in scheduling so many trains. The Sierra Club, for instance, has brought suit to force a thorough environmental impact study of a proposed 116-mile coal route through Wyoming.[22]

One solution is to build slurry pipelines which pulverize coal and add water to it so that it flows easily. There are cost advantages of such lines over long-distance rail transport of coal but these proposed lines face serious environmental barriers. Again there is the question of available water to operate the lines.

In sum, I project that in the 1980s we shall increase coal production from today's level of about 625 million tons annually to perhaps 850 million tons in 1990. Coal will obviously not become our near-term solution to the energy problem. Over the longer range, however, I see its use growing with the development of new technologies. Given new technologies to mine, ship, liquefy, and convert to gas and oil, our coal reserves could make the United States a giant "middle east" of the twenty-first century.

The Outlook for Nuclear Power

Dr. Porter: That's encouraging. Now, how about our nuclear situation?

Dr. Engineer: We have in the United States 72 operating nuclear reactors. They produce about 12.5 percent of our nation's electricity and about four percent of our total energy consumption. Not long ago it was generally conceded that the United States would be leaning heavily on nuclear power in the 1980s and that, as a result, we would have no energy problem. The accident at Three Mile Island in March 1979 marked a major turning away from that dream. Even before that accident great questions concerning nuclear power sharply slowed new plant construction plans.[23] At the time of the Three Mile Island accident the Nuclear Regulatory Commission suspended new licensing of nuclear plants, but that ban was lifted in September 1979. This change in policy, however, will not stop opposition to the construction of nuclear power plants.

Unfortunately, there seems to be a stalemate with respect to nuclear power. There are many strong proponents of nuclear power and they are opposed equally strongly by others. Reputable scientists, political scientists, and laymen find themselves on opposite sides in the controversy.

Those who oppose nuclear power plants have a long list of reasons. They range from known health hazards in mining uranium to potential accidents that can spew radioactive dust which can cause death over a wide geographic territory. There is plenty of reason, say the opponents, not to trust the government. For a long period of time the government played down the hazards of radiation and rejected any liability in deaths caused by government programs, such as leakage of radioactive wastes in temporary dumpsites. Opponents also cite a long list of questions to which there are no answers today but which, they say, should be answered before nuclear power expands. For example: Granted that technically superior nuclear power plants emit only very low levels of radiation, what are the effects on people over a long period of time? What is the real probability of a major accident to a nuclear power plant? What would be the effect of such an accident on health? How are we going to dispose of nuclear waste products so that we can be absolutely sure there will be no adverse impact on human beings for the thousands of years required for the waste to lose its radiation? Nuclear power plants have a life of perhaps 40 years. Will they be radioactive? How are we going to dispose of them? Added to those concerns one finds, of course, blind opposition to a technology that is not understood and that has been responsible for great loss of life, namely, the use of atomic weapons in World War II.

On the other side are those who answer the technical questions. It is asserted that a full meltdown with consequent release of radioactive gases is an eventuality that is highly unlikely. That has never happened and with the tightened safety measures imposed on power plants following the Three Mile Island incident its probability becomes very remote. Even at the Three Mile Island accident there were fewer millirems of radioactivity present than there are on any day of the year at high altitudes, such as Denver, Colorado, or in a jet airplane. Proponents point out that every day people are exposed to far greater risks than nuclear power plants. For example, many people face higher risks of death from a collapsing dam than from nuclear power. Certainly the risks on the highways are much greater to one's health and safety.[24]

Disposal of nuclear trash is a problem of a different dimension. Contrary to popular belief there are, in the opinion of reputable scientists, very safe ways to bury the trash so that it will not harm anyone. Not only are there safe places but technology exists to recycle unburned fuel. Furthermore, there is research under way to use spent reactor fuel to treat sewage sludge and to extract valuable metals from it. The question is: At what point should a firm policy decision be made about what to do with nuclear waste? What should the decision be?[25]

The central issue here is that we have a new and important industrial risk. Experts disagree on the degree and probabilities of risk. The public is confused about the argument, except those who approach it purely from an emotional point of view. We have no suitable mechanisms in the Congress to appraise the risks involved and make appropriate trade-offs.

Stobaugh and Yergin come to this conclusion, with which I agree:

> In the United States there is simply no reasonable possibility for "massive contributions" from nuclear power for at least the rest of the twentieth century. In fact, unless government and industry leaders start now to work with the nuclear critics, many existing plants will run out of spent-fuel storage within four years. The federal government will then face a very difficult choice: shutting down the plants or riding roughshod over the nuclear critics. The time available to avoid the choice is short. *In any case, nuclear power*

offers no solution to the problem of America's growing dependence on imported oil for the rest of this century.[26]

There will be some increase in nuclear power output as the plants now under way become operational. However, nuclear power will not fulfill the hope many people had for it only a few years ago. Department of Energy Secretary Schlesinger said this in his farewell speech: "Quite bluntly, unless we achieve the greater use of coal and nuclear power over the next decade, this society may just not make it."[27] I believe we will achieve the required level of outputs, but just barely.

The Outlook for Solar Energy

Dr. Porter: Well, John, is there any important relief in solar energy over the next decade?

Dr. Engineer: The answer is affirmative but how much is in doubt. To begin with we should understand that solar energy includes a wide range of technologies. Included is power derived directly from the sun, as in solar heaters; wind power; hydroelectric power; ocean thermal electric power; and fuels from biomass, such as plant matter. The unifying concept is "that solar energy is the energy that arrived on the earth from the sun 'recently'—during the last hundred years or so."[28]

President Carter's goal for this nation is to produce enough solar energy to supply 20 percent of our needs by the year 2000. That seems to be an ambitious goal but I believe it is achievable, especially when you define solar broadly. Reaching this goal will, however, encounter many problems and necessitate many choices. To give you one little example, solar home heating systems are not competitive with other fuels in industrial and commercial buildings for many reasons. One is that fossil fuels and electricity are tax deductible as operating expenses while the capital investment for a solar installation must be depreciated over the life of the machinery. We will need many changes in laws governing financing, use, design, construction, pricing, and repair of solar systems before usage will rise significantly. I believe we shall make changes in these areas that will stimulate solar energy production.

We have vast reserves of energy in natural surroundings—trees, plants, crops, algae, seaweed, and garbage. This is referred to as biomass. It can be burned to provide heat or to generate electricity. It can be made to yield alcohol. It can be made to produce methane gas and oil. It is estimated that our trees and plants contain 15 times as much energy as we annually import as oil.[29] Unlike oil and gas, biomass is rapidly renewable. If managed well it is inexhaustible.

The big problem is what choices are to be made in using the biomass. Attention has currently focused on gasohol. Gasohol is one part grain alcohol (ethanol) made from grain, sugar crops, and almost any starchy plant, and nine parts goasoline. The cost is four or five cents more than gasoline and it works very well in engines. Think through, however, the implications of our seeking enough ethanol to provide a 10 percent additive to our gasoline consumption. If we wanted to produce that ethanol from corn we would have to double our production of corn. Imagine the problems that would create.

We have abundant wood supplies in this country and in some areas wood is currently cheaper than heating oils. People therefore are turning increasingly to wood as a partial source of house heating. However, as wood usage increases so will the price, and at some point the wood cost will be higher than heating oil.

Geothermal technology is progressing to the point where it is estimated that in 1985 it will replace the equivalent of 250,000 barrels of oil a day. By the year 2000 it may be supplying five percent of our energy needs.[30] However, it is not without its problems. Explorations around Yellowstone Park, for example, have raised the enmity of environmentalists because they fear geothermal exploration within miles of the park may damage irreparably the geothermal displays in the park, such as Old Faithful.

There are infinite possibilities for new energy in this general solar area. They include new types of windmills to generate electricity, ocean farming of kelp to make methane gas, the use of hydrogen as energy, and ocean temperature changes to generate electricity. Since deep ocean temperatures are at least 37 degrees cooler than surface temperatures there is an opportunity to generate electricity through ocean thermal-energy conversion processes.[31]

For much of the energy in this area costs are a barrier to be overcome. Although power from the sun is free, equipment to catch it is expensive. Also, as I have noted, we will need many changes in laws as well as styles of living. But much is going on. Most of it is localized, is conducted in small projects, but in the aggregate adds up to significant contributions to our energy supply. There is increasing potential here.

The Potential of Conservation

Ms. Govern: I agree with what Dr. Engineer has told us. I would like to add that our major source of energy in the future is conservation.

Stobaugh and Yergin conclude in their study that if we make a serious commitment to conservation in a few years we could consume 30 to 40 percent less energy than today and still enjoy the same or even higher standards of living. They assert that savings would not depend on new technology but only modest adjustments in the way we live and work and play. The possible savings, they conclude, "would be the equivalent of all imported oil—and then some."[32] That is a bright note in our energy future. This is a conclusion confirmed by a study of the Office of Emergency Preparedness published in 1972. That study showed in the greatest detail how we could conserve energy and save 7.3 MBPD by 1980.[33]

We are a wasteful people but given a clear goal, a need, and incentives it is surprising what people will accomplish, as has been proven so many times. For instance in late 1973, at the time of the Arab embargo, the Department of Water and Power of the City of Los Angeles asked people to reduce their energy usage by 10 percent. Industrial users were asked to reduce theirs by 10 percent, and commercial users by 20 percent. Stiff penalties were to be levied if targets were not met. Residential users cut their energy by 18 percent, industrial by 11 percent, and commercial by 28 percent.[34]

There are all types of incentives that might be applied, from taxes to bonuses. Increasing taxes to discourage consumption is generally frowned upon. This is not, of course, a novel idea. OPEC in effect has taxed energy consumption heavily in the United States.

Possibilities for conservation abound. They range from unnecessary usage of energy to replacing or redesigning machinery and buildings that waste energy. They involve better scheduling of the use of vehicles and improved maintenance of vehicles. They include more efficient means to transport larger numbers of people; and they include recycling of waste, such as aluminum. There is no one "big fix" that could meet our conservation potential but thousands and millions of individual efforts can achieve it.

Dr. Margin: I would like to agree with Ms. Govern and those she quotes about what we can and are likely to do by way of conservation. The possibility is there but will we do it? Will we have the type of national leadership that will really lead and motivate our people? I cannot help but believe that what happens in the energy area will depend significantly upon the characteristics of our Presidents during the next decade.

Other Plans for Dealing with the Energy Problem

Dr. Porter: With this background let's turn now very briefly to other ideas for resolving our energy crisis. Jim, I know you have some ideas.

Dr. Margin: I certainly do. There are eight policies that I propose, as follows:

First, I would decontrol all gas and oil prices immediately or at the very least on a much more rapid time schedule than the government proposes.

Second, establish a Presidential Commission and/or Congressional Oversight Committee to identify and make recommendations concerning all government regulations—federal, state, and local—that in one way or another reduce energy output and/or inhibit conservation.

Third, relax environmental controls and constraints and at the same time speed up environmental assessments. Provide a mechanism, as envisioned in President Carter's proposed energy mobilization board, for arbitrating conflicting interests.

Fourth, continue to develop a strategic petroleum reserve.

Fifth, eliminate all import quotas.

Sixth, strongly encourage widespread conservation of oil and natural gas.

Seventh, forget the windfall profits tax but, perhaps, make sure that a maximum part of the windfall, after taxes, goes into new energy investment.

Eighth, let the free market allocate resources. Depend on the free market to resolve our energy crisis.

Dr. Porter: Thanks, Jim. I know that many of these points are controversial. Before opening a debate about them, however, are there any other ideas for resolving our crisis?

Mr. Plummer: I'm not convinced we have a crisis. I still think oil and gas companies are withholding supplies and that when the price gets high enough we shall get plenty of oil and gas.

─────────────────── **EXHIBIT 2** ───────────────────

U.S. ENERGY SUPPLY, ACTUAL 1977

AND PROJECTED FOR LATE 1980s

(millions of barrels daily of oil equivalent)

	1977	Late 1980s
		Balanced
	Actuals	Program
Domestic (excluding U.S. exports)		
Oil	10	10
Natural Gas	9	9
Coal[a]	7	11
Nuclear	1	2
Subtotal, "Conventional"	27	32
Solar, Including Hydro[b]	1	4
Total Domestic	28	36
Imports		
Oil	9	9
Gas	0[c]	1
Subtotal	9	10
TOTAL	37	46
Extra Conservation	–	8
GRAND TOTAL	37	54

[a]Estimates for late 1980s exclude estimated exports of one million barrels per day of oil equivalent. DOE estimate for late 1980s includes new technology—liquefaction and gasification.
[b]1977 excludes biomass, principally wood, used by the forest products industry. Late 1980s includes biomass beyond that used in 1977, all active solar hot water and space heating, passive solar heating, and all hydroelectric.
[c]Slightly less than 0.5 mbdoe.

Sources: 1977 from Energy Information Administration, *Annual Report to Congress, Volume III, 1977* (Washington D.C.: Government Printing Office, 1978), pp. 5, 23, 51, 145. Conventional program from middle-demand, middle-supply scenario in *Volume II, 1977,* pp. 28, 119, 206, 216, 229, adjusted for the National Energy Act and more recent nuclear estimates—obtained from DOE news release on National Energy Act, October 20, 1978, and recent discussions with DOE officials. Balanced program developed by authors, based on Chapters 2–7.

Ms. Sierra: My prescription is to nationalize the oil companies. They have shown that they are incapable of managing our oil and gas resources, not to mention bringing to market new energy sources such as solar energy. Only the government can act in the public interest.

Ms. Newham: Several of the presidential candidates have suggested that we establish a North American Common Energy Market which would pool the resources of Canada, Mexico, and the United States.

Dr. Engineer: I believe that our salvation lies in a much closer joint business-government partnership. Part of a new relationship—in sharp contrast to past and current antipathy on both sides—would be direct partnership relationships as envisioned in the President's energy-security corporation to develop synfuels.[35]

Dr. Margin: Our time is very limited so we cannot discuss these proposals in detail, but I would not like to pass without some comment. It is difficult to support Mr. Plummer's observation after all that has been said here today. Ms. Sierra's proposal to nationalize is absurd. Do you want to have our oil and gas industry run like the post office? Now, I'll grant that we do not have as much information as we should to know precisely how efficient and effective are the oil companies, but foreign experience makes it abundantly clear that government-owned oil companies have no special regard for consumers and are considerably less efficient than privately owned and operated companies. If Ms. Sierra is suspicious of the oil companies, and there are millions of others in her camp, the solution is not to nationalize. There are other ways to protect the public interest. One might be to pass a law putting a government observer or representative on each board of directors of each oil and gas company.[36] The common market idea seems attractive, but I have heard no jubilation about the idea in Canada and Mexico.[37] Furthermore, once we get over the energy crunch in the next decade we may not be particularly enthusiastic about joining a common energy market with our neighbors. I guess I agree with the partnership idea but I am a little uneasy with it.

Summary of a Proposed Balanced Energy Program for the 1980s

Dr. Porter: I wish we had time to debate the many ideas for resolving our energy problems, but time presses. As a final topic of discussion I would like to present, in Exhibit 2, our actual energy supply situation in 1977 and what a balanced program might look like in the late 1980s, according to Stobaugh and Yergin. My question to the conference now is: What do you think of the balanced program? Where do you think it is in error and why?

CASE QUESTIONS

   1. Do you agree that we have an "energy crisis" in the United States? If not, why not? If so, what are the dimensions of the crisis?

   2. If you believe we have an energy problem of major proportions, do you think it is serious enough to modify some of our environmental regulations to increase our energy output? Explain your position in detail.

   3. In your view, who is really to blame for our current energy problems? Explain.

   4. Evaluate each of President Carter's July 1979 energy proposals. Explain what you believe the implications for each one are in terms of resolving our energy problems, who benefits most, the inflationary impacts, and the environmental implications.

   5. If you do not particularly like the President's plan, or parts of it, what do you suggest? Explain.

   6. What did the Congress do with the President's plans following the writing of the case in September 1979?

7. Do you approve of what the Congress did?

8. Should the oil companies be deprived of all windfall profits resulting from price deregulation? If so, explain how that would benefit society.

9. During World War II the United States rather quickly built a synthetic rubber capability to replace natural rubber supplies. The question is now raised; why can't we do the same thing with synfuels and thereby quickly reduce our dependence on imported oil? What is your view about this? (See Ronald Alsop, "War, Rubber and Synfuels," *Wall Street Journal,* July 24, 1979.)

10. Examine the projections in this case for each of the major contributors to our energy supply and explain whether or not you agree with the assessments made?

11. Appraise the eight-point plan suggested by Dr. Margin.

12. When you have reevaluated the projections what numbers would you put in Exhibit 2 for the late 1980s?

13. Do you believe that nationalizing the oil industry would improve our energy sources and lower prices?

14. If you were asked by the President to set forth a program of effective partnership between business and government in dealing with our energy problem what would you suggest?

15. What is your view of the suggestion made by Dr. Margin to place a representative from the federal government on each board of each oil and gas company? If you like the idea, what authority, behavioral patterns, restrictions, and accountability would you suggest for such representatives?

16. Do you believe we should try to establish a North American Energy Common Market?

Notes

1. "Sergio Koreisha and Robert Stobaugh, "Limits to Models," Appendix in Robert Stobaugh and Daniel Yergin, *Energy Future* (New York, Random House, 1979); and Daniel L. White, "America's Energy: Policies and Prospects," *Business,* May-June 1979.

2. *Ibid.,* p. 14.

3. *Energy Policy Project of the Ford Foundation, A Time To Choose: America's Energy Future.* Cambridge, Mass., Ballinger Publishing Co., 1974.

4. *U.S. News and World Report,* July 30, 1979, p. 25.

5. Stobaugh and Yergin, *op. cit.,* pp. 36–37.

6. See for example, David A. Stockman, "The Wrong War? The Case Against a National Energy Policy," *The Public Interest,* Fall 1978.

7. Walter J. Mead, *Energy and the Environment: Conflict in Public Policy* (Washington, D.C., American Enterprise Institute, 1978).

8. Bart Holaday, "Oil: More Pitfalls Than Payoffs," *Business,* May-June 1979, p. 26.

9. Congressional Budget Office, *The Decontrol of Domestic Oil Prices: An Overview* (Washington, D.C.: U.S. Government Printing Office, May 1979).

10. Stobaugh and Yergin, *op. cit.,* p. 217.
11. Open letter printed in various newspapers.
12. Stobaugh and Yergin, *op. cit.,* p. 44.
13. *Ibid.,* p. 43.
14. *Ibid.,* p. 44.
15. Peter Nulty, "Shale Oil is Braced for Big Role," *Fortune,* September 24, 1979.
16. Stephen J. Sansweet, "An Oil-Shale Industry Appears to be Nearing, But Problems Remain," *Wall Street Journal,* August 16, 1979.
17. *Ibid.,* p. 78.
18. Stobaugh and Yergin, *op cit.,* pp. 70–71.
19. Edmond R. du Pont, "The Current Status of Natural-Gas Regulation," *Business,* May-June 1979.
20. James T. Rogers, "King Coal Is Just a Commoner," *Across the Board,* June 1979.
21. *Ibid.*
22. Stobaugh and Yergin, *op. cit.,* p. 89.
23. *Life,* May 1979, p. 26.
24. For a discussion of such arguments pro and con see A Panel Discussion, "Nuclear Power: Can we Live With It?" *Technology Review,* June-July 1979.
25. Edmund Faltermayer, "Burying Nuclear Trash Where It Will Stay Put," *Fortune,* March 26, 1979.
26. *Technology Review, op. cit.,* p. 135.
27. In *Wall Street Journal,* August 23, 1979.
28. Stobaugh and Yergin, *op. cit.,* p. 185.
29. Gene Bylinsky, "Biomass: the Self-Replacing Energy Resource," *Fortune,* September 24, 1979.
30. *U.S. News and World Report,* August 13, 1979, p. 36.
31. *Ibid.,* p. 36.
32. Stobaugh and Yergin, *op. cit.,* p. 137; Chapter 6.
33. Office of Emergency Preparedness, *The Potential For Energy Conservation* (Washington, D.C.: Superintendent of Documents, U.S. Government Printing Office, 1972).
34. Stobaugh and Yergin, *op. cit.,* pp. 144–145.
35. W. W. Rostow, "A New Energy Partnership," *Wall Street Journal,* June 1, 1979.
36. Ernest Conine, "Government in the Oil Business? No Way," *Los Angeles Times,* September 3, 1979.
37. Herbert E. Meyer, "Why a North American Common Market Won't Work—Yet," *Fortune,* September 10, 1979.

DISCUSSION GUIDES ON CHAPTER CONTENT ───────

1. The authors mention that there is widespread dissatisfaction with excessive government controls. What do they mean? Do you agree with the textbook on this matter? What can and should be done to remedy the main deficiencies in current government controls?

2. Opinion polls seem to point to a majority approval of more reliance on the free market mechanism. Why then do you think government controls are moving in the opposite direction?

3. Discuss the relative merits and demerits of command and incentive controls. Which would you prefer? Explain.

4. There have recently been some instances of deregulation of business, such as civil aviation and heavy oil. What is your assessment of the consequences of these measures?

5. What are the principal reasons for resistance to the deregulation of business? Should all regulation of business be abolished?

6. Comment on the energy policy of the government as it relates to the regulation of business.

7. What is the rationale for certain activities being better performed by the government and others by business? What is your view regarding the activities currently being undertaken by the two sectors—is the division of labor equitable or lopsided?

8. How would you go about reforming the regulatory process of the government? Comment on the suggestions made in the textbook in this respect. What further proposals can you think of to reform this process?

9. How can the principle of marginal social cost-benefit analysis be applied in assuring a better relationship between government and business?

10. What other guides would you suggest for bringing about and maintaining a proper relationship between business and government?

11. Do you agree with Galbraith that the solution to regulatory reform is to socialize industry?

MIND-STRETCHING QUESTIONS

1. How much faith do you think can be placed in business in general to act in the public interest, through competition and responsible behavior, in lieu of governmental regulations?

2. What do you think are the prospects of the free market mechanism being allowed to flourish in this country as it did in the past?

3. Can you think of some basic guidelines for introducing new regulations, so that the business-government relationship is put in proper balance?

4. What do you think will happen in the United States in the 1990s if we do not reform the federal regulatory process and if we do not slow the expansion of federal regulation of business? Do you like what you project? Explain.

25
THE POLITICAL ROLE OF BUSINESS IN PUBLIC AFFAIRS

A) PANPAC AND THE SENATE CANDIDATE

Jonathan Conrad, Republican candidate for the United States Senate, paced nervously back and forth in his dimly lit, downstairs study. His campaign for high office in a southern state would draw to a close in less than two weeks with the general election, but the most difficult decision of the campaign, indeed of his career, loomed before him. Now, with the house nearly darkened, his wife and two children in bed, Conrad discovered that the repose and detached reflection he had promised himself were not forthcoming.

Conrad, a native son and prominent big-city banker in his state, had been a reluctant candidate. Although he had served on the city council in his home town for four years, been elected to the State Assembly for a term, and spent an additional year as chairman of the state's Republican Central Committee, his reputation as a fair and reliable politician stemmed partly from lack of ambition for higher office. He earned a yearly salary of $70,000 as president of Midland City Bank. This was supplemented by income from several businesses in town that he owned plus the earnings of bank shares in his name. He led a gentleman's life and valued the time he was able to spend away from politics with his family.

Several years ago, however, state leaders became concerned about the growing influence of Alvin "Big Toe" Weaver. Weaver had captured the sentimental attachment of the voters in a race for a seat in the House of Representatives by touring his district in shoes with holes in the front to dramatize the plight of poor sharecroppers who would be displaced from their land by construction of a dam. Weaver, a Democrat, had so skillfully exploited this issue in speeches filled with purple oratory that he was elected by a margin of almost two to one.

The landslide fed Weaver's ambition, and during three terms in the House of Representatives he curried the favor of party professionals and placed cohorts on party committees across the state. Two years ago, when Joshua Ironwright, the popular Democratic senior Senator from the state, announced his retirement at age 81, the dominance of the so-called "Weaver machine" in Democratic party politics assured Weaver's nomination for the seat.

In anticipation of the forthcoming election Weaver had spent more time at home than in Washington during the last year and a half, criss-crossing the state with a proposal to cut unemployment in the state's huge pool of unskilled labor. In speech after speech Weaver proposed a three-step plan, which he referred to as "a new Bill of Rights for the working man." Step one would require all major corporations operating in the state to reinvest capital gains from state operations in programs for training and hiring the hard-core unemployed. Step two called for each business that employed more than 25 workers to hire an additional labor force of not less than five percent of the total number of workers. Step three provided for the establishment of a "Citizen Overseer Body" to enforce reinvestment and the hiring of minority workers.

Businesspeople, including Conrad, had opposed this plan by calling it unworkable, inefficient, and probably unconstitutional, but Weaver persisted in its advocacy and his charismatic appeal met with success. A statewide polling organization determined that as a result of Weaver's canvassing, 55 percent of the voters approved the plan, 30 percent disapproved, and 15 percent were undecided.

Approximately a year ago, however, doubts about Weaver began to grow—even among Democrats. He launched a bitter attack against businesspeople, educators, and politicians who opposed the plan by branding them bigots and exploiters. The issue, already hotly debated, developed dark racial overtones. It was then that a bipartisan committee of state politicians, businesspeople, and professionals had come to visit Conrad.

Weaver was dangerous, they explained. His ability to incite the base emotions of the population on the race issue was feared. Furthermore, there were unconfirmed but widely circulated rumors that Weaver was mentally unstable. Aides reportedly swore he had delusions of grandeur and late at night would lock himself behind his office doors and rage at the demons that tormented him. "We have come to you," the committee spokesman explained, "to enlist your service to the state. We want you to oppose Weaver in the upcoming senatorial race because your reputation for fair play and popularity with voters make you the only candidate with which to oppose a demagogue like Alvin Weaver." Conrad had consented, but now he half-wished he had not.

With the support of all factions of his party and the endorsement of some prominent Democrats, Conrad breezed through the June primary. The first polls of the Conrad-Weaver match-up in early July, however, showed Weaver leading in voter preference with 64 percent and Conrad trailing miserably with only 28 percent and 8 percent undecided. With only three months until the general election the situation seemed bleak.

Conrad chose a staff, set up headquarters operations in the capitol, and conducted fund-raising campaigns netting a total of $450,000. Throughout the remainder of July and well into August he conscientiously attended teas and rallies, spoke before large but reserved audiences, and earnestly solicited funds.

Much of the money was allocated for staff expenses and mass mailings. Volunteers went door-to-door and telephoned voters. Billboard space was purchased to insure that Jonathan Conrad became a household name. Some radio and television spots were purchased, but emphasis was placed upon reaching "influentials" in the electorate, or community leaders who supposedly could swing others' votes.

This effort produced inadequate results. A poll in the first week of September revealed that Weaver still held a substantial lead, although the margin had narrowed somewhat to 61 percent for Weaver versus 33 percent for Conrad and 5 percent undecided. Throughout September Conrad's attempts to diminish the large gap, although successful in a small way, lagged behind projections and it appeared that Weaver's magnetic personality was sufficient in itself to overcome even the most concerted effort and widespread party support. Then it happened.

Weaver and Conrad had shared a platform together at the dedication of a new textile plant. At the conclusion of his speech Conrad had pivoted to return to his chair when an angry Weaver jumped up and confronted him. With noses barely inches apart a debate between the two ensued much to the delight of the roaring crowd. Then, after an angry exchange of words, Weaver spat on Conrad in full view of the audience. This action was greeted with a loud chorus of boos and Weaver's bodyguards were forced to struggle to lead him to safety.

The incident was widely reported in the press, and the public—its sense of fair play violated—began to listen to what Conrad had to say. His measured tones and carefully thought-out proposals suddenly gained new support and now, 10 days from the November 5 election, the polls showed that he had closed to within five percentage points of Weaver. In a meeting with advisers earlier that day, however, there had been a feeling of impotence despite such great gains.

A privately commissioned poll showed that although Conrad had closed to within five points of Weaver, the gain capped a leveling off trend and the rise was not likely to continue without increased effort. It was time for a major media blitz to push Conrad over the top, but not enough money remained. Advisers estimated such a campaign would cost $215,000, but the cost was academic since campaign coffers held only $48,610. It seemed too late for further fund-raising efforts.

After the meeting with his advisors Conrad returned home, where he soon received a phone call from an excited aide at his campaign headquarters. The aide indicated that PANPAC, a political action committee of the Pacific National Oil Company, had just committed $200,000 to run pro-Conrad messages on radio and television stations around the state. Pacific National was one of the nation's largest oil companies and had several big refineries in the state. The money had not been solicited by either Conrad or members of his staff, but had been committed "independently" by PANPAC.

The aide suggested a meeting the next day to plan a new campaign strategy to take advantage of this unexpected windfall. But Conrad told the surprised caller he was not sure he would accept the help. Conrad said he would call back in the morning with a decision that could, if it were negative, be immediately relayed to PANPAC and end the group's effort on his behalf.

CASE QUESTIONS

1. If you were in Conrad's position, what would you do?
2. If Conrad accepts the help and is elected will he be beholden to the

oil company interests when he votes or otherwise exercises his influence as a senator? in all areas of public policy? in some?

3. Are present campaign financing and spending laws adequate to regulate practices that might later lead to subtle forms of political blackmail?

4. Do businesses and people with great wealth have the right to translate their economic power into political influence? Do federal laws properly control them?

References

Murray W. Bradford, "How To Get Business Heard in the Political Arena," *Management Digest* (November 1978), pp. 8–9.

Edwin M. Epstein, "An Irony of Electoral Reform," *Regulation* (May-June 1979), pp. 35–41.

Fred Wertheimer, "Has Congress Made It Legal to Buy Congressmen?" *Business and Society Review* (Fall 1978), pp. 29–32.

U.S. News and World Report, "Pro and Con: Keep Business Cash Out of Politics," (April 30, 1979), pp. 53–54.

B) DEVELOPING A BUSINESS CONSTITUENCY

Mr. Reginald H. Jones, chairman of the board and chief executive officer of the General Electric Company, laid down the following challenge to business leaders in a speech given to the Wharton Club of Washington, D.C., on May 17, 1978.

> Business leaders are going to have to learn to think politically in a politicized economy.
>
> We will have to do it because there are so many public policy issues that affect business and its ability to meet the needs and expectations of the people. Inflation, energy, technology, foreign trade and investment, taxation, capital formation, job formation—all these are issues of vital importance to America's future. But the voices speaking out for a sensible, economically sound approach to these issues are very few indeed. Business leaders these days are trying to make themselves heard, and I think we are making some honest headway. But we will not get the serious attention of the Congress until we have the vocal backing of a solid constituency.
>
> "That is why we must raise these issues with our employees, our customers, our shareowners and others who have a direct, personal stake in the success of American business. They and their families number in the millions. Their potential as a base of support for sound policy is enormous. But we are not going to have their support unless we work for it as a politician works for it—earning their trust, discussing the issues, demonstrating how they are personally affected, and asking them, directly and persuasively, for their wholehearted support."

CASE QUESTION

The chairman of the Business Roundtable, a group of chief executive officers of the largest companies in the United States, believes that Mr. Jones's proposal is something that business leaders must heed. He asks you to develop a plan that can be used by chief executives of individual companies to do what

Mr. Jones suggests. He is willing to pay you generously for your work. What would you propose to him?

DISCUSSION GUIDES ON CHAPTER CONTENT

1. Does business have a right to exert political power?
2. What is the difference between business involvement in the electoral process and business involvement in day-to-day activities of government?
3. What major trends are discernible in the current political activities of business?
4. In what ways are local businesses exerting political influence in your community? Do you accept what is being done as in the public interest?
5. Develop a case to support the involvement of business in political activities. What is the case against it?
6. Where, and under what circumstances, does business in general have great power in government? Give examples of instances in which particular business interests have gotten their way in government. Cite also instances in which they have not.
7. Is it beneficial to business, and to the country, to have people from business move in and out of government as managers or staff experts?
8. Are business pressure groups evil? Explain your position.

MIND-STRETCHING QUESTIONS

1. Is it possible (or desirable) for pressure groups to act in the best interests of the public instead of in their own selfish interests?
2. It is the right and duty of every individual citizen of the United States to support political candidates of his or her choice. Yet, this is considered unethical for corporations which are regarded as individuals in the eyes of the law. Why? Is it right?

26
PROPOSALS FOR NATIONAL ECONOMIC AGGREGATE PLANNING IN THE UNITED STATES

DISCUSSION GUIDES ON CHAPTER CONTENT

1. What is meant by "planning" in government? How does it differ from corporate planning?

2. Describe the principal types of governmental plans. How does the concept of National Aggregate Economic Planning (NAEP) compare with some other planning approaches?

3. Comment on the essential features of the Humphrey-Javits bill, with particular emphasis upon the reasons why different meanings have been ascribed to the planning system described in the bill.

4. How was the French Five-Year Plan developed? Argue the proposition: The United States should prepare comprehensive national plans along the lines of the French system.

5. Discuss the pros and cons of National Aggregate Economic Planning and assess their relative merits.

6. On the assumption that the United States will not develop a single national plan, what do you think ought to be done to assure better planning by the federal government?

MIND-STRETCHING QUESTION

1. It is altogether likely that in the United States the federal government will work closely with private industry in undertaking major projects that neither can carry out alone. What basic principles would you suggest so that, as the two work more closely together, each will devote to an undertaking that influence which it is best able to make, and each will avoid potentially significant problems that such a partnership can easily bring?

27
MULTINATIONAL CORPORATIONS AND GOVERNMENT RELATIONSHIPS

A) NESTLÉ UNDER FIRE FOR HYPING INFANT FORMULA*

Introduction

In Zambia, dead babies' graves are adorned with empty Nestlé's Lactogen cans and baby bottles that were thought by the mothers of these dead infants to be indispensable to them. While Third World mothers believe that the powdered infant formula is essential to an infant's survival, critics allege that the infant formula product has led to the deaths of infants through consumer misuse.

Nestlé of Switzerland has been the major target of critics for allegedly engaging in misleading marketing practices to promote infant formula products in less developed countries (LDCs). Much of the criticism is directed at Nestlé due to its world leadership position in the infant formula business. It has a worldwide market share of 50 percent, and a penetration of over 70 percent in individual national markets.[1] Other major firms in the infant formula industry include American-based multinational corporations like Abbott Laboratories (a Ross Laboratories subsidiary), Bristol-Myers (Mead Johnson Laboratories), American Home Products (Wyeth Laboratories) and Borden. All these multinational corporations are accused by various international organizations, the medical profession, governments, journalists, church groups and others, of unethical sales promotion of infant formula products in the Third World.

AGGRESSIVE MARKETING PRACTICES IN THE THIRD WORLD

Marketing practices of the infant formula companies in the Third World involve massive radio and TV advertising, billboards, posters, calendars, and promotion in

*Prepared by Marjorie Chan under the direction of John F. Steiner

hospitals and clinics. Because much of the Third World is characterized by great poverty and illiteracy, the marketing of infant formula to women there should include proper warnings as to the fatal effects of its misuse. Instead, high-pressure promotion has tended to focus only on the product's advantages. The distribution networks of the formula companies are comprehensive, and infant formula is spread to both cities and rural areas.

Commercial Advertising

Mike Muller, in a study undertaken in 1976 of commercial advertising of infant formula in Africa, reports that the following advertising message of Nestlé, sung in the different languages of Sierra Leone with the accompaniment of fast-paced music, was on the air almost five times a day in 1974.

> Bring up your baby with love and Lactogen.
> Important news for mothers! Now Lactogen is even better, because it contains more proteins plus vitamins and iron, all essential for making your baby strong and healthy. Lactogen Full Protein now has an even creamier taste and is guaranteed by Nestlé. Lactogen and love.[2]

The nutritional value of the product in terms of "protein" and "vitamins and iron" is stressed in most other advertising messages of Nestlé. These terms are enmeshed in the emotional appeal of the advertisement to capture audience attention. Furthermore, the infant formula companies very often advertise their products together with various attractions like a free gift scheme, premiums, and the establishment of baby clubs. This is done to elicit the involvement of consumers.[3] An advertisement of the Nestlé baby club in Dakar, Senegal, can be found in the newspaper *Le Soleil* for January 6, 1972. It reads: Nestlé sends very pretty presents to the most beautiful babies, and the best photo received each week is publicized in the papers.[4]

Medical Promotion

To gain access to hospitals and clinics, the infant formula makers donate various gifts to these medical organizations and their staffs. The companies sponsor medical conferences and pediatric courses, and offer postgraduation grants to doctors. This is termed "manipulation by assistance" by Dr. Derrick B. Jelliffe, presently head of the Division of Population, Family and International Health, University of California at Los Angeles, and a leading critic of the infant formula companies. Hospitals and clinics are not only provided with a free supply of infant formula by the companies, but with free samples of the product as well. Since it is common hospital practice to separate newborn infants from their mothers for the first few days, these babies are fed with the baby formula by hospital staff from the moment of their birth until the end of their stay in the hospital. By the time the mothers are ready to leave the hospital, their breast milk has dried up. So they continue to feed babies with free formula samples. Consequently, formula feeding replaces breast feeding.

By feeding newborn infants with baby formula during their stay in the hospital, and distributing free samples to new mothers, hospital practices and the attitudes of hospital staff encourage formula feeding. In addition, education posters on formula feeding donated by the infant formula companies can be found hanging on the walls of hospitals and clinics. Their use has been a popular gimmick of Nestlé. Mike Muller discusses a Nestlé series of five posters in *The Baby Killer.*

> One on pre-natal care; another on cleaning and dressing the baby; one devoted to ways of preparing the baby's first solid foods; a fourth devoted to breast feeding. The last used to be incorporated with a guide to bottle feeding which has now been made into a separate poster.
> The only hint of commercialism in the posters is the Nestlé feeding bottle illustrated and the mention of CERELAC, a Nestlé product, in the solid food poster. And of course the company logo in the upper right hand corner of each poster.[5]

Another promotional gimmick involves the use of "milk nurses," that is, female sales representatives who may or may not be qualified nurses, but who dress in nurses' uniforms to promote infant formula in hospitals and the private homes of new mothers.

Promotional efforts like the aforementioned create the illusion that formula feeding is endorsed by the medical profession. This endorsement by association is condemned by critics. "Whether it is intended to or not," says Muller, "much of the promotional, or educational material used by the milk companies, will, to the illiterate, appear to endorse bottle feeding. And the association of this material with clinic or hospital can only reinforce this impression."[6] Leah Margulies, director of the infant formula program for the Interfaith Center on Corporate Responsibility, criticizes "milk nurses" for the same reason. Says Margulies: "Capitalizing on the respect given a nurse . . . implies a connection between the health care profession and the commercial product.[7]

In conclusion, critics charge that misleading promotional efforts lead gullible mothers in LDCs to turn from breast feeding to formula feeding, and misuse of the infant formula product begins.

Distribution

Major markets for Nestlé's infant formula product are Europe, Africa, Latin America, and Asia. The company does not sell this product in North America, the United Kingdom or Holland. It has established local food processing plants for manufacturing the formula product in LDCs, and often participates in joint ventures in developing nations to achieve economies of scale with integrated production facilities.[8] The product is distributed in LDCs through hospitals, clinics, pharmacies, government and private health services, and food stores. From the information presented in a bulletin on Thailand put out by Nestlé in 1971, Ted

Greiner of Cornell University noted that Nestlé distributed its products to even the most remote areas in Thailand. He also described the following organization.

> It [Nestlé] kept 1–3 agents per town and 10 trucks and one boat for other regions. Although its products were sold in 200 luxury shops and 10,000 cafeterias, the most important segment of the market was the small shops, 10,000 of which were visited monthly by Nestlé 'vending forces.'[9]

Supporting evidence of the penetration of the infant formula product to even remote areas of the Third World is found in testimony before the Senate Health Subcommittee hearings by Reverend Daniel Driscoll, Fatima Patal, and Leah Margulies.

Reverend Driscoll spent 11 years in Venezuela. He found that the infant formula companies gave free samples to a hospital in Cagua, which is located in a jungle-like area three hours from Caracas. Reverend Driscoll found that many babies in this hospital suffered from diarrhea, and the nurse there told him that "all the babies who came in used Nan—a Nestlé product—all of the babies who had diarrhea used Nan."[10]

Fatima Patal, a voluntary public health nurse with the Canadian University Services Overseas, stated that there are light planes that connect the cities with the most remote areas of Peru. Young people from the remote villages, who hold menial jobs in the cities, bring baby formula back to the villages when they come home for vacation. Nurse Patal also remarked that, "formula feeding bottles have invaded even the most remote part of the 'Green Hell' [jungle] where civilization and basic health education is still sadly lacking and living conditions leave much to be desired."[11] Margulies learned from an investigator who returned from Kenya that infant formula products are found in even the remotest areas of Kenya.

FATAL EFFECTS OF FORMULA FEEDING IN THE THIRD WORLD

Much of the Third World is characterized by poverty, illiteracy, poor sanitation, and inadequate basic health care. Thus, the misuse of infant formula may be inevitable. Water is often obtained from a highly polluted river or common well, and it is carried back to homes in contaminated containers. Fuel is extremely expensive, and a refrigerator is a luxury item that the lower socioeconomic class cannot afford. Consequently, the powdered formula is mixed with contaminated water, feeding bottles and nipples are not properly sterilized due to the shortage of fuel, and the prepared formula is not refrigerated. Furthermore, afflicted with poverty, Third World mothers dilute the powdered formula with a great deal of water so it will last longer. All this leads to excess infant morbidity and mortality.

Examples of incidents that illustrate the linkage between formula misuse and infant morbidity and mortality were described by Dr. Allan Jackson and Reverend Driscoll in their testimony before the Senate Health Subcommittee hearings. Dr. Jackson described the malnutrition suffered by two exclusively bottle-fed infants whom he had treated in a Jamaican hospital. The 18-month-old baby girl and her 4-month-old brother weighed 12 pounds and 5 pounds respectively. Dr. Jackson stated that one can feed a 4-month-old baby with one can of baby formula "for something just under 3 days."[12] Yet for this particular case, the mother diluted the formula so that one can of baby formula was used to feed the two infants for a fortnight. The mother was poor and illiterate, and she lived with 12 children in a place with no running water or electricity. Reverend Driscoll showed a picture to the Senate Health Subcommittee of what he saw in the emergency ward of the children's hospital in Caracas. It illustrated the following:

> In this room, there were 58 babies, 53 of whom had diarrhea. Of the 58 babies who were there, all were bottle-fed, although the hospital does not know which formula they are taking. The doctor checked the records, and all had been bottle-fed.
> As you can see in this picture, which is on one side of the wall, three of the babies are receiving intravenous feeding which, of course, in babies they receive through the head.[13]

The afflictions resulting from formula feeding were summarized by nurse Patal as follows:

1. *Severe malnutrition—Kwashiorkor, Marasmus:* Mainly caused by the overdilution of the formula to make a tin of milk powder last longer.
2. *Vomiting and General Upset Stomach:* Due to overconcentrated feeds if the given instructions cannot be followed because of illiteracy.
3. *Gastro-Intestinal Infections:* Ingestion of contaminated formula, causing severe diarrhea, vomiting, cramps, and colic. With the rapid loss of body fluids—dehydration leading to death.
4. *Respiratory Infections:* Low resistance to infection due to malnutrition—bronchopneumonia, pneumonia, tuberculosis, etc.
5. *Inner Ear Infections:* Otitis media, caused by the drainage of formula into the eustachian tubes while formula feeding in the unnatural position with the bottle propped up.
6. *Infectious Diseases and other Infections:* The infant's health remains poor, and he gets frequently ill due to the malnutrition and low resistance of his body to infections, such as the usual infantile ailments like measles, chicken pox, whooping cough, scarlet fever, and mumps. He takes much longer to recuperate.[14]

The linkage between overly aggressive marketing practices of the infant food companies and infant excess morbidity and mortality through product misuse was described by Dr. Jelliffe as "commerciogenic malnutrition,"[15] that is, malnutrition which results from thoughtless marketing practices of the infant food industry. A moral issue is raised by Dr. Jelliffe, who asks:

> For example, is it ethical to advertise, using modern techniques of motivation and persuasion, infant foods in a population that has no chance financially or hygienically of being able to use them in adequate quantities? Should infant milk foods be widely advertised in regions where breast feeding is currently practiced?[16]

Due to problems of nutrition and infection associated with bottle feeding, medical experts and various critics call for a reemphasis on breast feeding in LDCs. Dr. Jelliffe states that, "human breast milk is an active anti-infective biological system, which cannot be duplicated in any way whatsoever by a formula."[17] Similarly, Dr. Michael C. Latham, professor of international nutrition at Cornell University, has summarized the advantages of breast feeding this way.

> The advantages of breast, over bottle feeding, include the ready availability and convenience of breast feeding (breast milk comes in excellent containers); the adequacy of nutrients in breast milk; the greatly reduced likelihood that it will lead to infant obesity; the economic advantages for the family and the nation (breast milk is the one available low cost high protein food of animal origin); the good mother-child relationship fostered by breast feeding; the immunity conferred by the globulins in breast milk; the fact that the chances of developing diarrhea are reduced by breast feeding and enhanced by bottle feeding; and the contraceptive effect of breast feeding.[18]

He also stressed the fatal effects of bottle feeding in these words:

> Although breast feeding has advantages everywhere, it is now recognized that for about two thirds of the world's population bottle feeding of infants is highly undesirable, and in many instances placing an infant on a bottle might be tantamount to signing the death certificate of the child. Bottle feeding is responsible for a huge amount of childhood illness and for many, many deaths.[19]

INTERNATIONAL ATTENTION TO THE ISSUE

The possible linkage between allegedly unethical sales promotion of infant formula and infant morbidity and mortality through product misuse has been under close scrutiny since the early 1970s. This problem has been discussed by medical professionals, industry representatives, and government officials in various international conferences on health and nutrition.

Journalists have also taken interest. Public awareness was heightened with the 1974 publication of *The Baby Killer* by a British charity organization, War on Want. In this pamphlet Nestlé of Switzerland and Unigate of Britain were the prime targets of attack for engaging in ill-considered marketing activities in Africa. In 1975, a German translation of the pamphlet with the title changed to *Nestlé Kills Babies* resulted in a lawsuit in Switzerland by Nestlé against the publisher for defamation. Though Nestlé won the case, the court advised the firm to review its marketing practices.

RAMIFICATIONS OF THE NESTLÉ TRIAL

One side effect of the Nestlé trial in Switzerland included intensified efforts in the United States against the marketing of infant formula in LDCs. The leaders in this cause are the Interfaith Center on Corporate Responsibility and the Infant Formula Action Coalition (INFACT). While the former is an agency related to the National Council of Churches, the latter is a national coalition, formed in 1977, of health-care professionals, church activists, Third World activists and other concerned individuals. Starting in 1975, stockholder resolutions have been filed with Bristol-Myers, Abbott Laboratories and American Home products by church activists. These resolutions have called for a critical review of the companies' infant formula marketing practices in LDCs.

Since United States church groups do not own Nestlé stock they have made no stockholder resolutions to the company. One major tactic they have employed is to try to stop Nestlé's infant formula promotional efforts. Another tactic is a nationwide boycott launched by INFACT of all Nestlé products. One result of all these efforts was the decision of the U.S. Senate Health Subcommittee, chaired by Senator Edward M. Kennedy, to hold hearings in 1978.

INDUSTRY RESPONSES TO PUBLIC CRITICISM

The International Council of Infant Food Industries (ICIFI) was formed in November 1975 by nine manufacturers with Nestlé, American Home Products, and Abbott Laboratories included. ICIFI members established a code of marketing ethics:

> In recognition that sound nutrition during infancy is essential for normal growth and development, the members of the INTERNATIONAL COUNCIL OF INFANT FOOD INDUSTRIES subscribe to the principles and the primacy of the medical and paramedical professions' roles in supervising the dietary intake of infants. These principles affirm that breast milk is the preferred form of nutrition for infants not needing special diets for metabolic purposes, and support the recommendations of the United Nations Protein-Calorie Advisory Group and of the World Health Organization.
>
> Breast-milk substitutes meet essential needs when used appropriately in the feeding of infants. Breast-milk substitutes are intended to supplement breast milk and for use when mothers cannot or elect not to breast-feed for medical or other reasons.
>
> Therefore, the members of the INTERNATIONAL COUNCIL OF INFANT FOOD INDUSTRIES hereby pledge that:
>
> 1. As providers of essential supplies for infant nutrition, the members of ICIFI accept responsibility for the diffusion of information which supports sound infant feeding practices and for services consistent with the application of this Code.
> 2. Product information for the public will always recognize that breast milk is the feeding of choice with the recommendation to seek professional advice when a supplement or alternative may be required.
> 3. Product labeling will affirm breast-feeding as the first choice for the nutrition of infants.
> 4. Product claims will reflect scientific integrity without implication that any product is superior to breast milk.
> 5. To insure optimal nutritional intake, explicitly worded instructions and demonstrations for product use will be provided for the hygienic and correctly measured preparation of breast-milk substitutes.
> 6. In cooperation with health authorities, professional communications and educational materials will be provided to caution against misuse and to inform mothers on the importance of and methods for obtaining safe water for the preparation of breast-milk substitutes.

7. Members' personnel will observe professional ethics and established rules of conduct in medical/nursing centres, maternities, and physicians' offices and in all contacts.

8. Members will employ nurses, nutritionists and midwives whenever possible to perform mothercraft services. When professionally trained personnel are not available, high educational standards and experience commensurate with prevailing conditions will be required. Training of these staffs will be in keeping with scientific standards for infant nutrition to emphasize the importance of breast-feeding and the appropriate use of breast-milk substitutes.

9. Individual contacts by mothercraft personnel and issuance of complimentary supplies of breast-milk substitutes will be in consultation with medical or nursing personnel in the institution or the area.

10. Mothercraft personnel will support doctors' and nurses' prerogatives in counselling mothers on infant feeding and will not discourage mothers from establishing or continuing breast-feeding.

11. Nurses' uniforms will be worn only by persons who are professionally entitled to their use. The attire worn by mothercraft personnel will bear the identification of the respective ICIFI member. It is recommended that an ICIFI emblem be worn.

12. Compensation of mothercraft personnel will be on a basis of quality and level of services performed and without relationship to sales.

13. Adherence to this Code will be obligatory on all members of ICIFI except when precluded by the laws or regulations of a given country.[20]

ICIFI also monitors business practices of firms in the infant food industry, studies scientific research on infant nutrition, and communicates precise infant formula feeding instructions with the aid of visual materials so that illiterate mothers can understand correct use.[21]

In response to criticism that the ICIFI code is not stringent enough, Abbott Laboratories, Bristol-Myers, and Nestlé each established a company code that goes beyond the ICIFI code. Abbott Laboratories had been very critical of the ICIFI code, and it withdrew from ICIFI. The company established for itself a code which calls for restrictions on consumer advertising and the marketing of infant formula only to upper- and middle-income groups. In addition, "milk nurses" can no longer wear uniforms even if they are qualified nurses. Bristol-Myers, which has not been a participant in the health conferences on the infant formula issue or a member of the ICIFI, also has established a more stringent company code of marketing ethics than the ICIFI code as a direct result of a two-year stockholder lawsuit against misleading statements in the company's proxy report initiated by a group of stockholder church activists. The code obliges Bristol-Myers to restrict its distribution of free samples to doctors, to ban direct contact with consumers, to communicate to Third World mothers the superiority of breast feeding and to give warnings on all labels. The company also proclaimed the discontinuance of its milk nurses at the Senate hearings in May 1978.[22]

Nestlé, too, has drawn up a more stringent code of marketing ethics for itself. It subjects its marketing practices to regular, critical review, and modifications are made in line with its marketing policies. The company has recently discontinued commercial advertising of the infant formula product in LDCs so as to reexamine the educational role of advertising media. In order to conduct worldwide implementation of the company's code, governments and medical professionals are consulted with respect to the ethical quality of its marketing practices.[23]

THE NESTLÉ BOYCOTT

INFACT has launched a nationwide boycott of all Nestlé products to stop the firm's infant formula promotional efforts in the Third World. INFACT'S boycott list includes the following Nestlé items; Nescafé, Nestea, Taster's Choice, Nestlé's Quik, Nestlé's Crunch, Libby, McNeill and Libby products, Souptime, Stouffer products, Crosse and Blackwell products, Maggi products, Swiss Knight Cheese, Deer Park Mountain Spring Water, and L'Oreal cosmetics.[24]

The demands of INFACT on Nestlé are:

1. STOP the use of "milk nurse" sales personnel, in or out of starched uniforms;
2. STOP distributing free samples of formula to hospitals, clinics, and the families of newborn babies;
3. STOP promoting formula to the health professions and through health care institutions;
4. STOP promotion and advertising of artificial milk formula aimed at Third World mothers who can't use it safely, as recommended by the World Health Organization.[25]

United States church groups have exerted pressure on American infant formula companies by sponsoring shareholder resolutions. This tactic is deemed necessary because self-regulation on the part of the infant formula companies with respect to marketing conduct is suspect. Douglas Clement, coordinator of the INFACT Coalition Clearing-house in Minneapolis has stated:

> Management's will to self-regulate was cast into doubt when it was learned at the May Senate hearings that no formula company has conducted thorough research on the socioeconomic backgrounds of its Third World Market populations to see if formula is, as the companies repeatedly state, being sold only to those who can use it safely. Such studies are essential to the implementation of effective codes of ethics, but apparently because they are not essential to market growth, they have not been done. In this context, asking the infant formula industry to regulate itself is like asking Colonel Sanders to babysit your chickens.[26]

Publicity generated by the boycott has tarnished Nestlé's corporate image and has created pressure on the company to deal with the infant formula issue. Due to extreme pressure, Nestlé has reevaluated its marketing strategies in the Third World.

NESTLÉ'S DEFENSE AGAINST CRITICISM

Henry G. Ciocca, assistant secretary of Nestlé, defends the company by addressing infant morbidity and mortality problems as an international issue that calls for cooperation among representatives of governments, industry, and the medical profession to come up with a solution. He thinks that the infant formula controversy is really a controversy over the basic question of how best to solve the infant malnutrition problem. The question is one of how best to alleviate problems of poverty, ignorance, poor sanitation, and inadequate basic health care in LDCs. The basic question is *not* unethical product promotion as critics allege.[27]

Ciocca points out that it has never been Nestlé's position to sell infant formula as a substitute for breast milk; rather, it is a supplement to breast milk.[28] The Human Lactation Center, the Nutrition Foundation, Inc., and the World Health Organization agree that breast milk alone is not sufficient to sustain an infant during the first year of life. Therefore, a supplement to breast milk is required. The Human Lactation Center states:

> Very early in our work, we became aware that infants in underdeveloped countries who breast feed from undernourished mothers require additional food to supplement breast milk by the time they are three months old. When they do not get it, their development is inhibited. Soon they are undernourished, then malnourished. They weaken, become susceptible to disease or die. . . . The claim that Third World women can breast feed exclusively for one or two years and have healthy, well-developed children is outrageous and dangerous.[29]

Similarly, a report by a group of experts to the Nutrition Foundation, Inc. states: "Even under good conditions a diet of breast milk alone is likely to become insufficient within four to six months after the birth of the baby."[30] Furthermore, the World Health Organization says that "a food supplement is likely to become necessary after the age of three months if the energy needs of the baby are to be met."[31]

Ciocca also comments on the fact that no matter what kinds of supplementary food are used, they are all subject to problems of contamination and sanitation; therefore, the question that arises is why not use infant formula as a supplement due to its high nutritional value as opposed to "thin starchy gruels" which are of questionable value, but are often used by Third World mothers to supplement their babies' diets.[32] A group of medical researchers, M. G. M. Rowland, R. A. E. Barrell, and R. G. Whitehead, support Ciocca's point. They say:

> Microbiological contamination is clearly not just confined to commercial baby milks and feeding bottles. It is found equally in traditional weaning foods and the simplest of feeding containers. . . . Apart from microbiological contamination, traditional Gambian weaning foods, like those of many other countries, are nutritionally inadequate.[33]

Critics allege that formula feeding has led to excess infant morbidity and mortality in the Third World through product misuse, and they campaign against formula promotion in the developing nations. Yet there are occasions when formula feeding is indispensable, and Dr. Adeoye Adeniyi, a Nigerian pediatrician, enumerates them as follows:

1. Infants whose mothers die during or shortly after childbirth.
2. In cases where breast milk fails or is inadequate.
3. In cases where breast feeding is contraindicated as in severe maternal illness.
4. In rapid growth after three months of age when the need to supplement infant feeding is crucial to normal nutrition status in early childhood.[34]

Various hospitals also have expressed their appreciation of the donation of infant formula products by Nestlé, for these products are essential to infants whose mothers have insufficient breast milk. The Franciscan Sisters' Hospital in Kenya states:

> This has been a very hard year for us here in Kitui District for famine has been wide-spread, and so our people have not had the necessities of life. The Lactogen you have given us in the past has been a great help to us as the people are so poor here. We give it to the most needy, especially to newly born babies whose mothers have very little milk.[35]

Similarly, the Catholic Mission Hospital in Kenya comments:

> You have no idea the relief and pleasure it gives us to be able to feed our little pre-mature babies with your products. Otherwise, as I explained before, they would just die as the mothers haven't sufficient breast milk and are too poor to buy baby food.[36]

Dr. Adeniyi also comments that "the high incidence of Kwashiokor, marasmus and general protein-energy malnutrition" is not found in the "educated classes of Nigerians" who use formula products properly. Therefore, he opposes demands on the formula companies to stop selling them to Third World nations and advocates that these companies should take on an educational role. He states:

> If Africa will not continue to be a target for malnutrition, if our babies should ever have a chance, correct nutrition and supplementary feeding in relation to milk and other feeds must remain available . . .

Instead of a destructive criticism which is aimed at depriving Africa of the milk products, efforts should be directed at *EDUCATING* African mothers on the correct use of these products . . . . We are pleased that Nestlé Products has responded favourably. They have appointed trained nurses who visit clinics in towns, villages and hamlets to help with educating the masses. They also have put out pictures encouraging mothers to breast feed their babies and announcements to this effect put out on mass communication media of radio and television. This I believe to be commendable and morally justified.

It is also important to stress that the economic development of Nigeria has produced *"The Working Mother."* The Nigerian woman of today is at work and *NO PROPAGANDA* can stop this. It will be criminal to deprive her of the only sensible means of feeding her baby while she is at work. Rather than pursue this puerile propaganda, a programme geared to educating her in the proper use of the products is both right and moral. Lastly, it will be unfortunate for Africa if a company that has done so much and has come such a long way to meeting the needs of Nigerian mothers and infants is made to suffer in any way or libeled as murderous. Rather, it and others should be encouraged to inprove their efforts to the overall advantage of our children.[37]

In support of Dr. Adeniyi's view, Dr. Aykroyd, one-time Director of Nutrition at the Food and Agricultural Organization (FAO) of the United Nations, states:

"The effects of eliminating infant formula foods would be to raise the proportions of malnourished infants in the population and the infant mortality rate. It would not increase the numbers of infants satisfactorily fed at the breast."[38]

Though critics have alleged that infant formula is available to even the remotest part of the Third World where misuse is most likely, Ciocca suggests that it has been Nestlé's intention to sell the infant formula product to only the urban upper- and middle-income groups in LDCs, and not to the rural poor there. "It would be economic suicide," he says, "to concentrate any sales effort in rural areas, where people can't afford our product."[39]

Douglas Groner, director of corporate responsibility at the New York office of Nestlé, states that, "it does not make economic sense for a company to sell a product to people who can't afford them," in support of Ciocca's above statement. "Though the infant formula product might be found in a small general store somewhere in a rural area," he says, "this product is certainly not found everywhere as the critics have alleged." He mentions also that he has learned from conversations with various doctors who work in the bush areas that the infant formula product is not found in the areas where they work. He states that virtually 100 percent of the Third World mothers in the bush areas breast feed their babies for at least six months, and at the end of the year, around 90 percent of these mothers still breast feed their babies. When supplements are used, local traditional foods like fermented corn and maize are used.[40]

Nestlé indicates that increase in the demand for infant formula is not created by commercial and medical promotion, but is due to the following factors.

1. Third World mothers do not have sufficient breast milk to feed their babies more than three months.
2. Instead of using local traditional foods as supplements to their babies' diet, Third World mothers are looking for more nutritional supplements for their babies.
3. A greater number of Third World mothers are in the urban work force, and they can afford to buy more nutritious supplements for their babies.[41]

In order to prove the point that the demand for infant formula is not created by promotional tactics of companies, Nestlé states the following:

As proof of the fact that the demand for infant formula is *real* and not created, many state-controlled countries which do not allow commercial companies to advertise, promote, sample or distribute their products nevertheless buy infant formula in large quantities and distribute it themselves to hospitals and stores. The governments of India, Chile, Mexico and Algeria themselves manufacture and sell infant formula products.[42]

As a defense to the charges by INFACT, Nestlé stated its company policies in a letter to a number of American clergymen dated May 11, 1979, as follows:

1. The company no longer engages in commercial advertising of the infant formula to consumers in the Third World.
2. Nestlé's medical representatives are not allowed to have direct contact with mothers without the authorization of the medical professionals, and they are not permitted

to render free formula samples to mothers. Their chief duty is to provide informa-tion about Nestlé's formula products to health professionals, and sometimes they assist the latter in educating mothers on the details of breast feeding, health care and the proper use of the infant formula.

3. The Nestlé medical representatives give to health professionals in the Third World free formula samples, which are used by the latter to instruct mothers on the correct use of the product so that when the occasion arises that a supplement is required to fulfill the nutritional needs of an infant, this educational process will ensure proper usage of the formula product.

4. Nestlé donates samples of the formula product and equipment to hospitals and clinics whenever the request on the part of these organizations "is reasonable and represents a community-wide benefit," . . . Nestlé also sponsors conferences on infant nutrition.

These policies are in line with recommendations of the Protein Advisory Group of the United Nations as specified in its Statement #23. This statement consists of the only official directive from the United Nations to industry, governments, and health professions with respect to the proper promotion of supplementary foods.

Nestlé has played an essential role in educating Third World mothers about the proper use of infant formula. In a statement before the Senate Health Subcom-mittee, Oswaldo Ballarin, chairman of Nestlé-Brazil, stated the following in 1978.

Nestlé recognized that even the best products will not give the desired results if used incorrectly. We, therefore, placed great weight on educational efforts aimed at explaining the correct use of our products. Our work in this field has received the public recogni-tion and approval of the official Pediatric Associations in many countries. Such educa-tional efforts never attempt to imply that our product is superior to breast milk. Indeed, we have devoted much attention to the promotion of breast-feeding, and educational material has always insisted that breast-feeding is best for the baby.[43]

Nestlé has also put out a booklet entitled *I Am Feeding My Baby*, which not only encourages breast feeding, but provides all pertinent information with respect to successful breast feeding. Douglas Groner states that "the approach taken in this booklet is, by the way, the same approach taken by our medical representatives when they are asked by local health authorities to conduct clinics for mothers."[44]

Credit has been given to the infant formula companies for educating mothers on successful breast feeding, proper use of the infant formula and basic health care. Dr. Jerzy Lukowski, chief gynecologist of Menelik Hospital in Ethiopia, approves of Nestlé's medical promotional efforts. Dr. Lukowski says:

We note with pleasure that you employ a fully qualified nurse and that during discus-sions with mothers she always encourages breast-feeding, recommending your products only when natural feeding is insufficient or fails.[45]

Dr. Elizabeth Cole of the Human Lactation Center states:

Health care in many parts of the world is very scarce and milk nurses, while promoting a particular product, are providing more public health care and information than the mother receives at any other time. In some instances, they are doing more to promote infant survival than is the local government.[46]

On the whole, Nestlé's views with respect to infant malnutrition in the Third World are summarized by Ciocca as follows.

- Lack of sufficient food after the baby's third month is a major cause of morbidity and mortality whether or not the infant is breast fed.
- Infants born into the higher socio-economic groups, whether bottle fed or breast fed, are healthier than infants in the lower socio-economic groups.
- Breast fed babies appear to develop better and suffer from fewer illnesses than bottle fed babies, as long as the breast milk is available in sufficient supply.
- Even where breast feeding is universally practiced, as in poor traditional cultures, infant mortality is far higher than in urban areas, where breast feeding is on the decline.[47]

Finally, one of the strongest statements in defense of Nestlé is made by Sister Silvia Probst, R.N., of Ibana Hospital in Uganda.

I have been surprised to see that your firm has been accused of killing babies in the developing countries. I have been in Africa for 18 years and have personally treated over 800,000 children and have handled health reports on an additional two to three million children. These accusations bear no relation to the truth. . . . I am certain that Nestlé does not kill babies; it has saved millions.[48]

CASE QUESTION

Do you agree with the public criticisms of Nestlé's promotion of the infant formula in the Third World? Why or why not?

Notes

1. James Post, *Corporate Behavior and Social Change* (Reston, Virginia: Reston Publishing Co., 1978), p. 262.
2. Quoted in Ted Greiner, *Regulation and Education: Strategies for Solving the Bottle Feeding Problem* (Ithaca, New York: Cornell International Nutrition Monograph Series, No. 4, 1977), p. 7.
3. *Ibid.,* p. 7.
4. *Ibid.,* p. 7.
5. Mike Muller, *The Baby Killer* (London; War on Want, 1974), p. 9.
6. *Ibid.,* p. 9.
7. Leah Margulies, "Bottle Babies: Death and Business Get Their Market," *Business and Society Review,* No. 25 (Spring 1978), p. 45.
8. U.S. Congress, Senate, Committee on Human Resources, Subcommittee on Health and Scientific Research, *Marketing and Promotion of Infant Formula in the Developing Nations,* Hearing, 95th Congress, 2nd Session, May 23, 1978 (Washington, D.C.: Government Printing Office, 1978), Supplementary testimony presented by James Post, "The International Infant Formula Industry," pp. 222-234.

9. Greiner, *op. cit.,* p. 18.
10. Subcommittee on Health and Scientific Research, *op. cit.,* transcript of testimony by Reverend Daniel Driscoll, p. 15.
11. *Ibid.,* transcript of testimony by Fatima Patal, p. 21.
12. *Ibid.,* transcript of testimony by Dr. Allan Jackson, p. 6.
13. *Ibid.,* transcript of testimony by Reverend Daniel Driscoll.
14. *Ibid.,* testimony by Fatima Patal, *op. cit.,* pp. 21–22.
15. Derrick B. Jelliffe, "Commerciogenic Malnutrition?" *Food Technology,* Vol. 25, No. 2 (Feb., 1971), p. 154.
16. *Ibid.,* p. 154.
17. Subcommittee on Health and Scientific Research, *op. cit.,* transcript of testimony by Dr. Derrick B. Jelliffe, p. 42.
18. See the Introduction by Michael C. Latham found in Ted Greiner, *The Promotion of Bottle Feeding by Multinational Corporations: How Advertising and the Health Professions Have Contributed* (Ithaca, New York: Cornell International Nutrition Monograph Series, No. 2, 1975), p. i.
19. *Ibid.,* p. ii.
20. International Council of Infant Food Industries, "Code of Ethics and Professional Standards for Advertising, Product Information and Advisory Services for Breast-Milk Substitutes," Nov. 20, 1975, amended Sept. 14, 1976.
21. *Ibid.*
22. James Post and Edward Baer, "Demarketing Infant Formula: Consumer Products in the Developing World," *Journal of Contemporary Business,* Vol. 7, No. 4 (1979), pp. 25–26.
23. Henry G. Ciocca, "The Infant Formula Controversy: A Nestlé View," *Journal of Contemporary Business,* Vol. 7, No. 4 (1979), p. 40.
24. The Newman Center, Infant Formula Action Coalition (INFACT), "The Nestlé Boycott," a newsletter to supporters signed by Douglas A. Johnson, National Chairperson of INFACT, 1979, p. 4.
25. *Ibid.,* p. 3.
26. Douglas Clement, "Nestlé's Latest Killing in the Bottle Baby Market," *Business and Society Review,* No. 26 (Summer 1978), p. 64.
27. Ciocca, *op. cit.,* pp. 37–40.
28. *Ibid.,* p. 39.
29. "Breastfeeding and Weaning Among the Poor," *The Lactation Review,* Vol. III, No. 1 (1978), p. 3.
30. Quoted in an in-house publication of Nestlé titled "Nestlé and Infant Formula: Facts and Fallacies," April, 1979, p. 4.
31. *Ibid.,* p. 4.
32. Ciocca, *op. cit.,* p. 51.
33. Quoted in "Nestlé and Infant Formula: Facts and Fallacies," *op. cit.,* p. 11.
34. Subcommittee on Health and Scientific Research, *op. cit.,* statement by Dr. Adeoye Adeniyi, "The Place of Artificial Feeding in Africa," p. 1038.
35. Quoted in "Nestlé and Infant Formula: Facts and Fallacies," *op. cit.,* p. 9.
36. *Ibid.,* p. 9.

37. U.S., Congress, Senate, Committee on Human Resources, Subcommittee on Health and Scientific Research, Statement by Dr. Adeoye Adeniyi, "The Place of Artificial Feeding in Africa," *op. cit.,* p. 1038.
38. Quoted in "Nestlé and Infant Formula: Facts and Fallacies," *op. cit.,* p. 3.
39. "A Boycott Over Infant Formula," *Business Week,* April 23, 1979, p. 140.
40. Interview by the writer with Douglas Groner, director of corporate responsibility at the New York office of Nestlé, July 1979.
41. "Nestlé and Infant Formula: Facts and Fallacies," *op. cit.,* p. 5.
42. *Ibid.,* emphasis in the original.
43. Subcommittee on Health and Scientific Research, *op. cit.,* statement of Oswaldo Ballarin, chairman of Nestlé-Brazil.
44. Personal correspondence dated July 17, 1979, from Douglas Groner, director of corporate responsibility at the New York office of Nestlé, to the writer.
45. "Nestlé and Infant Formula: Facts and Fallacies," *op. cit.,* p. 7.
46. *Ibid.*
47. Ciocca, *op. cit.,* p. 46.
48. "Nestlé and Infant Formula: Facts and Fallacies," *op. cit.,* p. 1.

B) FLEXON CONSTRUCTION COMPANY

Virginia Hazard, president of giant Flexon Construction Company, was preparing to make some policy decisions about questionable payments in foreign countries. New federal statutes and public pressure made it imperative that large firms such as Flexon develop guidelines for their employees on this touchy subject or risk jail terms for employees and widespread censure from constituent groups.

Flexon was a worldwide construction firm engaged in the building of highways, oil refineries, airports, dams, transit systems, nuclear reactors, model cities, and anything else that construction technology could give birth to. Its revenues were over $5 billion dollars in 1980 and it was undertaking 75 different projects in 25 countries on every continent. Headquarters were in New York.

The company had always adhered to high ethical standards in United States operations, but since its founding in the 1920s its leadership had been pragmatic about bending to local custom overseas. While Flexon employees had not actively sought out foreigners with offers of bribes and gratuities, neither had they shrunk from the facts of life of overseas business when approached by foreigners on the take. Company executives had maintained the position that Flexon was a guest in foreign countries and should accommodate local habits. In addition, there was widespread agreement among the management that if Flexon did not pay, other American or foreign companies would do so and business would be irretrievably lost.

During the 1970s Senate hearings on "payoffs" and blaring media coverage necessitated keeping such publicly unacceptable views in low profile at Flexon. The company had been informally probed by the Internal Revenue Service and the Securities and Exchange Commission, and had even weathered a suit brought by public interest group representatives owning a few shares of Flexon stock. Passage of the Foreign Corrupt Practices Act of 1977, designed to curtail questionable payments by American firms overseas, had brought minor changes in Flexon policy, but Flexon's management had resisted a rethinking of past practice. Now, Virginia Hazard had been installed as President, bringing new managerial philosophies and a new management team in with her. She intended to rethink systematically Flexon's ethical stance in this area.

Still, purity was easier to contemplate than achieve. She disliked the idea of payoffs. They were unsavory, costly, potentially embarrassing, and they often involved kickbacks to Flexon employees. One payoff set the stage for blackmail and was often the first in a long string of payments. Still, the fact was that local custom often demanded these payments and big contracts sometimes hinged on pecuniary presentations as much as performance criteria. The range of problems was wide. She thought of five current examples.

First, a construction project in a small, Central American "banana republic" had been slow to progress because dockworkers and their leaders in a nearby port demanded small payments to handle crates of machinery and building supplies transported in by Flexon. Without these payments crates were "lost," "accidentally" dropped or simply left on the pier exposed to the sun and rain for prolonged periods. The payments demanded amounted to less than $1,000 a month and nobody ever was given more than $50 at one time. This was a paltry sum compared to the cost of "losing" even a few crates. The manager in charge of the operation had asked for permission to develop a schedule of payments and keep the project moving with a little regularly applied "grease." While such payments were not, strictly speaking, legal in the country, the practice was endemic and authorities looked the other way.

Second, a hotel construction project on a small island in the Caribbean had run afoul of the widespread local practice of buying favors by giving favors-in-kind. The project manager had not bribed anyone with cash, but had requested permission to provide free rooms at expensive resort hotels to local officials, to put on lavish banquets for local bureaucrats and their families, to provide an apartment in the apartment complex housing Flexon workers and their families for a mistress of the local Minister of Interior (who controlled levers of power that could facilitate construction), and to do other favors such as loaning company vehicles to island officials for hunting trips. In return, Flexon would certainly be given priority consideration for building permits and the local labor unions would be quiescent.

Third, a project director in a Latin American country was being denied an exit visa to attend a meeting at New York headquarters unless he paid a gratuity to an official in the local customs office. He requested permission to pay the small amount from his personal funds rather than use company money and jeopardize Flexon's legal standing.

Fourth, Flexon was negotiating for a $20 million contract to install electronic navigation and guidance systems at three airports in a Middle Eastern country and seemed about to close the deal. Flexon's chief negotiator, however, had recently wired that he had been approached by an official in the government's Transportation Minstry and informed that a five percent "administrative fee" payable to him would be required when the deal finally closed. This was not illegal in the country and European competitors in the bidding were likely to pay without thinking twice. The chief negotiator had requested instructions.

Finally, and perhaps worst, a member of the president's cabinet in an Asian country had approached Hazard personally on a recent trip there. In no uncertain terms the cabinet minister had demanded a payment of $10 million to the President's forthcoming political campaign and implied in a threatening way that unless the payment were made two oil refineries owned and operated by Flexon in that country would be expropriated by the government. The two refineries were worth far more than the $10 million contribution; indeed, they brought in about 10 times that amount in yearly revenues.

Since the laws of the country proclaim that extortion is illegal, Hazard knew that such a request was contrary to the law. On the other hand, the law would never be enforced because the president held near-dictatorial powers over a weak judiciary in the country. In addition, she knew that in a country the size of this one, $10 million was probably enough to insure the reelection of the tyrant to another five-year term. Even without it, though, she thought he would probably be able to get a safe majority in a rigged election.

All these problems reflected common dilemmas for executives in the international construction trade and they had cropped up many times before. The circumstances changed but the generic problems remained the same.

CASE QUESTIONS ──────────────────────────────

1. In your opinion, is it necessary for companies operating overseas to make questionable payments in order to have profitable operations? What are your reasons?

2. Consult the references below and other recent publications and familiarize yourself with the Foreign Corrupt Practices Act of 1977. What decisions should Virginia Hazard make on each of the five requests being made of her if she wishes to follow the law?

3. Write a draft of a "Questionable Payments Policy Statement" which could be issued by Flexon's top management to provide a guide for ethical behavior to Flexon employees around the world. Be sure to take into consideration such factors as public opinion, competitive forces, federal law, host country laws and customs, and your own personal moral predispositions.

References

Hurd Baruch, "The Foreign Corrupt Practices Act," *Harvard Business Review,* Vol. 57, No. 1 (January-February 1979), pp. 32–50.

John S. Estey and David W. Marstow, "Pitfalls (and Loopholes) in the Foreign Bribery Law," *Fortune* (October 9, 1978), pp. 182–188.

Richard A. Hibey and Benjamin P. Fishburne III, "The Foreign Corrupt Practices Act: 'Knowledge' Most Vexing Problem," *Boycott Law Bulletin* (June 1978), pp. 148–152.

Neil H. Jacoby, Peter Nehemkis, and Richard Eells, *Bribery and Extortion in World Business* (New York: Macmillan, 1977).

Barry Richman, "Can We Prevent Questionable Foreign Payments?" *Business Horizons,* Vol. 22, No. 3 (June 1979), pp. 14–20.

DISCUSSION GUIDES ON CHAPTER CONTENT

1. How would you define a multinational corporation?
2. Why do American companies invest in foreign production facilities?
3. Explain some of the major sources of conflict between multinational companies and the host countries in which they do business.
4. What are the more important conflicts that the federal government has with multinational companies whose headquarters are in the United States?
5. Do you believe that multinational companies export jobs? Explain.
6. What is the case for free trade? for tariff protection?
7. How would you go about assuring that there are no more foreign payoffs by American companies? Do you believe that would be easier to achieve than curbing domestic corruption?
8. All things considered, do you see the multinational corporation as beneficial or harmful?

MIND-STRETCHING QUESTIONS

1. There are many observers who think that in the next 30 years a few hundred of the largest multinational companies will virtually control world trade and production. Others think that the problems facing the multinational corporation will bring about an important decline in its influence. Which side are you on? Explain.
2. There are many observers who think that the multinational corporation has virtually unlimited capacity for doing "good things" in the underdeveloped countries of the world. What good can a multinational company do and still keep its stockholders happy?

28
FULL
E 1PLOYMENT POLICY

A) PRO AND CON—MANDATORY WAGE-PRICE CONTROLS

The Case For*

Q. Professor Lekachman, why do you favor mandatory wage and price controls?

A. Largely because there are industries in which either you have concentrated market power—as in automobiles, aluminum, pharmaceuticals, chemicals, food processing and a long list of others—or, as in the health sector, you have what one might characterize as a form of market failure. In a major share of the American economy, conditions even approximating classical competition simply do not operate.

That means a great many private judgments are made, quite different from those that follow automatic obedience to market signals. I would prefer to have those decisions made by officials who are responsible to elected congresspersons or to the President because, to put the matter bluntly, you can throw out the rascals at the end of their terms. The public can't get rid of the largely anonymous chief executive officers of large corporations.

Q. Do you want to put controls on the whole economy?

A. No. Where a market is operating reasonably competitively, I'd leave it alone. By and large, retailing is an example of reasonably workable competition. I wouldn't try to fiddle with retail prices. I rely upon Gimbels to keep an eye on Macy's.

Note that by excluding retailing, one greatly simplifies the process of control because at one sweep you reduce the size of the business population to be regulated by 80 or 90 percent.

Q. Why zero in on the other industries?

A. If you go down the list of major manufacturing industries, you'll find that in the bulk of them the market is controlled by the top four or eight firms.

Let me give you an example: Back in the rather turbulent months which followed the Organization of Petroleum Exporting Countries' oil embargo in '73 and '74, and in the minidepression of '74–75, auto sales shrank very sharply. Neverthe-

---

*Robert Lekachman, "Pro and Con Mandatory Wage-Price Controls?" *U.S. News and World Report,* June 18, 1979.

less, the major auto companies raised the average price of passenger vehicles in the two selling years '74 and '75 by an average of $1,000.

Now, I'm not quarreling with the rationality of General Motors'—the price leader—reaching a decision to sell fewer cars at higher average prices and profits rather than more cars at lower prices and lower per-unit profits. What I am suggesting is that this is an excellent example of the power of a price leader in a concentrated industry to make a choice of price-and-product strategies.

It's not a choice that a competitive seller can make. The little garment manufacturer on Seventh Avenue in New York does not have the choice of selling a few dresses at high prices or more dresses at low prices. He meets the market price, or he sells zero dresses.

Much of American industry is organized nearer to the automobile model than it is to the Seventh Avenue model.

Q. Wouldn't controls simply postpone inflation until later?

A. This is fair comment if you regard controls as the whole of economic policy and, paradoxically, also if you regard them as just a temporary emergency measure.

If you use controls intelligently, if you accept them as a permanent tool of economic management, you accept them in conjunction with appropriate fiscal policy and appropriate monetary policy as well. And it is in that sense that I advocate controls.

Q. Why do you want these controls to be permanent?

A. We need the ability at any moment to impose controls. Whether or not the controls would be imposed would depend on price behavior. It would be superfluous to impose controls on an industry which wasn't raising its prices. But the ability to control should always be within the President's discretion. I assume this would have a profoundly moderating effect upon pricing strategies.

Q. What makes you think workers would be willing to go along with wage controls without big strikes?

A. For what it's worth, you have the stated position of the executive council of the AFL-CIO, which has declared its preference for mandatory controls of incomes as well as of prices.

But my main hope is a very simple one: The unions are perfectly aware that too-large settlements threaten to accelerate the movement of work away from unions to nonunion labor. Unions have also been, on the whole, amazingly restrained in their demands. My assumption, based upon this sort of evidence, is that if prices were put under control, unions would bargain for essentially noninflationary settlements.

Q. What good would selective controls on big companies do when most of the inflation in the last year or two has been from soaring food, fuel and housing costs?

A. On energy, I would go to rationing along with more effective price controls than we have now.

You can do something about food, not by anything as simplistic as putting a flat price on hamburgers, but by recasting agricultural policy, allowing more of certain imports to come in, amending acreage controls and so on. This would be tough going. I recognize the politics.

Another important source of inflation is the whole health sector. Reorganization, largely through movement toward some kind of national health program with very tough cost controls, is probably required to put this under control.

Q. If prices were held down, wouldn't that lead to shortages by dampening a company's incentive to expand production?

A. The point would be more plausible if the investment behavior of American business had been more buoyant in this current expansion. There has been very little effort to restrain the price behavior of sellers, and yet it has only been in the last six months or so that capital investment has begun to seem really buoyant.

The Case Against*

Q. Mr. Gramley, why do you oppose mandatory wage and price controls?

A. They don't work. Our experience with mandatory wage-price controls in the early 1970s gives ample evidence of that. They don't work, because they do not deal with the fundamental problems that give rise to inflation.

While controls are in effect, they tend to sow the seeds of their own destruction because of the resource misallocations and the inequities that they create. Inevitably, after controls have been on a while, the forces to remove them become so great that they're ultimately stripped off, and then the submerged inflation re-emerges.

Q. What do you mean when you say that controls don't deal with the fundamental causes of inflation?

A. The fundamental causes of inflation fall into three general bailiwicks. One is special factors such as food shortages or energy shortages or changes in the international value of the dollar which drive up inflation.

Another source is demand pressures in the economy which pull up prices. Mandatory wage-price controls clearly do not deal with that at all.

The third source is the momentum that develops once an inflation is under way. Wages and prices keep chasing one another. That problem can be dealt with to some degree by mandatory controls—but not effectively, because the mandatory controls give rise to widespread beliefs that each individual group is being treated inequitably. So once the controls come off, the pressures emerge again.

Q. Some argue that Nixon's controls didn't work because they didn't last long enough and weren't enforced strictly—

A. What happened when controls were on from August of '71 until late 1974 contradicts that. Throughout that whole period, we had continuing shortages because of what the control program was doing: Of food, of particularly critical products that were not being produced here because it wasn't profitable to do so, of products being sold in export markets that were in very short supply in the U.S. because it became more profitable to sell them abroad.

The forces that evolved blew that program right out of the water. The Nixon

---

*Lyle E. Gramley, *Ibid.*

administration didn't have much alternative but to take the controls off. I think that same experience would be repeated.

Q. Wouldn't controls prove the government was doing something about prices, thus encouraging people to show restraint?

A. It might have some psychological effect at first. But I'm not at all sure that the effect would be beneficial.

One of the things we learned in the fall of 1971 and early 1972 was that sometimes the psychology developed by a control program leads people to euphoria— and therefore to greater spending, to more demands on aggregate supply and, hence, to a fundamental worsening of the problem.

Q. Some proponents of controls say that they are the only way to restrain prices in industries dominated by a few big firms—

A. I don't think that's true. Competitive pressures differ among industries, but if market forces that complement voluntary guidelines are maintained, the overall workings of the economy will handle the situation.

Q. But those in favor of mandatory controls contend that there isn't enough competition to hold down inflation—

A. History doesn't support that statement. We've had significant periods in the past in which market forces, given the degree of competition we have in our economy now, have been sufficient to hold down the rate of inflation.

We're simply looking at a situation now in which inflation has become deeply embedded into decision making on the part of businesses and labor alike. It takes a long time to unwind from that. But we shouldn't lose our patience.

Q. Couldn't you simply put controls on a few large industries and avoid the problems of policing myriad retail prices?

A. I don't see how you can control just a subset of prices and then expect to make any significant progress on your inflation problem.

The experience of the voluntary control program since last October indicates quite clearly that careful monitoring of the prices of a few large firms is not enough. The experience in the early months of the program, when the economy was growing strongly, indicated that, unless we undertook a very intensive and careful monitoring across the board, we were not likely to be successful.

Q. You said that controls create inequities, but one argument made is that mandatory controls assure equal treatment for everyone, making it unnecessary for labor and management to feel they have to catch up with inflation—

A. If everyone were in exactly the same situation, that might be correct—but they're not. Productivity trends in different industries have proceeded at different paces. They always have. Raw-materials costs go up faster in some industries than in others.

Labor unions and nonunion workers are caught, at any one point in time, in different positions relative to where they have been in the past.

So anytime you put on a set of controls, you find complaints from various groups that they're not being treated equitably. And they're not, because the initial conditions in which they find themselves have not been taken adequately into account. In a mandatory program, there isn't enough flexibility to deal with these situations.

Q. Are there times when mandatory controls are justifiable?

A. In a complete wartime situation, such as we had in World War II, you can't avoid them. Then it's of utmost importance to get every ounce of production you can get out of your economy. So you deliberately do things that you know would be adverse to the functioning of a free-market economy to get critical materials for national-defense production and civilian needs.

But we are certainly not in that situation today.

CASE QUESTIONS

1. Which of these arguments are most persuasive to you?
2. In making a decision whether or not to control wages and prices do you believe that economic arguments are more important than political considerations? Explain why you believe as you do.
3. Is the justification for wage-price controls the same or different as between wartime, such as the Korean War and World War II, and peacetime?
4. Do a little library research and compare the success of wage-price controls in wartime and the 1971–1974 period.

References

Herbert Stein, "Price-Fixing as Seen by a Price-Fixer," *Across the Board,* December 1978: and Center for the Study of American Business, *Alternative Policies to Combat Inflation: Proceedings of a Conference Cosponsored by the Center for the Study of American Business and the Federal Reserve Bank of St. Louis* (St. Louis, Missouri: Washington University, January 1979).

DISCUSSION GUIDES ON CHAPTER CONTENT

1. What is meant by "full employment policy"?
2. Have the objectives of the Employment Act of 1946 been met?
3. How do the provisions of the Humphrey-Hawkins Bill amend the Employment Act of 1946?
4. What were the fundamental causes of price inflation in the United States following 1965? Were the actions taken by the federal government to counteract inflationary forces effective? Explain.
5. Are you in favor of direct wage and price controls to contain inflation? Explain.
6. Do you find President Carter's 1979 Anti-Inflation Program satisfactory? Explain your reasons.
7. Is future inflation inevitable in the United States?
8. There are many people today who believe that the rate of growth of this

society should be slowed. What are the arguments they give? What are the major criticisms of these arguments? What is your evaluation of the arguments?

MIND-STRETCHING QUESTION ──────────────

1. If it is a question of having full employment at the cost of inflation or slowing the rate of economic growth, what would be your choice? Explain.

29
ECONOMIC CONCENTRATION AND PUBLIC POLICY

DISCUSSION GUIDES ON CHAPTER CONTENT ⎯⎯⎯⎯⎯

1. How do the views of business executives, lawmakers, economists, and political theorists differ concerning competition? In what ways are they similar?

2. Identify: the Sherman Act; the Clayton Act; the rule of reason; conglomerate; price competition versus other types of competition; concentration ratios; reciprocity; entry barriers; and horizontal versus vertical mergers.

3. Identify the most significant Supreme Court decision up to the 1960s concerning firm size and mergers.

4. What is the difference between the structural school of thought concerning mergers and size, and the performance and behavior school? Which side are you on? Explain.

5. Is aggregate concentration growing or remaining relatively constant? How about micro concentration?

6. It has long been accepted conventional economic wisdom that market concentration is indicative of monopoly power, collusion, price inflexibility, high prices, and high or excessive profits. More recent data do not confirm this. Explain.

7. Explain the reasoning of the Supreme Court in the Brown Shoes case. Do you think the decision was right?

8. Has it been proven or disproven that conglomerates lessen competition, add to aggregate concentration, and are less efficient than smaller companies?

9. Outline those basic public policies that you think should govern the growth and merger of business enterprises.

MIND-STRETCHING QUESTION

1. The business ethic of the United States has always stressed efficiency, becoming the best in one's field, and outstripping the competition. Why then, when a company does just this and eliminates all or most of its competition, do we penalize it for becoming a monopoly?

VI
FUTURE RELATIONSHIPS AMONG BUSINESS, GOVERNMENT, AND SOCIETY

30
REFORMING CORPORATE GOVERNANCE

A) THE PUBLIC DIRECTOR

Robert Townsend, former chairman of the board of Avis and a critic of corporate management, recommends that guardians to protect the public interest should be placed on the boards of directors of all corporations with assets over $1 billion. His suggestion is that the federal government require such full-time board members to be seated.

Each public member would, according to Townsend, be given a fund of $1 million, to be paid by the company in question. The member would pay himself $50,000 annually and would, of course, have enough left over to pay for staff. He and his staff would be responsible for making studies of what the company was doing. Each member would be obliged to call at least two press conferences a year and to report on the company's progress or lack of it on issues of interest to the public.

Each member would have an office in the company and would have access to all meetings conducted by the company.

A group of distinguished national legislators who had occupied vice-presidential positions or higher in nonfamily-owned businesses would choose for these jobs people who met at least four criteria: (1) knowledgeable about large-company behavior, with at least 10 years' experience in line jobs; (2) wealthy enough to be objective and incorruptible; (3) energetic; and (4) reasonably intelligent. Once such a pool of people was formed, public directors would be chosen for a particular corporation by lot and at random. After selection, they would rotate every four years.[1]

CASE QUESTIONS

1. Argue the foregoing case pro and con.
2. Are such guardians as Townsend recommends to be viewed as the final word on whether or not the company is serving the public interest? Argue the case pro and con.
3. Can you suggest alternative methods to insure that the public interest is met by large companies?

References

"Arthur Goldberg on Public Directors," *Business and Society Review/Innovation,* Spring 1973, pp. 35–39: "Responses to the Goldberg Proposal on Public Directors," *Business and Society Review,* Summer 1973, pp. 37–43.

Note

1. See Robert Townsend, "Let's Install Public Directors," *Business and Society Review,* Spring 1972, pp. 69–70. For a comparable but more conservative proposal, see John A. Patton, "The Working Director—Management Middleman," *The Conference Board Record,* October 1972, pp. 36–39.

DISCUSSION GUIDES ON CHAPTER CONTENT

1. What is meant by "corporate governance"?
2. There is a wide range of proposals for corporate reform, from conservative to radical. Which specific proposals appeal to you? Why?
3. What is the central function of the corporate governance system? What are the major issues involved in corporate reform?
4. Do you favor federal incorporation of businesses? Explain.
5. Do you agree with the statement that managers have tended to exercise more power than boards of directors in recent times? Explain your position.
6. Make an evaluation of the various proposals for reforming corporate boards of directors made in the textbook.
7. What are the general considerations you would keep in mind while suggesting or undertaking corporate reform? How much value would you place on maintaining traditionally efficient structures of doing business, on the cost of carrying out reforms, and on overcoming resistance from entrenched powers?

MIND-STRETCHING QUESTIONS

1. How would you assure that corporate boards of directors act in a responsible manner? Are there any reforms you have in mind to achieve this?
2. To what extent do you think the special interest groups in society and in an organization should be given representation on the board of directors? How much democratization of decision making is appropriate?

31

FUTURE FORCES AND PATTERNS IN THE BUSINESS-GOVERNMENT-SOCIETY INTERRELATIONSHIP

DISCUSSION GUIDES ON CHAPTER CONTENT

1. What is meant by "alternative futures exploration"?
2. What is a "surprise free" scenario? What does it mean in terms of the premises upon which such a scenario is based?
3. The authors say that "institutional lags" could prevent the solution of many social problems. What do they mean? Do you agree?
4. If we can land a man on the moon and bring him back safely, why can't we better manage our socioeconomic problems?
5. What are your views on the future of capitalism? Do you agree with the analysis made by the authors? Explain.
6. A number of alternative futures have been presented in the textbook. Appraise the probability of each for the year 2000. the year 2050. the year 2100. Explain.

MIND-STRETCHING QUESTION

1. Which of the relationships that exist in the business-government-society nexus in the year 2000 will be most different from today's? What relationships will be much like those of today? Explain your position and the premises upon which it is based.

FIELD RESEARCH: BOARD OF DIRECTORS AUDIT COMMITTEE

In recent years increasing pressures have been placed on publicly held corporations to improve the governance performance of boards of directors. One result is the creation in more and more companies of board of directors audit committees. The thrust has been to name three or more directors to such committees and to have a majority of outside directors on them.

The New York Stock Exchange in January 1977 required that "Each domestic company with common stock listed on the Exchange . . . establish no later than June 30, 1978 and maintain thereafter an audit committee comprised solely of directors independent of management." The Securities and Exchange Commission endorses the idea that publicly held corporations should have audit committees dominated by outside directors but has not mandated this for all corporations. In recent years, however, the SEC has required companies to establish audit committees as a result of its enforcement proceedings and has imposed an extensive list of duties relating to such matters as recommending an independent accounting firm as auditor and reviewing its activities, reports, and recommendations; reviewing all public releases of financial information; and auditing activities of officers and directors in dealing with the company.

Visit a local corporation having an audit committee on its board of directors and discuss with a member of the committee and/or management how the committee operates and what functions it performs. Review the following publication and report on the organization, duties, and responsibilities of audit committees: Deloitte, Haskins and Sells, *Audit Committees: A Director's Guide,* Deloitte, Haskins and Sells, 1979.

George A. Steiner is one of the leading pioneers in the development of university curriculums, research, and scholarly writings in the newly developing field of business, government, and society interrelationships. After receiving his B. S. in business administration at Temple University, he was awarded an M. A. in economics from the Wharton School of the University of Pennsylvania and a Ph. D. in economics from the University of Illinois. He is the author of many books and articles. His latest books are *Strategic Planning: What Every Manager Must Know, Management Policy and Strategy* (with John B. Miner), and *Business and Its Changing Environment* (ed.). In recognition of his writings, Temple University awarded him a Litt. D., honorary degree. Professor Steiner has held top-level positions in the federal government and in industry, including boards of directors. Past president of the National Academy of Management and founder of *The California Management Review,* he is currently Harry and Elsa Kunin Professor of Business and Society and Professor of Management at UCLA.

John F. Steiner teaches courses in business and society and in management at California State University, Los Angeles. He received his B. A. from Southern Oregon College and his M. A. and Ph.D. from the University of Arizona. The author of papers and articles on business ethics, political science, management, and social policy, John Steiner is co-author of *Issues in Business and Society* and *Business, Government, and Society* (both with George A. Steiner). He is the producer of a continuing series of educational videotapes on business, government, and society topics used in university classrooms around the country. As a consultant on business ethics, he has developed an ethics training program used by corporations.

NOTES

NOTES

NOTES

NOTES

NOTES

NOTES